More P

"This is a must read for anyone who w   :e predictable success in this industry.   1s and choices that are part of the journey, and learn how to effectively incorporate the 3-Step Success Pattern through masterful storytelling. Thank you for tying a bow around the Ri Training Program, which was the missing link that our team so craved. Because of Ri Training, we are now experiencing explosive personal and team growth!"
—*Reagan Dean, National Marketing Director, Juice Plus+*

"This book gives you every step to producing residual income, if you take action and follow the simple practical system Clay has shared here. I would highly recommend sharing this book with your team members; it will teach them the right way to build a solid business."
—*Diane Walker, Senior Executive, Send Out Cards*

"*Six Figures in Six Months* is the first systematic approach to success in network marketing. Personal development is the backbone of success, and Clay is clear and concise about the road to growing your network marketing empire! It has nothing to do with luck but everything to do with following this blueprint. Read this book. Apply its principles. You will succeed."
—*Andy and Natalie Goddard, Blue Diamonds, doTERRA*

"This book is an inspiration! With the clarity and focus of an effective coach and the direction of a wise mentor, Clay Stevens not only provides practical guidance for building a six-figure income in six months, but he does it while keeping us engaged in the lives of the characters he has so wonderfully developed. As you join this journey with Steve, Sara, Jen, and the entire cast, you will learn the lessons of the 3-Step Success Pattern right along with them. Thank you Clay for this outstanding book. May all who read it quickly become six-figure earners themselves."
—*Cheri Alguire, Business Coach, Author of* 13 lessons in 13.1 Miles

"Finally, a road map to success for direct sellers! Clay's three-step process is easy to follow and takes the guesswork out of how to build a successful business. If you're serious about building your own business, *Six Figures* is THE book for you. It has inspired me to stop wasting time on luck and chance and do it the right way! A great book that will help thousands. You can't afford **not** to own this book."
—*Tony Lloyd, Communications Director, Freedom Rocks*

"The best network marketing book I have ever read. It was incredible to go through the emotions of the ups and downs of the different phases of building a network marketing business. The three phases of building are powerful and have taught me a piece of the process I have been missing. What a great tool to have in our arsenal. Grab a pen because you will want to write notes."
—*Dave Smith, Executive, Send Out Cards*

"WOW! *Six Figures in Six Months* is one of the best books I have read for training in network marketing. Over the years as a trainer of thousands of salespeople, oh how I wished I had a book like this that so clearly outlines the three-step pattern of success in building a business. This book is for anyone thinking about getting in or out of network marketing. If followed diligently, there is no doubt that you can find the success you so rightly deserve."
—*W. Viggo Madsen, President, Invest in You*

"One of the greatest teaching books in the industry. As a 20-year veteran I can say that everyone should read and re-read this book."
—*Rhonda Voss, Senior Executive Unit Leader, Avon*

"Perfecto! Network marketing magnificently explained! Whether you're a novice or ready to leave your legacy, *Six Figures in Six Months* will invigorate and stimulate your thought process. I can hardly wait for the movie!"
—*Tony E. H. Serna, Founder and CEO of Precision 3*

"*Six Figures in Six Months* is right on! It's for the brand new and seasoned distributor. I love the 3-step system that helps set people up for success from the first step all the way through to becoming the leader of a successful team. *Six Figures in Six Months* will help anyone in this business to get people moving toward you and then with you, and take the appropriate actions toward success."
—*Kim Olson, Crystal Executive, 4-Star Golden Circle, Isagenix*

"*Six Figures in Six Months* is what I have been trying to say for the last 25 years but didn't quite have the verbiage. There is no book in this industry that puts it all together so anyone can understand it like this. Everyone in the industry should read and re-read this book."
—*Brad Doyle, former Amway Diamond and Director of Training, Unique Advantage*

"*Six Figures in Six Months* had me captivated. It mapped out what it takes to be successful in network marketing, especially for those who have no sales experience. The characters in the book came to life and made it easy to understand why people fail in the business and what they need to do to succeed. I plan to implement the process in the book with anyone on my team who is willing to commit to the 3-Step Success Pattern. Thanks Clay for writing this awesome book and for creating the tools to go along with it."
—*Cathy Hazzlerigg, Certified Relationship Coach and Trainer*

"Alarmingly poignant in its authentic portrayal of the only REAL long-term team building technology that exists in our industry."
—*Matt Peterson, CEO, Wake Up Now*

"WOW! If you will just follow this simple yet effective system you will create predictability in your business and all the success that you desire."
—*Terry Johal, CEO, World Financial Group*

SIX FIGURES
IN
SIX MONTHS

Three Steps to Six Figures

Clay Stevens

SIX FIGURES
IN
SIX MONTHS

Clay Stevens

Acknowledgements

Special thanks and grandest appreciation goes to all the people who believed the dream of *Six Figures in Six Months*.

I received help and encouragement from my wife, Carol, as well as from mentors, family, friends and business partners. Notably Kevin Hoggan, Dean Koerner, John Davidson, Jim Hickey, Frank and Ruth Harmon, Lillian Heil, and William Black have been invaluable in the creation of this book.

Furthermore, Mary Ellen Stevens, Heather Seferovich, and Carole Warga worked tirelessly editing and Carol Stevens shared her expertise and commitment in designing and creating a publishable product. Lastly, I also want to acknowledge the team at Hedgehog Solutions for their dedication and expertise, especially for meeting impossible timelines.

The true stars of this book, however, are the characters. Without them there would be no story to tell. They are a composite of many people who have been willing to try something different, and to learn, practice, and apply the principles that create predictability and success in this industry.

I

Introduction

"Success is not a matter of chance, it's a matter of choice. Success most often occurs by making correct choices in their proper sequence according to a proven, established pattern of success." —Clay Stevens

Have you ever watched people who are really good at putting jigsaw puzzles together? To the casual observer it looks like an art form the way they seem to be able to find the corner and edge pieces. Glancing from time to time at the accompanying picture on the puzzle's box, they put pieces that seem not to belong anywhere in the general area where they will ultimately go when the puzzle is finished. However, accomplished puzzle masters are not randomly placing pieces and experimenting with vague ideas of where each piece goes. They follow a process that enables them to recreate the picture on the box in a short amount of time. The really good puzzle masters can rapidly put puzzles together, even without a picture to follow.

How do they do it? They follow three bedrock principles that produce success in any endeavor. First, they start at the start—not in the middle. Second, they build personal effectiveness before doing the visible work. And third, they follow a proven success pattern that creates predictable outcomes.

For most people, building a network marketing business looks like someone throwing a thousand-piece jigsaw puzzle onto a table and trying to put it together without the picture to follow or any real strategy to help them put the pieces into place. In most cases, people who try to complete a puzzle this way soon give up and quit. Why do they do this? Because it's frustrating to spend so much time figuring out what pieces go where and which ones fit together without a picture for a reference. Some can get the corners and edge pieces, but the interior pieces—forget it! They sigh a few times and then surrender.

I have watched and participated in the seemingly odd charade of network marketers enrolling with high hopes of a bright future, hoping that the pieces of the puzzle will somehow fall into place for them if they stay at it long enough to figure it out. But without a framework for success, most give a sigh and then surrender their dreams, goals, and passions to failure. They quit working on what could be a magnificent collage pieced together to create the life they desperately want. Why? Because they lack the knowledge of a success pattern and the skill to do the required work effectively.

The good news is that network marketing, like all other endeavors, has a systematic formula that will predictably get you from wherever you are to wherever you want to go. Yes, you read that right; I used the words *predictable* and *network marketing* in the same sentence. Without predictable formulas, frameworks, structures, programs, processes, systems, or success patterns in everything we do, we would be left to the follies of chance, luck, and guess work. These follies have led to success strategies like "enroll, hope, and replace," "throw mud at the wall, some is bound to stick" and "just keep doing what you're doing and it will eventually work," to name a few.

Chance, luck, and guess work leave us to try to put our network marketing puzzle together without a picture. And without a picture or a predictable success pattern, most will quickly become discouraged and quit. Those who are willing to endure may eventually discover the magic framework for success, like Thomas Edison did when he invented the light bulb. However, most will never get it and will struggle until one day they throw in the towel and simply give up.

Formulas, frameworks, structures, programs, processes, systems, or success patterns are the keys to success. They give us power to not only imagine life by design, but to take appropriate action in its proper sequence to systematically achieve our greater causes and higher purposes.

The predictable framework or success pattern in network marketing has three steps, parts, or phases that reliably create success. The problem is that until now, no one has been able to articulate the process and the critical skills within each step that actually produces the promise of the industry: duplication, residual income, and generational wealth.

This book was written to bring clarity to the industry of best opportunity, to help anyone who wants to succeed in network marketing to do so predictably and with less frustration. The predictable success pattern and its underlying principles, skills, and knowledge taught in this book are necessary to build a strong and profitable business. This book contains the precision and focus of an effective coach and the direction of a wise mentor. This book not only provides practical guidance for building a six-figure income in six months, but it does so while engaging you in the lives of the characters who are wonderfully developed. As you join the journey with Steve, Sara, Jen, and the entire cast, you will learn the lessons of the 3-Step Success Pattern along with them.

You will learn that when you began your business, you enrolled in an intensive personal improvement course, and that it's not enough for anyone just to go through the motions of recruiting, training, and retaining people on a team. You also will learn that success is not based on how long you have worked, or the number of times you have repeated some task, as if they were deposits in some sort of cosmic success account. Through this book, you will learn that success in this business comes from the effective application of correct knowledge and skills in their proper sequence within a predictable three-step success pattern: Improve Yourself, Build a Team, and Become a Leader.

You will experience the cause and effect of working for the sake of working. You will see firsthand the results of massive action taken by people with low personal effectiveness. And you will be an eyewitness to the unintentional and unreliable consequences that come from what often masquerades as progress.

This book is intended to help you engage in appropriate work in a calculated sequence to become a professional business owner. In any career or business, you must learn and practice the critical skills and knowledge unique to the industry before you can effectively apply them in the real world with your family, friends, and colleagues.

Knowing the secret framework and mastering its underlying principles has helped thousands of people in this industry predictably create job-dropping residual income and generational wealth. All high achievers become superior performers within distinct areas that give them a credible claim on the success they have achieved. They master critical skills embedded within a framework of success, and they teach others to do the same.

Decades of industry data show that knowledge by itself is not enough. It is not enough to know what to do; everyone knows what to do. But the missing link is the when and how to do it. Think of it this way: Would you get into a plane where the pilot had learned to fly by reading Flying for Dummies™, or attended a workshop where someone talked about how to fly, or simply watched someone fly a few times? No way!

Network marketing is a unique craft. And learning a few tips and tricks is simply not enough for those who want to achieve greatness. The process of achieving success requires an understanding of how all the pieces fit together within a business context, then confronting and overcoming areas of personal weakness that allow you to increase your effectiveness beyond your current ability. Sounds easy, right? Just learn the process, practice the critical skills, and eureka!

The proven predictable process detailed in this book is based on three bedrock principles that most people are completely unaware of. These principles are like an operating system to the success pattern, or the ingredients that allow the success recipe to consistently create the same positive result. The three-step Improve Yourself, Build a Team, and Become a Leader success pattern will help you become aware of your strengths and weaknesses. It points out precisely how to improve in specific skills and knowledge areas that are holding you back.

So why does any of this matter? Well, most associates don't know or understand the 3-Step Success Pattern, so they try to build a team without any skill or knowledge. This appears to have the same effect that jumping into the deep end of a swimming pool without the skill or knowledge of how to swim. Some people drown rather quickly just trying to learn how to tread water. That is to say, they quit soon after they enroll because either they can't enroll anyone or can't enroll enough people to make any measurable progress. And most of those who last long enough to tread water rarely learn to do more than tread water; they rarely learn how to swim.

Mastering the 3-Step Success Pattern contained in this book will give you a supersonic way to gain the foundational knowledge and skills of the business and practice them in a real world way, like policemen, firemen, astronauts, airline pilots, and soldiers in the military are able to do. This pattern serves as a road map and a way to measure progress in every phase of the business.

Six Figures will give you experience that transcends reading. You will receive life-long lessons, a set of principles, and practical skills that will motivate you and your team to build businesses on purpose with purpose. Your personal effectiveness will increase with every page and chapter as you learn how to eliminate distractions and gain intolerance for things that don't pay off by seeing the cause and effect of decisions, actions, and results of the characters in this story.

See for yourself what creating success in this industry is really like through the lives of Steve and Sara Thoms, Glenna Hanks, Gary Kirk, and fifteen other characters as they learn, practice, and apply the principles that actually create six-figure incomes. Discover the power of the predictable pattern of success, including the critical skills and how to employ them in their proper sequence to accelerate your ability to achieve your greater causes and higher purposes. Begin to piece together your future empire by following the example of the cast of characters in this book. Become a network marketing puzzle master, and make your life whatever picture you envision.

1

The Promise of Tomorrow

Tomorrow is the day I have been waiting for. It is the day I have been working for and the day I have been dreaming of my whole life. Tomorrow, Coach Curtis of State University is going to officially offer me a full scholarship to play baseball. State is a sure stepping-stone to the major leagues and a life of riches and fame.

As I lie here in my bed trying to go to sleep, I can hear the sound of the pen as I sign my name, Steve Thoms, on the dotted line. Tomorrow the dream life will begin to come true: fancy cars, big houses with swimming pools, no worries about money, awesome vacations, boats, parties, housekeepers, and yard workers. I can see the sights and sounds of a big league stadium, fans cheering, reporters welcoming me to the team club house, the smell of freshly cut grass, the vendors yelling, "Hot Dogs, get your hot dogs here," or "Ice Cold Beer here." As the crowd roars, I get a thrill as I see my name and picture on the giant score board in center field. I imagine looking hall of fame pitchers in the eye, as if I know something they don't. Then I hear the crack of the bat as I rip one down the line and stretch a double into a triple. Evening sports anchors show my hit as a highlight! As I drift off to sleep I relish the fact that very soon I will be playing a kid's game for millions of dollars and having more money that I can ever spend.

The alarm goes off at 6:00 AM, just as it does everyday. But today I was up and ready to go at least a half hour earlier. My dad and I were supposed to meet Coach Curtis at the school at 9:00 AM. The local newspaper, radio, and TV guys are supposed to be there to interview us and take some pictures and video. I could hardly wait. I hurried through breakfast, hoping that my pace would somehow influence time to speed up as well.

We met Coach Curtis at the school. In front of reporters and school administrators he made his formal offer. I then put on the State

University hat and we posed for pictures. After a few interviews, the reporters left, and Coach Curtis excused himself to get on a plane to resume his other duties.

When the commotion died down, my dad asked me a few questions about baseball and how it would affect my education. We frequently had this conversation and, rolling my eyes again, I thought, "Education! Doesn't he know that I am going to be playing baseball?" Classes and studying were the farthest things from my mind. I had gotten through high school okay, how much more difficult could college be? And besides, I was a baseball player at one of the premier schools. The school would certainly help me make sure I was in good academic standing, wouldn't they?

Dad reminded me that I hadn't exactly been a stellar student and that on many occasions I had had to do extra work or pass a test on game day to remain eligible. He also rehearsed the numerous times he and the coach had to invent ways to clear my name at the attendance office for skipping school. My dad was a successful businessman. He had what he wanted in life: a nice house, a swimming pool, some race horses, a membership at the local country club, and a set tee time on Wednesday afternoons and Sunday mornings. Now it seemed like he was about to rain on my parade. I didn't know exactly what he was going to say or do, but I felt like the dark clouds of doom were gathering in his tone of voice.

Dad told me very matter-of-factly that I shouldn't go to State and play baseball; if I did, I would be home in just a few months. At State I would have to take classes, real classes with teachers who didn't care if I came to class or not, and who certainly weren't going to make sure my homework was turned in. He insisted that my lack of academic preparation and motivation would cause me to fail in one semester and that I would never have an opportunity to play baseball in the spring. His words felt like ice water being poured over me at the time.

Dad suggested, then encouraged, and finally told me that I needed more discipline to be truly successful in life. He helped me remember how easy it was for me to be the star of the team; how easy it was for me to stand out among my peers in our local community; how easy it was for me to piggyback on his name and reputation to get summer jobs. He pointed out that at State University and beyond, others had had to work harder than I had and that they had had to sacrifice everything to get there, and that they would be competing with me for the same things I wanted. "You need to be more disciplined," Dad repeated.

He had a way of making his point so plainly that it often cut me to the core, and this was one of those times. So, as was customary for me, I took the rest of the day off from school. I drove around town for a while then went for a drive to the mountains; it was there that I had a profound experience. I felt inspired for the first time in my life, somewhat unexpectedly, I felt inspired to follow my dad's counsel.

I contemplated my father's main concern: "You need more discipline," he said. As I drove I asked myself "Who teaches discipline?" The only thought that came to my mind was the military. When I got home I immediately called the athletic department at State University and declined the scholarship offer. Then I jumped in my car and went to the military recruiting center.

A few weeks later I found myself in boot camp. Soon after I moved on to a permanent-duty station. I played baseball and football for the base team, and before I knew it, three years had passed. The lesson of discipline was emblazoned in my heart, mind, and soul in true military fashion. My objective had been met, so I left the military and enrolled at a local junior college.

I tried out for the baseball team and made it. I was a starter, but not a star by any means. These kids were good, really good. And every one of them was hungry and dedicated to making it to the four-year college level, or the minor or the major leagues. Their ambition was no greater than mine. I trained hard and worked as hard or harder than anyone else.

My first year I had a slow start, but I attributed it to my absence from real competition for three years while I was serving in the military. My second year wasn't going much better. I had a low batting average and was in danger of losing my starting position. "How could this be happening?" I wondered. I had gained the one thing I was certain was missing—discipline—but it still wasn't happening. As the year went on, I discovered that I really didn't have the natural talent to compete at this level. Everyday I was reminded that if I couldn't compete at this level, the major leagues were definitely out of the question.

Day by day the dream that I had allowed myself to imagine that one night several years earlier was fading. By the end of the season, the reality of the situation had grown into devastation. I turned to God again, and he instructed me to serve in my church. I was assigned to live and work in the housing projects of East Los Angeles.

This was a far cry from cheering crowds, adoring fans, fancy houses, and loads of money. My dad had been right. I didn't have the discipline to succeed. But more than that was what he hadn't told me that day at the school. He hadn't wanted to tell me that I didn't have enough talent to compete. He hadn't wanted to crush my dream. He wanted me to discover it myself when the time was right, when it wouldn't lead to my complete downfall. He had been just and merciful at the same time.

During my church experience in Los Angeles I met my wife, Sara, an incredible woman from a great family. They worked hard and served others. Two years after we met we were married. She encouraged me to pursue my love of baseball by becoming a coach and a teacher. A few years later, I got my first job and we began our career in the school system. I loved helping kids learn the game I had such a passion for. They were so eager to learn and had fun playing. In the first four years we won two state championships. But one thing took me completely by surprise: I loved being in the classroom. Maybe it was the fact I hadn't spent much time there as a kid, or maybe it was the freedom to really connect with students who were eager to discover how the world around them worked. No matter the reasons, the classroom was exhilarating. There was no daily grind. It was something new each day. But every month, I was reminded of the down side of this work—compensation, or lack of it.

Sara and I welcomed four children to the family in six years, including a set of twins. I wanted desperately to give them a nice house to grow up in. I wanted a safe and reliable car for Sara to drive. I wanted to provide my family with nice clothes, new toys, music lessons, sport camps, the best health care, college funds, and big weddings. I also wanted to be able to help them out when they needed it. However, my chosen profession was always in conflict with my fatherly dreams. I had neither time nor money to adequately provide for my family. In short, I was so busy making a living that I didn't have a life. So I decided to become the very best at some part of my life. I followed my father's example and became the best at my profession. I applied what I had learned from my parents and coaches and achieved my first teaching goal: I became Teacher of the Year. But much to my dismay, Teacher of the Year honors didn't provide any bonuses or raises. The reward for being the best teacher in the district was very much the same as all the other accolades of teaching—emotional gratification accompanied by a certificate to hang on the wall.

I further immersed myself into teaching and coaching to show that I could be truly successful at some part of my life. But I ended up spending more time with other people's kids than my own. While driving to and from school and practices, I often thought about my own small children who were essentially fatherless. I thought about the teachers they had that were spending their time with my kids. They were the ones defining success and teaching my kids how to achieve it.

Sara and I had made the decision when we first got married that she would stay at home and take care of our children. As the single money earner, these concerns weighed heaviest on me. I laid awake at night, staring into the darkness and wondering how I would ever make it financially on a schoolteacher's salary?

I thought about my relationship with Sara and was reminded that, even when we went on our weekly date, we were limited to fast food or dollar movies. We had to limit our time away from home to an hour or two at most, because we didn't have much money for babysitters. This gnawed at me. I wondered, how is it possible to be a great teacher and a championship coach, and not even have enough time to go on a decent date with the one I love?

My pain grew when Sara invited me on a date to the grocery store. I thought, "Why are we going on a date to the grocery store?" It finally dawned on me that we didn't have any money for a "normal" date, and we needed food; so, in Sara's tactful, loving way, she found a way to have a date and get what she needed for the kids.

During our tour of the store I watched her shop. I noticed that she carefully picked up each can of soup, each bar of soap, each tube of toothpaste. She compared the cost of every item she put in the cart, making sure that she got the best deal she could. At the checkout counter she gave the clerk coupons she had cut out of the newspaper. For the first time, I got to experience Sara's daily challenge of running a household and raising healthy, happy children on a schoolteacher's salary. I asked her how she felt about this? She smiled and responded that this was her financial contribution to our family. Every time she could stretch a dollar, she was adding to our ability to make it to the end of a month.

The bloom had definitely fallen off the rose. The cold reality of our situation struck me like a ton of bricks. No matter how successful I became as a teacher and a coach, at my current level I simply couldn't make sufficient income to meet my desires to provide for my family without putting Sara to work somewhere and the kids in day care.

So, like all other "successful" teachers, I got an advanced degree. Two more years of hard work and yet more time away from the family. But I was committed to making the extra money the added degree would bring us; thinking that the few hundred dollars a month raise I would earn would somehow solve my income problem. However, a family of six can eat up a few hundred dollars with no problem. Once again Sara supported me in this, hoping that, somehow, we would be able to spend more time together as a family and be able to do the things the parents of my players did. But after years of hoping and supporting me, she was losing hope of anything changing and started to suggest that I do something else.

During one of our many "discussions" about the fact that something must change, she suggested that if I wanted to continue teaching and coaching, she might need to go to work. If that wasn't a possibility, then I needed to make more money doing something else or something extra. Then came the final straw; she told me that she had received a letter from her father that day and it had a check for $1,000 in it. When she opened the letter her heart sank. She said that she felt so bad for me that she was reluctant to say anything. She knew that I was working as hard as I possibly could to provide for her and the kids. But she did deposit the check. Never had I felt more humiliated. Not only was I unable to take care of my family, but now my father-in-law felt it necessary to contribute to the care of his daughter and grandchildren.

The feeling I had felt with my dad that day in high school returned. I was devastated. Only I couldn't go for a ride around town or up to the mountains—I didn't have enough money for the gas. I told Sara I was going for a walk. As I walked around town, I thought, pondered, and prayed that somehow a solution could be found. But how?

As I passed by the park, I took a seat on one of the swings, remembering the vision of screaming fans packed into huge ballparks. The smell of freshly cut grass was in my nose again. "Ah there's nothing like it," I thought, taking a moment to reminisce. Just then a couple of kids running to the swings brought me back to reality; screaming kids instead of screaming fans, a swing in the city park instead of swinging a bat in a major league ball park. What a hopeless mess this was turning out to be. A feeling of anger started to rise within me. How could things have come to this? I should have fame, houses, and money in the bank; instead I had a mortgage on a forty-year-old house. I loved my children and Sara, but I felt like a failure. The only thing that seemed to be going right was my baseball team; not much consolation when compared to the life I had wanted so badly to provide for Sara and the kids. Feeling more defeated than ever, I headed home.

About five minutes after I got home someone knocked at the door. It was Doug from the school district office. I wondered what was wrong? After everything else, what could Doug possibly want? Was my job in jeopardy? Was I in trouble from some complaint from a parent of a student or team member? This was turning out to be a perfectly bad day.

2

What's It All About?

Doug began by reaching out to shake my hand and asked, "How are you Steve? I know I may be intruding, do you have a minute?" I replied, "Sure. What is going on? Is there a problem?" "Oh no, I just wanted to drop by say 'Hi,' and see if everything was okay." "Okay," I responded still upset from the events of the past couple of hours! "What makes you think something is wrong?" "Well, at the game yesterday I noticed that you were pretty impatient with the Jacobsen boy when he made a base running mistake. It seemed like you lost your cool a little and it surprised me, that's all."

"Sorry for snapping at you," I said. "It's the end of the month and once again there's more month than money; you know how it is. I earned Teacher of the Year honors and two state championships, and still I can't pay my bills. Why can't a schoolteacher, even the very best schoolteachers, make a decent living?" I continued, raising my voice a little. He chuckled and said, "Not how you envisioned your life at thirty-five, huh? I know the pain," he said. "I used to imagine what my life would be like if I won the lottery, or if suddenly they gave us all corporate salaries. Tell me what your life would be like if money wasn't a problem anymore, Steve."

I was taken back by the question. I hesitated for a moment because I had been thinking about this on those long bus trips with twenty-five kids who all had parents making more money than I was, who had nicer cars and didn't seem to worry about how much their kids spent on candy, pop, and chips at the store after games. "Well, without boring you with all the details," I said, "I would at least be able to pay all of my bills and my father-in-law wouldn't have to send me money to take care of his dau...." I stopped short realizing that the stress of money, or the lack of it, was really getting to me. In the seconds that followed, nanoseconds really, I got lost in my own thoughts and fears.

Time seemed to stop. It was like one of those scenes from a movie when everything slowed down to stress every detail of the moment.

I recalled several examples during the last few months when I had become impatient and lost control of my emotions. I replayed incidents with my players and situations with Sara. I felt ungrateful for the gift that my father-in-law had given us, and I wasn't hiding it well either. The very reason for Doug's visit was caused by a public display of emotional outburst. To top it off, I had just finished telling a relative stranger that I didn't have any money, that I couldn't pay my bills, and that my father-in-law was sending me money. I was in trouble. I was reacting to things instead of doing things on purpose, with purpose, as I had been taught growing up.

This wasn't me, I knew better. I spent most of my growing-up years learning to make a plan and execute it with absolute precision. I knew that as my emotions went up, my intelligence went down. Those who react to things inevitably lose. And losing wasn't what I was used to. But losing the financial game was becoming all too familiar lately.

I reflected on my dad. He had taught me to act for myself and not to be acted upon. And I felt that unfamiliar but, recently, more frequent sting of failure. I was failing at the core level to behave in a way that produced an intentionally positive outcome. What a knucklehead I was! Even a simple visit by a concerned colleague turned into an uncontrolled outburst. "I need help," I thought, but from whom: my dad, my father-in-law, Doug? And what was anyone going to be able to do? I suddenly realized that I was detached from the conversation and didn't really know how much time I had been on a mental vacation.

Apparently not enough time had passed for the situation to be awkward. Doug continued by asking how serious I was about making more income? I thought but didn't say, "What difference does it make?" Instead, what came out was, "On a scale from 1 to 10—about a 40!" Then Doug said something I will never forget. He told me that he thought he found something that could help me with my money problem! He said that he had met a successful businesswoman who was teaching a few people how to take control of their finances, and that he was going to a meeting on Tuesday at her home to hear more. It should last about an hour and he was thinking that maybe I would like to go with him. I asked if Sara could go with me as well; he quickly agreed and told me he could pick us up at 6:30 PM if we needed a ride.

I accepted his offer. I didn't really want to show up to a meeting about finances in my twenty-five-year-old car.

Doug's visit had lifted my spirits a bit. He gave me some hope that my prayers were at least being heard. The night was still young. Sara and I could still go on our weekly date. I didn't want to completely blow our only weekly time to be alone, away from the daily challenges of marriage, children, mortgages, and yard or housework. We packed up a few goodies and went to the park down the street. I pushed Sara in the same swing I had been sitting in an hour or so before. It reminded me of our college days. No money and no cares in the world; our whole future was ahead of us. For the first time in weeks we had fun! Not the kind of fun you have when you win a game or get an "A" on a test, but real enjoyment. The kind that lasts, the kind that lifts your spirit by just living and being with the ones you love.

I told Sara about my talk with Doug and his invitation to the meeting with the mysterious businesswoman. She asked me what it was all about, who was this woman and how had Doug met her? I, of course, didn't know any of these details, but I asked her to go with me. She told me that she wanted to, but our oldest daughter had a piano rehearsal and she wouldn't be able to. She did encourage me to go, however, and take good notes and let her know everything after the meeting. I think she saw the stress begin to lift from my face as I talked about the meeting. She smiled and gave me a reassuring hug as she whispered in my ear, "I believe in you!"

That night I had a hard time sleeping. My mind was racing with ideas of what I could do to improve my situation. Selling the house and renting an apartment would certainly reduce our expenses. I could quit coaching and take a second job. Coaching was paying a whopping thirty or forty cents per hour. Not exactly a significant part of any wealth strategy. When I thought of life without coaching, my stomach turned a bit. I didn't want to quit, but maybe it was time to turn my focus on my own family and what they needed instead of everyone else's kids. Still I didn't want to quit. A comment my dad made to me one day while we were mending a fence in a pasture for horses (that I didn't give a darn about) came to my mind. I had complained that I didn't want to work on the fence and that I had other things I wanted to do instead. Dad reminded me that I *did* like to eat everyday and sleep in a warm bed every night. He told me that he wasn't asking me if I wanted to help him repair the fence—wanting to would be an added bonus. He had simply asked me to help him get the job done!

Those words stung me again as I contemplated what I was going to do about my situation. Now it was time to do what needed to be done, not what I wanted to do. There were people in my life who were depending on me. When I got over the emotional pangs of "wants" versus "needs," I remembered the offer that Doug had made to me, to learn from someone who was financially successful. I thought about the possibilities of financial success and what that could mean.

My dreams were pretty meager. I wanted Sara to go to the grocery store and buy what she wanted instead of what I could provide on a schoolteacher's salary. I wanted the old car in good enough repair to start every time she went to drive it. I wanted to be able to pay doctor's bills on time, and to pay off those student loans ahead of schedule. For a moment I even thought of what it would be like to have a pickup of my own to drive to school, or to take baseball equipment to and from the field every day. That seemed like it was so far away I quickly dismissed it as even possible, given our current circumstances.

Morning came and I was thinking that this was the last week of baseball practice and that the state tournament was the next weekend. School would soon be out and I needed to make some serious decisions about the future, about the future of *my* baseball program. I was feeling more peaceful about my dad's counsel from so many years before. During the day I felt impressed to relinquish my duties as "The Coach." The thought seemed strange because I didn't have any plan in place to replace the time or the income associated with coaching. I wondered how to tell Sara, but as I looked at her sitting next to me, somehow I felt like she already knew!

When we got home she told me that she had been thinking about what Doug had said and shared her thoughts that, "Somehow I feel like it might be something really good for us. I don't know much about what it was that Doug was talking about but, somehow, I know it is something we should pay close attention to. I want you to feel better about being a good father and husband. I know that the stress is eating you up inside; I see it in your face everyday when you come through that door. So, take good notes, ask lots of questions, and then let's see if this is the answer to our prayers."

The decision to retire from the baseball program was made, but

I didn't dare let anyone know publicly yet. It would be better to wait until after the season. We didn't even tell our kids for fear that in their regular unfiltered conversations with their friends, it would get out and then I would get pressure to stay or have to answer questions about what I was going to do instead. I already had enough on my mind without having to deal with all that.

I arranged my practices for the week to end early. The kids wondered what was going on with shorter, but more intense practices the week of the state tournament. But no one asked directly. I needed to start getting into the swing of a different schedule. I also thought the change would be a good preparation for the state tournament and I did need to be ready for my Tuesday meeting with Doug.

He picked me up at 6:30, just as he had promised. He took me to the nicer part of town and as we drove, he was listening to a CD about success resulting from making proper decisions and taking effective action in the proper sequence. It was interesting, and I lost myself in the voice telling me how success is just the right opportunity and a decision away. We turned up the driveway and headed toward a very nice home with perfectly manicured landscaping. There was a small water fountain by the front door. The door was open a crack, indicating it was okay to just walk in. There were a few people already there helping put chairs out and filling cups with juice and water.

Doug introduced me to the woman who owned the home we were in. "Steve," he started, "This is Glenna Hanks, she is the financial guru I talked about the other day." She insisted that I call her Glenna. She had a powerful confidence that jumped out at me when we shook hands. She was very nice and welcoming, but I sensed that somehow Doug was uneasy. A few minutes later, a couple Doug had invited appeared in the driveway and he seemed to relax a bit. A man and his wife got out and Doug met them at the door.

I knew the woman, her name was Cindy. She was a successful, local real estate agent. She had sold Sara and me our home when we moved to town. Doug introduced them to Glenna, and again she was very gracious in her welcome.

Doug got everyone's attention and invited us all to sit down. There were about twenty people there. Glenna must really be something to draw a crowd like this. On back-to-school night I was lucky to get five parents to come. He welcomed us all to the meeting and began to introduce Glenna as a very successful entrepreneur and financial wizard who had been teaching him and a few others in the room about a method for taking control of the future doing what most of us were already doing. I was puzzled at this statement. "Doing what I was already doing?" How could I take control of my future by teaching and coaching? Glenna thanked Doug for the polite introduction and self-assuredly welcomed all of us to her home. She told us that a few years ago she had been invited to a meeting like this one. She sat in a living room and listened to a man talk about business, finances, and the stress of everyday life, trying to make a living and not having a life. That night she told us was the beginning of a fairy tale story for her. She had taken the information that the man had shared, implemented it, and now had the lifestyle she could have only dreamt of before.

She explained that she had taken advantage of a predictable business system that anyone could do. This reminded me of some of the talks I had had with my team when I taught them how to execute a "hit and run," or "double steal," or a "run down." The word "predictable" seemed the most important word to me. I took notes to share with Sara when I got home and I circled the word *predictable.*

Glenna spent the next few minutes asking people what their life would be like if they didn't have time or financial challenges. I learned in the military not to volunteer for anything; but a few people did weakly speak out. "I would get a new car," one man said, another offered that he would quit his job, and a third added that she would go on vacation to Hawaii or the Bahamas. The woman sitting to my left whispered that she would get a housekeeper and remodel her kitchen. Glenna then asked about our prospects for making these things happen doing what each of us was doing now?

The room was silent for an uncomfortable amount of time when the woman, who had so carefully arranged the cookies, said that there was no way she could ever get what she wanted most by working for someone else. Glenna smiled and agreed. The comment and Glenna's smile relieved the tension in the room. She then spent the next thirty minutes or so explaining how a company called XL-8 provided opportunities to people who were interested in taking control of their finances. She detailed the products and services offered by XL-8 and then highlighted how partners were compensated for the work they did to advertise and market XL-8 products and services. She showed how time could be leveraged and residual income was made by doing what we were probably already doing; referring our family and friends to the company.

She finished by inviting us to evaluate our lives and financial wellness and consider the choices we had made that created those results. She thanked us for coming, then encouraged us to direct questions to the person who had invited us there. Glenna said that if any of us were ready to get started, the person who invited us would have enrollment forms. She told us that if we needed some time to think about what we had seen tonight, that was okay as well.

After the meeting most every one took a cookie and talked to the person who had invited them. Cindy, her husband, and I gathered around Doug. He was so excited that we were both interested. Cindy and her husband asked a few questions about the cost of products and different enrollment options. I was listening from a few feet away so as not to intrude on what might include personal information. Doug asked what they had been thinking when Glenna asked about their dream life without time or money constraints. Doug became transformed right before my eyes. I hadn't seen anything like this outside the locker room before. I referred to this as *hype* and *hopium*. Doug told them that they shouldn't wait to get started working for their dream life, that big money makers all take immediate action. Cindy and her husband decided to enroll and Doug gladly accommodated them. As they were filling out the paperwork, he talked about how their program would create thousands of dollars of income, or millions if that's what they want. This could be accomplished in a short amount of time and they didn't need any special skills, schools, or tools. He went on to say that this could happen as fast as they could talk to about a hundred people.

Glenna noticed that I was standing off to the side while Doug was talking to Cindy. She came and talked to me for a few minutes and asked about my family and what I had liked most about the presentation. She was curiously interested in me. I told her that this might be a way to increase my income by leveraging my standing and contacts in the community. I wasn't sure though, my head was spinning with the possibilities. I told her that I would talk it over with my wife, and then make a decision. I asked her how often she had these meetings. She told me once a week and said that I was welcome to bring or invite others to the meeting, like Doug had brought Cindy and me.

She asked me what questions I had about the products, the company, or the compensation plan. I told her that I needed some time for this to sink in and to formulate my questions. I liked Glenna, she had a way of helping people take action that helped them move toward their goals in a very matter-of-fact way.

Susan, the cookie arranger, came over to us to ask Glenna a question. I excused myself and sat down to complete some notes for my conversation with Sara. Everyone was gone by now except me, Susan, Doug, and Cindy. He was talking to Cindy just loud enough for me and everyone else to hear him without really eavesdropping. He was telling her to make a list of at least a hundred people; then she should start inviting them to either come to next week's meeting or to make an appointment to show them what she saw tonight.

Glenna and Susan moved to the other side of the room, but still within earshot. Glenna was talking to Susan about Doug. It turned out that Susan was Doug's cousin. He was enrolled in the business, but for some reason he chose to sign up under someone else. Even though he had not enrolled with her, Susan seemed genuinely interested in his success. She was asking Glenna if there was anything she could do to help him build his business better. Glenna started talking about what she called a "3-Step Success Pattern" when Doug walked up. Glenna told Susan to call her tomorrow to finish the conversation. Doug interrupted without even being aware that he had. He told them that Cindy and her husband had enrolled. Glenna and Susan congratulated him, and Glenna gently reminded him that he really needed to make sure that they were engaged in the system that she had put together to help them make the business predictable. He assured them both that he would, hugged Susan, shook Glenna's hand, and with enrollment form in hand, asked me if I was ready to go.

I looked at my watch and to my amazement it was after nine o'clock. Not that late in the grand scheme of things, but I got up at 4:30 every morning to help Sara get ready for the day and to exercise. Doug and I talked in his car for another hour about my feelings and what I was most interested in about the business. It was hard not to be excited. Doug was excited. Cindy had been excited and for the first time in a long time I was genuinely excited about my future.

Doug gave me a couple of websites to visit with information about the products and the company. I told him I wanted to go to next week's meeting but that I could drive myself. He agreed and we said goodbye. Sara was already asleep and, because it was after 11:00 by the time I got to bed, I didn't wake her. In just five and a half hours the alarm was going to go off and, ready or not, the day was coming.

But the excitement of possibility was just too much. I couldn't go to sleep. I was exhausted, but my mind would not stop racing. It all seemed too good to be true. And that would be the test when I talked to Sara in the morning. My mind shifted from if it could be true and how it could be done, to all that I wanted to give Sara. What would our life look like if this actually worked? I allowed myself to drift into "what if" land. Sara could shop without hesitation. We could go on dates without worrying about money for babysitters, or if the movie we wanted to see was playing at the dollar theatre. I might be able to enjoy teaching without the stress of payday. The pile of bills in the tray by the phone would be gone. We could go on vacation to somewhere besides grandma's house. The little things that don't work on her car could all be fixed. Sara could get a housekeeper, and maybe I could get my own car or truck.

The last thing I remember was looking at the clock and realizing it was 4:47! Sara let me sleep in a little. When I came downstairs I found Sara in the kitchen reading over my notes from the meeting. Through my sleepy eyes I apologized for coming home so late.

I don't know why I thought she would be upset; the good news was that she wasn't. She said that she figured that it must have been going well if I was out past ten o'clock. "So how did it go, what did you think?" she asked. I was still dragging from the lack of sleep, but my excitement shined through. I wasn't quite sure where to begin, so I started with my general impressions to test the waters of what I thought might be skepticism on Sara's part. "I thought the products and services they talked about were of high quality and provided an incredible value to normal everyday people like us, and there is a money back guarantee," I said. I told her that the idea of leveraging your time and energy seemed awesome. I hadn't seen a way to leverage myself like that before. "Pretty much the idea is to build a team of people who are all trying to create success. I like being around people who are positive and going somewhere in life." Sara saw through my smoke screen and said, "Okay, out with the details that I am reading about in your notes. Is this a way for us to overcome our challenges? Can we actually make money working with them? Come on, fill in the blanks from the notes."

"The company we would represent is called XL-8. Essentially what I think we do is use their products and services, then market, distribute, or advertise those products to people we know. When someone buys from us, we get a commission. When someone decides to partner with us we can get commissions from the work they do and sales that they make, like an insurance agency," I answered. Sara quickly caught my excitement. She hadn't seen me be excited about much of anything for a long time, and this was certainly a welcome change.

"I met some really great people there. Doug of course was there, and the host's name was Glenna. We met at her home. She was articulate and genuinely happy to see us there. She gave the presentation and afterward she answered a few of the questions I could think of right off hand. She invited me to call her if I had any other questions. She seems to be very successful in the company," I added eagerly. I asked Sara if she remembered our real estate agent Cindy. She nodded as I continued, "Cindy and her husband were at the meeting and they enrolled. I didn't do anything myself yet. I wanted to talk to you and let you meet the people for yourself before I did anything. But I did overhear Doug telling Cindy that she needed to make a list of a hundred people who she could talk to, and when she got through the list she would be making over 10k per month. That's $120,000 per year! And the income comes in any time the people we refer to the company buy anything. This creates what they were calling *residual income*."

Sara was getting a bit more excited now and the sleepiness left me as well. She asked why I circled the word *predictable*. "I thought this was a very interesting word that Glenna used. She said it a few times and it impressed me that this wasn't about luck or chance, but about implementing some kind of system that made the growth of the business predictable," I answered. I invited her to come to the meeting at Glenna's house next week and she agreed—I had my first yes!

School was a bit challenging because of the lack of sleep and, of course, baseball practice was already scheduled to end early. The Jacobsen boy was the last to leave the locker room. He drove away in the beautiful new four-wheel drive pickup his dad had bought him for his sixteenth birthday. I was a bit envious that a sixteen-year-old would have such a nice truck while I was riding my bike home. The passenger side brake light in my twenty-five-year-old car needed to be replaced. I was going to fix it yesterday, but instead I was at the meeting.

When I got home I began to think about what I had seen at Glenna's. I could hardly wait to get more information so I could make some decisions about the rest of my life. As the night went on, the desire to get more insight overcame me and my fear and politeness of not wanting to bother Glenna went away. I gave in to the urge and called her to set up a meeting for the next night; the day before we left for the state baseball tournament.

I wondered at the wisdom of this since I probably wouldn't sleep again that night, and for the next three days I had to manage twenty-five teenage boys, get them to play their best baseball, and keep them out of trouble. But I could not let go of this feeling of needing to know more!

3

The Meeting

Glenna was presenting at a larger meeting in a town about an hour away. I wasn't able to finish baseball practice, go home, change my clothes into something presentable, and drive the hour before her meeting started; so we agreed to meet at a diner after her presentation.

I wanted so much to impress her and to let her know that I was serious about really succeeding. I prepared a list of questions so I would be ready to get down to business. I thought about one of my college professors as I drove. He had given us an assignment one day with a week to complete it: "If you could ask three questions to anyone in the world, what would they be, who would you ask them to, and why would you ask those questions to that person?" I had a feeling this was one of those rare opportunities to ask a guru a few questions and get unfiltered answers. However, I didn't have a week to think about what to ask. I referred to my memory of the meeting and the word *predictability* came to mind.

I started to formulate the first question. "You said a few times during the meeting that this business is predictable. What makes it predictable?" I rehearsed it in my mind a few times until I was satisfied I could easily ask it when I was feeling nervous. Then I thought of more. "What are the rules of the game? What does a person do when he or she enrolls? How do we keep score? What is the role of mentorship? And how does personal improvement fit into success?" These questions were coming so quickly now that I couldn't rehearse them; I couldn't organize them, heck, I couldn't even remember them all. I looked frantically for a piece of paper to write on. The best I could do while driving was the back of a scorecard from baseball practice. I wrote as fast as I could. But no matter how fast I wrote, my mind was going at supersonic speed and my hand was stuck in first gear. I ignored the notion that I was limited to three questions. I wrote everything down that came to mind. I figured that if I hurried I would have a couple of minutes to at least refine or organize them before I would ask Glenna *the* magically insightful questions. To my dismay, Glenna had arrived exactly at the same time I did. No time for formal improvement to the questions, but at least I had something to talk about.

We sat down at a booth. Glenna ordered a small meal and I had only water with a slice of lemon. The truth was that I had spent money I didn't have on gas getting to this meeting. There wasn't any money for dinner. The waitress left, and we got down to business. I didn't want to waste Glenna's time with too much small talk so I started in with my questions by asking about the founders of the company and her upline mentors. She smiled, seemingly aware of my desire to be quick and respectful. She let me ask, but her response took me a bit by surprise. She responded with a couple of questions of her own.

She began by asking me about why I wanted to meet with her, and before I could answer she asked what I wanted to accomplish by starting my own business? I suddenly felt like I was being called on by the teacher to answer a question that I knew the answer to, but now that I was on the spot, I couldn't think straight. Glenna continued to press me for my goals or aspirations for the business.

I struggled for a few minutes to explain what I was feeling and how I wanted desperately to change my circumstances, beginning with creating enough income so Sara could go to the grocery store and buy what she wanted, instead of what I could afford as a schoolteacher. Glenna pressed for something bigger, more impressive or longer reaching. I recounted what I had been through over the past few years and made a stand on having my dreams beat out of me by life. I reiterated that grocery shopping was about as far as I could really allow myself to dream at this point. She sighed and told me she had been in a similar circumstance earlier in her life and that she could empathize with me. She had made a determination that money would no longer make decisions for her when she began her career with XL-8.

Glenna had been making six figures for a long time now; but her goal was to achieve the highest level in the company and that would happen by helping one more person become a leader in the business. She wanted desperately to make a real difference to people in developing countries by helping to end hunger and get clean water in those places where there are life-threatening challenges. She longed to teach self-reliance and provide opportunities to people in every aspect of their lives. For her to make a significant contribution, she would have to stand on the stage with all the other big leaders in the company. And then there were those prestigious trips the company offered to the very best producers; they would be incredible as well. As I listened, she sounded as serious about this goal as I had ever been about playing in major league stadiums, marrying Sara, winning state championships, or changing my current circumstances.

She caught herself in mid-dream and quickly changed the subject from her goals and dreams to what I had wanted to discuss with her. I handed her the questions I had scribbled on the back of a scorecard. She read for a moment and contemplated how she would respond. Then she grabbed the napkin on the table and started to draw a diagram. As she drew, she shared a story about how she learned what she was about to tell me. She told me about her mentor David McKay, a Double Platinum in XL-8. He told her that all success comes as a result of tapping into, or creating systems that have proven to predictably produce results.

David told her if she wanted to create debt, want, lack, and stress, use the established systems that predictably produce these results. Namely, working for someone else at some job somewhere, making someone else's dreams come true. If she wanted financial freedom, the ability to pursue her passions, and to control her future and the decisions of her everyday life, then she needed to master a specific set of skills embodied in a system that creates those results. He went on to tell her that every system creates a result; so choose what result you want, pay the price to learn how to optimize that system, and predictably move through its success pattern to the greatest rewards of that system. For example, Glenna continued, "The education system is one that rewards you emotionally when students do well. So if it's emotional support you need, then the education system produces that result. But if it's wealth, riches, and financial security you desire, then the greatest reward of that system will never be more than subsistence living." She expressed her gratitude for having had a mentor willing to share this with her from the start of her career.

When she finished the story, her diagram had three sections with the headings "Improve Yourself," "Build a Team," and "Become a Leader." She called this diagram the "3-Step Success Pattern" because David told her, without drawing anything, that there were the three steps: (1) Improve Yourself, (2) Build a Team, and (3) Become a Leader. There were personal effectiveness requirements that went along with each step. She continued, "Over the last few years I have further developed the diagram as I have been helping my team to grow to a six-figure income. David preached three underlying principles that made what I call the '3-Step Success Pattern' work, and they are critical to implement. Principle number one is to start at the start. Many people skip right over this step and end up quitting or starting over. So he told me starting right is always better than starting over. Principle number two is to build personal effectiveness before building the team. He taught me that higher PEPs equal higher checks. And principle number three is to follow the proven pattern that creates predictability. All of these principles are kind of like the operating system to the success pattern, the ingredients that allow the recipe to consistently create the same loaf of bread," she explained.

Below each heading there were some numbers associated with the letters *PEPs* (whatever that meant) and then "Critical Skills," "Time Allocation Focus," "Business Characteristics," and lastly, "Goals" for each section.

3-STEP SUCCESS PATTERN™

IMPROVE YOURSELF	BUILD A TEAM	BECOME A LEADER
0-30 PEPS 14-30 Days	31-45 PEPS 60-120 Days	46-70 PEPS 10 Leaders
*20 Critical Initial Skills	*20 Critical Building Skills	*10 Critical Leadership Skills
Time Focus	Time Focus	Time Focus
Action Items	Action Items	Action Items
		Goals
	Goals	
Goals		

Of course I didn't understand any of what she wrote. She began explaining the answer to my questions about the rules of the game; predictability, mentorship, how to know if I was winning, and the place of personal improvement, were all contained in this diagram.

She discussed each section of the success pattern; that PEPs, or personal effectiveness points, were a measurement of a person's skill and knowledge in the critical skills, and that there were specific critical skills to master in each section of the success pattern—just as there are critical skills in each aspect of baseball, or teaching school, or anything else for that matter. She went on to explain that PEPs tell us whether we are prepared to take the next step in the process of creating job-dropping residual income. She even had a clever saying about this —"Higher checks come from higher PEPs." I chuckled at this saying. It seemed so obvious and yet somehow foreign at the same time. She also told me there were certain characteristics or activities that I needed to pay attention to in each phase, as well as goals specific to knowing when I was ready to advance to the next level of success.

She took a deep breath, paused for a moment, put down her pen, took a drink of water, and told me that she would share the details of the whole diagram as it became relevant. The beauty of the success pattern was that it helped people understand the most important part of the business: "You must get people to move toward you and then with you. Enroll people who want to succeed, and then teach them how to think and take appropriate action to succeed."

Glenna caught herself, realizing that I wasn't even in the business yet, and slowed the pace, not wanting to overwhelm me all at once with too much information. But she did let me know what the "Improve Yourself phase" was all about. She explained that I needed to take an on-line assessment called the Personal Effectiveness Profile or PEProfile. She needed to get a read on what skills I was already competent in, what skills I was adequate in, and what specific skills I needed to work on.

"An on-line assessment of my skills," I responded. "I have always been taught that tests are often used to classify and label kids, and I don't really want to be labeled or pigeon-holed as a specific kind of person." Glenna told me, "There are not right and wrong answers on the assessment and there are no labels from it. It's simply a snapshot of your current abilities and knowledge in the critical skills contained in the success pattern. It's the only way that you can know what you are good at and what areas you need to pay specific attention to in order to grow your business faster and with less frustration. This will greatly help me in counseling you, and for you to get through the Improve Yourself phase in as little as fourteen to thirty days. Without it you are left to chance and luck, instead of choice and meaningful, appropriate action taken in its proper sequence."

She explained that one of the ways to establish what I needed to do when I enrolled was to look at the PEProfile report and then take action based on results and facts instead of emotion. The report would give her great insight as to exactly what I needed to read, listen to, and what to practice. This way I could start building my business with purpose through effective action. Otherwise, I would be implementing what she called the "enroll, hope, and replace" strategy, which is to run around enthusiastically telling all your friends that you found something great, and that they should let you tell them about it!

Glenna said that effective action leads to long-term success; security and generational wealth is built on a foundation of skill and knowledge along with a team of capable partners who can build the business with or without you. Financial freedom and generational wealth come from calculated, consistent work applied toward meaningful goals. She told me that I would hear many people talk of quick riches without work, struggle, or personal growth. The notions, such as the average guy can succeed in this business, mud slinging, and faking it till you make it, are all artificial methods intended to get people out the door and motivated to work—whether they are ready to do the work or not.

The results of my profile report would tell us which phase of the 3-Step Success Pattern I was in, and what specific areas I should focus on. Glenna told me that, of course, the first step to success is to enroll in the company with Doug as my sponsor. But that was only a first step. She looked to me for some kind of confirmation that I was willing, able, and committed to at least take the first step. I nodded my agreement and then she did something I hadn't expected at all. She offered to mentor me! My heart skipped a couple of beats. How could she be willing to take that kind of chance on me, someone she had only briefly met once before, and only a second time now in a restaurant? My reaction must have tipped her off to my anxiousness of her seemingly generous offer. Then she clarified the conditions under which she would invest her time and expertise with me. She agreed to mentor me if, and only if, I agreed to take the PEProfile before the next weekly meeting, get on product autoship, purchase tickets to the next monthly event in four weeks, commit to come to the weekly meetings and Saturday trainings at her home, to do exactly what she told me to do and, lastly, embrace and religiously follow the success pattern. I felt a little like I had when I asked my father-in-law if he would give me his blessing to ask Sara to marry me.

I took a drink of water to buy myself a moment to contemplate what it all might mean and what the down side could be. I gulped and then as if I had just made the greatest trade in the world, I held out my hand to shake on our deal. Glenna told me she would give me the next assignments as we worked together. But first things first; she gave me the link to the PEProfile, encouraged me to take it as soon as possible and to enter her email address as the upline mentor. I was not to worry about what any of it meant until she could review it with me next week after the meeting.

I told her that I had overheard Doug and Cindy talking after the last meeting and I asked her why Doug hadn't told Cindy to do these things. (He had simply instructed her to make a list and begin talking to the people on it.) Glenna confided in me, "Doug has spent his whole life taking short cuts; he has heard different speakers on CDs and in various events talk about taking massive action and throwing mud at the wall to see if some sticks. So he follows what he thinks is the easiest and shortest way to enroll people, thinking that somehow enrolling people will create long-term success."

In all the excitement of the evening, I completely lost track of time. I looked at my watch and, to my surprise and horror, it was 1:30 in the morning! I shot out of the seat as if I had been shocked. I didn't want to seem disrespectful, but I had a bus to catch in just a few hours to the state baseball tournament. She told me she understood. "There was a time not too long ago when I had a job to get to as well." I thanked Glenna for her time, patience, and willingness to help me, then I excused myself.

4

A New Plan

On the way home I was anticipating the conversation I was going to have with Sara. How was I going to explain all that I had just agreed to, including spending our date money on a test that was going to tell me all the things I needed to work on to build this "simple" business that I haven't even enrolled in yet? I imagined her telling me that she could do that, she knows me better than anyone. No need to spend any money for what she could easily and gladly tell me for free.

When the alarm went off I had been asleep for only a few hours. I was scrambling to get ready to leave my classroom with a substitute, to live in a hotel for a few days, with all the equipment necessary for the tournament, and to keep the kids on track while living away from their parents. The bus came on time and a miracle of all miracles occurred, every kid was there with all his gear. During the bus ride I mulled over in my head the rules of the game. What was somewhat troubling was that I wasn't nervous about the tournament. I was thinking about the rules of the game as Glenna had explained them. The epiphany for me was that there were rules, which to me meant there was also predictability. It also meant that I needed to be just as patient and caring to people as Glenna had been to me. I got the feeling from her, that telling people what to do was probably not a great success strategy. I needed to appeal to what others wanted and what action they were committed to take to change their circumstances. This wasn't going to be like the military, my classroom, or the team.

We got to the hotel and changed into our uniforms, loaded the bus with the game equipment, and went to the fields to get ready for our first game. Because we had won our district tournament we were matched against an easier team. However, I couldn't tell the kids that. They needed to stay focused on playing and executing with precision. I reminded them that a loss anywhere in the tournament ended our team goal of winning a state championship. So we needed to stay focused and in the game at all times.

In our first game we were ahead by three runs in the fifth inning. But the other team was mounting a rally. There was one out, and runners on first and third, and the best hitter in the state was up to bat. I called time out and went to talk to the team. I was going to *tell* my pitcher and infielders what we were going to do, and when I was satisfied that everyone was on the same page, I gave the pitcher a pat on the back and retreated to the dugout. On the way back to the dugout something Glenna had said came to me. "The most important thing in this business is to get people moving toward you and then with you. Enroll people who want to succeed, and then teach them how to think and take appropriate action to succeed." What did this have to do with baseball? I wondered, and then shook it off. What I had told them to do worked, and we got out of the inning and won the game. Winning our first game gave us a break until that evening. We had to wait for everyone else to play their first game, and for the teams who lost their first game to play again in the consolation bracket.

I decided to take the kids back to the hotel where we could be in the air-conditioned rooms and eat a decent lunch, to get prepared for our second game. The weird thoughts I had while I was walking back to the dugout returned. "The most important thing in this business is to get people moving toward you and then with you. Enroll people who want to succeed, and then teach them how to think and take appropriate action to succeed." It suddenly dawned on me what this had to do with baseball. I had spent years getting these kids to fully enroll in my program—to do and think what I would think and do on every pitch. They had mastered the skills and knowledge to be successful. As I thought about the other coaches of the teams we had recently played, I recalled that their players didn't seem to be able to do anything without being told what to do every minute. I had actually mastered this success principle in my coaching career without even knowing it. And as a testament to what Glenna had taught me, it absolutely created success; two state championships in four years and still in the running for a third.

In our second game a similar situation came up. We needed to gather on the pitchers mound and make a strategic decision. Only this time I asked the pitcher and infielders what they thought we should do. They were shocked at the question. It was quiet for a minute, and then Dan Jacobsen gave his opinion with a question in his voice as if he was answering a test question in my geography class. "I was thinking the same thing," I said and we agreed. On the way back to the dugout it occurred to me that I had been teaching these boys for years now all that they needed to know to win—with or without me. For the first time I wondered if all the trips to the pitchers mound to bark orders was nothing more than a confirmation of what they already knew how to do. They executed perfectly, the threat was over, and we won as a result. The kids were elated, not only because we won, but because we were now in the championship game.

That night I thought about who could really lead this team if I wasn't there? Dan Jacobsen's name kept coming to my mind. I called his room and asked him to come and meet with me. I explained how I had admired his leadership skills and desire to set the proper example for the other kids. I told him the only reason I had ever chastised him was that I could see real greatness in him; I wanted him to reach his potential. He shared how he felt when I got on him about the base-running mistake in front of the whole town at the game a few weeks earlier—the time that had alerted Doug to my stress level. I asked him if he would mind making out our lineup for the championship game?

Dan was speechless. No one knew yet that I was going to retire as the coach and that, win or lose tomorrow, it would be my last game as head coach. I wanted this win to be theirs. They had worked and sacrificed as much as I had. They had given up a big part of their childhood. I justified this move by convincing myself that I just wanted to enjoy a game for once, looking on like a proud parent, teacher, and coach of capable young men who were willing and able to meet any challenge the other team could put before them.

They were ready. They didn't really need me, but I was like a security blanket for them. They knew what to do. Now on high school's biggest stage, they were going to prove it to themselves. The lineup wasn't exactly as I would have made out, but it did have merit, so we went with it. I even had Dan present the lineup card to the home plate umpire before the game. As a kind of ritual before each game, the home plate umpire explains any unusual ground rules to each team and wishes them good luck. Customarily, each team is represented by a coach—but not this time. Dan, our shortstop, was representing our team. The other coach didn't know how to react. Dan was nervous, but with a smile that reached from one ear to the other, he reached out and shook the hand of the other team's coach. The other kids gave him a little razzing, but he handled it beautifully. He just kept right on smiling as if the team was suddenly his, and no one was going to rain on his parade.

The championship game was a good one. We took an early lead and they came back to tie it up. In the top of the last inning we faced a challenge. Their best players were going to be batting after we had our chance to hit. So we knew we needed to score at least one run. Ben Chapman, the one kid who I wouldn't have put in the line-up, was the first batter we had coming up. Ben hadn't done much during the season and, as a kind of sanity check, I looked at Dan to see if he was nervous, maybe thinking that I should replace Ben with someone else. I decided to let him bat and then take things from there.

To all of our amazement, he got on base. Our eighth-place batter bunted him to second. With one out, our ninth-place batter hit a bloop fly ball. As soon as the ball was hit, Ben took off. Terror came over me when I saw him running. There was no way he could know if the ball would be caught by the shortstop, or the center fielder, or the left fielder. If any of them caught the ball, it would be an easy double play, then we would have to face their best hitters in a tie game. Ben was determined though. He ran as if his life depended on it. As it happened, the ball went just over the shortstop's glove and landed softly on the outfield grass. So determined was he that he didn't stop at third; he just kept on going toward home plate. No one on the other team had expected him to continue on such a shortly hit ball. Ben had caught them by surprise and by the time they realized what had happened, he had scored the go-ahead run. The other team was in such shock that they didn't do anything during their turn at bat. We won! And Ben had scored the game and championship-winning run. We won, and the kids knew they had made it happen. They had learned and now applied the skills and knowledge we had practiced in simulated games and practices for years. But in the end, they knew it was their effectiveness in the fundamentals of hitting, pitching, catching, and base running that made the difference on the field.

I learned as much in the past few days as any of the kids for sure. More than just learning, I had been able to see what a difference it made to teach success principles—let others govern themselves and take responsibility and accountability for the success they were pursuing. What a great way to end my coaching career. It overwhelmed me when I looked back on all that had transpired over the past half decade. Then I realized that this was not the end of my coaching career, it was only a transition from coaching high school kids to a new career of coaching adults to be successful in life. As I rode the bus home that night, the importance of the lessons I had already learned from Glenna and the responsibility of helping others to learn, practice, and apply success principles overcame me. I thought of the parents that I had dealt with as a teacher and as a coach. Not many of them knew or practiced success principles when I saw them. And these were going to be the very people I was going to be talking to about making their lives better. I wondered how this could even be possible? The best news of all is that succeeding in XL-8 will mean more than pats on the back and trophies in the school memorial case. It will mean a different life and lifestyle.

When we got to the outskirts of town, there was a group of cars lined up on Main Street. The welcoming committee intended to let the whole town know that we had arrived home victorious. Horns honked; people yelled and screamed as we drove to the school to drop off the kids; parents and friends greeted us as we got off the bus. It seemed like the whole town was there. The spoils of victory are often the memories and feelings of winning more than the trophies themselves. By the time everyone left, and I got the equipment put away and went home, it was after 3:00 AM. The light was on in the living room and there was a banner with streamers hanging across the far wall, congratulating me on a great year and another championship.

Sara and the kids were sound asleep. As I sat enjoying a good look at the banner hanging in my living room, I remembered my commitment to take the Personal Effectiveness Profile before the meeting on Tuesday. Immediately, the emotional issue of money came back to my mind. How am I going to break it to Sara that I have committed to spend money we didn't have on the assessment that Glenna had made me promise to take. I decided to tell her while she was sleeping, somehow hoping that in her half-conscience state, she would be more willing to agree. She stirred a little, congratulated me on the championship, and then, to my surprise, she approved of the expenditure. How could this be? Well, I wasn't about to question my luck so I left it alone and went back downstairs, wondering what this magical assessment was all about and if I would pass.

My oldest son was the first to wake up in the morning. He welcomed me home with a jump and a pounce. I opened one eye and his nose was about one centimeter from mine. He had a smile from ear to ear. He was so excited. I was his hero, the champion of the world in his eyes. He was so proud that we had won the state championship again. This was three years out of five. Essentially his whole life had been immersed in winning championships. The other children soon joined in. Sara looked so happy seeing her knight in shining armor rolling around on the floor with her kids. She stood there for a moment and then reminded us that we needed to get ready for church.

While we were getting ready to go, Sara told me that Glenna had called and welcomed us to the business while I was gone. She explained a few things like investing in the business and supporting each other in building it. "So when you got home I knew that you needed to take the profile. I was interested to see how you would tell me about it. However, I must admit I didn't think you would try to do it while you thought I was asleep. You know that I am fully behind you on this—if it's what you think we ought to do. I need you to tell me how to help you and what I need to do. I have already planned for a few dates that won't cost any money at all to offset the cost of some of the things Glenna told me about. She also encouraged me to go to appointments with you when there would be women so that I could help them see the business from a woman's point of view. I don't know how many of the meetings I can go to because of the kids and other commitments, but I will go at least a couple of times a week. I need a couple of product catalogues so I will know what we have. I will also make sure you have dinner and clean clothes for the business. I know you will be gone a lot and I am used to that, but I can also help you keep up with your appointment schedule. I will put a date appointment in the schedule for you each week so you don't forget, especially when you really get busy trying to fit people in. If there is anything else you need, you have to let me know at least a few days ahead of time," she said. What a blessing to have a supportive partner helping to keep me on track and build with me!

That Sunday morning was a bright sunny one—not a cloud in the sky and a pretty brisk breeze. We got to church and received congratulations from everyone. It was hard not to smile and feel extremely blessed: great wife, awesome kids, membership in the church, and a third state championship.

That evening after the kids were in bed and quiet, I was gazing at that banner again and began to wonder how and why I was going to give this up? At that moment a strong gust of wind blew through the open windows and knocked over the tray holding our mail. We affectionately called it our bill tray, instead of our mail tray. And when it hit the floor, it made a bang. That bang startled me back to the reality of my circumstances. No money, lots of debt, and a job that failed to meet our most basic needs as a family. I decided I would begin to take action on creating my new life beginning tomorrow by taking the PEProfile, studying the success pattern until I had it memorized, scheduling time for the Saturday training events and the meetings on Tuesday nights. I would enroll in the business. Sara and I had looked at the product line and decided what we wanted on our autoship order. If there was more to this, I was too tired to want to know about it then, and I drifted off to sleep on the couch.

During this time Glenna had been formulating a plan to get to the next promotion level. She was at the fourth of five promotion levels in the compensation plan and was making a six-figure income, but it wasn't producing the results she wanted most. She realized this was probably her best chance to see if the business and circumstances randomly chose winners and losers. She privately wondered if success was truly about predictability—a matter of skill and choices made in the proper sequence—or luck and chance. She decided to test her theory that knowledge and skill really do make a difference. Never before had she had students that she felt were more eager to learn and accept the challenge of success than Steve and Sara Thoms.

Glenna's old high school friend, Gary Kirk, was now the vice president of training at a Fortune 500 company. He didn't know anything about network marketing, so he wouldn't have any preconceived notions about it. His credentials were impeccable: three degrees from major universities, published in mainstream magazines, author of multiple books, and, best of all, he had a passion for designing systems that helped people from all walks of life succeed faster and with less frustration, which he had done in many different industries. Glenna arranged a meeting with him.

They exchanged a few pleasantries when she walked into his office. He invited her to sit down and she described her problem. As she began to talk, Gary's face lit up. This was just the kind of challenge he lived for. He listened for a few minutes and then began writing three phrases on the whiteboard in his office:

- What you focus on expands.
- People will do what you reward them for.
- People crave, even live for, recognition, far more than they love or want money.

To illustrate this he told her a story of how his father had been in the car business. Often his dad would have contests for the sales teams. He had offered money to them as an incentive for selling more cars, but no one seemed to be very excited about working harder for that kind of reward. Then he offered a television set as a reward for winning the contest, and suddenly everyone became excited. They came to work earlier, they stayed later. They came in on weekends; they called old customers; they called people right out of the phone book. Of course, the results followed with increased sales.

"So how does that story relate to your situation?" Gary asked. "Well, what behavior are you actually trying to get people to do, and what are the predictable results of that behavior?" Glenna had noticed that when people enrolled and then hurriedly made a list of the people they knew, followed by enthusiastically or excitedly talking to those people in an attempt to enroll them, about 85 percent of the time they stayed in the business for about sixty to ninety days and then quit. And often not only did they quit, but they were angry and bitter about the products, the company, and the industry.

At the same time, the people who stayed in longer than ninety days always seemed to spend time in the beginning learning, studying, and practicing what they had been reading and listening to; acting in a predetermined sequential way; and doing things in a specific progression. They mastered language, listening, and conversational skills, combining them with some basic knowledge about the products and compensation plan, then applying them to contact and invite others. When they made appointments, they called someone with more advanced presentation skills to take it from there. This process continued until they had learned and practiced more advanced skills, progressing to more and more of the business activities, until finally they could do everything by themselves.

"The problem with this discovery method is that only a few people are willing and patient enough to go through it. It takes years to do it this way. But once a person reaches competence, they are an awesome leader with an incredible income and lifestyle. And we put these people on the stage and they say 'If we could do it anyone can,'—anyone willing to pay the price can live like high achievers!" Glenna added, "If there were a way to shorten the amount of time it takes to get people to acquire skill and knowledge, so they could actually reap the rewards, that would be great. We do have some incredible tools at our disposal. We have the Personal Effectiveness Profile and a perfectly correlated audio library that correlates directly to the critical skills specified in the profile." She showed him a couple of profile report examples and then how the CDs were mapped to the profile. Gary was impressed that someone would have been savvy enough to put together this diagnostic assessment with a learning system.

"I don't think we need more tools," Glenna said. "I think we need more people to use the ones we have—to get them to buy into the cause and effect, and predictability, of a three-step 'Improve Yourself, Build a Team and Become a Leader' success pattern that I constantly talk about." Glenna wrote the diagram on the whiteboard beside Gary's bullet points.

3-STEP SUCCESS PATTERN™

IMPROVE YOURSELF	BUILD A TEAM	BECOME A LEADER
0-30 PEPS 14-30 Days	31-45 PEPS 60-120 Days	46-70 PEPS 10 Leaders
*20 Critical Initial Skills	*20 Critical Building Skills	*10 Critical Leadership Skills
Time Focus 95% on personal effectiveness 5% on recruiting	**Time Focus** 15% on personal improvement 50% on recruiting 30% on training new people 5% on retention	**Time Focus** 10% on personal improvement 15% recruiting 65% training people to become leaders 10% on retention
Action Items 1. Get associate# 2. Enroll on product autoship or autopay 3. Have tickets to next event 4. Take the PEProfile 5. Gain a firm knowledge and testimony of company and products 6. Memorize contacting scripts 7. Make an effective list of 200 names 8. Subscribe to education system 9. Have personal improvement plan	**Action Items** 1. 20-30 hours per week commitment 2. 8-10 personal contacts per week 3. 60% conversion rate on contacts and personal presentations 4. 90% conversion rate of follow-ups 5. Take PEProfile quarterly 6. Register team for education system	**Action Items** 1. Full time/professional commitment 2. Training using team PEProfile results 3. Enroll 2 new personals each month 4. Promote 1 new leader per month
Goals 1. Increase PEPs to30+ 2. Score green or yellow in first 20 skills 3. Enroll 1-5 customers/associates 4. Receive products for FREE	**Goals** 1. Increase PEPs to 45+ 2. Score green/yellow in team-building skills 3. 15-25 associates on team 4. 3-5 committed to leadership track 5. Break even and then earn at least $2,500 in residual income	**Goals** 1. Increase PEPs to 70+ 2. Score green or yellow in leadership skills 3. Increase team PEPs average to over 30 4. 250+ team members 5. 15 or more leaders 6. 20+ serious builders 7. 100 people on autoship or autopay 8. 100 in education system and events 9. 50 recognized on stage

"When I talk about this to my team, most of them look at me like I did when my mother would tell me to eat all my vegetables. I heard this so often that her plea became background noise to the other more interesting and relevant table talk."

Gary asked her at what point do people normally begin, if not at the beginning? Glenna quickly interjected, "They skip over the 'Improve Yourself phase' and go right to contacting, presenting, and selling." "And doing that results in them remaining in the business for about ninety days?" Gary asked. Glenna nodded her agreement. "So, back to my original points," Gary said, pointing at the whiteboard. "What are you focusing on in your training? Personal improvement and the natural result of it on income over time, or activity no matter what it results in?" Before she could respond, he asked the second question, "What are you rewarding them for, building a strong foundation of skill and knowledge, or a frenzy of activity? Remember my father didn't reward for activity in and of itself, he rewarded his sales people for sales."

Then the third principle came out. People live for recognition. Gary probed, regarding this more deeply. He asked about the kind of recognition a person gets for personal improvement, versus activity, versus results. What is the recognition for each and does a person get the same reward no matter which they achieve? Glenna was lost in a flurry of thoughts. For a moment she was caught in the first question, and then the second. She hadn't even heard the complexity of the last question, but she answered anyway. "Everyone is recognized on stage at our events for about the same amount of time, unless they achieve some really big milestone. And the only difference between activity and results are that we give a lapel pin for promotion level advancements based on sales volume. We don't recognize anyone at all for anything related to the Improve Yourself phase."

"No wonder no one engages in this first step in your success pattern. Why would they? Is it really a 3-Step Success Pattern or a Two-Step Success Pattern? The reason I ask is because you don't put any importance on the Improve Yourself phase. You don't focus on it except to nag them about it; you don't reward them for it, and you don't recognize them for doing it! Tell me more about this on-line assessment."

Glenna explained that it was a snapshot of the current level of mastery a person has in regard to skill and knowledge in critical areas sequenced in the success pattern. "How accurate is it?" Gary asked. "It's a little scary how close it is to what people really know about themselves, but don't want anyone else to know," she added. "And the audio library that is mapped to the assessment, who made it and why is he on the cover?" Gary continued. "The same guy who developed the profile produced the audios as well. He has been a six-figure earner in the industry and created these tools to help anyone in any company understand what to do," she added. "So this guy isn't in your company?" Gary inquired. "No. He's working to be an industry change agent instead of developing his own organizations," Glenna responded. Gary chuckled as he said, "Sounds like my kind of guy."

"Okay, I think I understand the success pattern and PEPs and that people need to take action in the correct order. But I'm not clear on how the business actually works, and what the key indicators of success are in the Build a Team and Become a Leader phases," Gary said. Glenna had no idea what Gary just asked. Gary saw the confusion in her face. Before she could respond, he clarified his questions by asking, "How do people make money? What do they do? What is the process people go through to create sales?" Confidently Glenna explained that normally they make a list of people they know, contact the people on the list, do a business or product presentation, follow up and enroll those who are interested in the products or business opportunity. Then they repeat this over and over again for themselves and help others to do the same.

"How do you track your team members' effectiveness in each of these areas?" Gary asked. "Well, we usually only keep track of enrollments and, to a vague degree, we suggest they do fifteen to twenty presentations per month to create some level of success," she answered. Gary told her that she must start keeping very close track of each of these numbers independently if she was going to create real predictability in a process for success. He continued by asking her how success was generally defined in the industry. She responded by telling him, "Most people talk of being millionaires from the stage, but I think it's more common to say creating a six-figure income." Gary asked for further explanation about how people are trained to be successful. Glenna sighed and said, "Reading books, listening to educational and inspirational CDs, weekly training meetings where the trainer stands at the front of the room and lectures, or sometimes we do role playing. We also have what we call 'phone zone'—where the downline calls people on their names list and the upline listens in on the conversation and then offers suggestions after the call is over," she continued.

"Any kind of real-world skill training in a simulated environment, you know like pilots and firemen use?" Gary asked. "No nothing like that," Glenna said, wondering where all this was going. "We assume that people can talk to each other and refer their friends and neighbors to use products that are better than they are using now. Most people are already doing what they would need to do now; they're just not getting paid for it," she added.

"Okay, I think I have enough information to get started," Gary concluded. "I'm sure what I come up with from this meeting will not be the whole program, but it will be a place to get started." He sat down and thought for a moment. The silence was uncomfortable, but Glenna didn't want to interrupt his thought process. He was staring at the whiteboard, drumming the fingers of one hand on the desk and quietly humming. After a few minutes he stood up and went to the board. He told Glenna, "We are going to call the project Operation Six Figures," he said with as much authority as he had. "Here is what I recommend we do." The word *we* caught Glenna's attention. Gary was on board with her idea. He would put his years of experience to work for her so she wouldn't have to invent this on her own. Gary continued, "We are going to use the PEProfile as a thirty-day challenge contest. Those who accept the challenge will take the assessment at the beginning and again at the end of the month. We will show the results to each individual as before and after shots," he continued.

"On stage we are going to recognize people for the most overall improvement and the greatest amount of increase in the Improve Yourself phase." Glenna interrupted and asked about the second and third phase improvement. Gary smiled and told her she was already recognizing people for this. "Remember your recruiting and sales volume awards," he reminded. "And we also want to make sure to recognize people who are coming to and embracing your weekly trainings." "The problem so far is that precious few are coming to the trainings," Glenna said.

"Okay then, we will begin to recognize people on stage for their accomplishments directly related to the training. We will also have a thirty-day contest and a three-month contest for the specific skills you teach, like edification; compensation plan knowledge; product, company and industry knowledge; commitment; goal setting; personal improvement plan; effective names lists; and anything else we can think of. But let's start with a few basics, and then if we need to expand we can," he brainstormed.

Glenna was excited to see her idea taking shape. Gary told her he had heard that she had become a very successful businesswoman. He wondered how it all worked, but he was confused why she hadn't implemented this before now. She told him there was a very established way of doing things in the industry and no one ever seems particularly willing to take on the tradition of those who have come before, especially those have been very successful in their own right. "The problem with most of the established leaders is that they can't really explain how or why they have become successful themselves. Kind of weird when you think of it," she explained.

"But the bottom line is that what I have been doing so far has produced the result I have been getting so far. I am almost at the top of my company's compensation structure, but not quite, and I am stuck at this level. I have three of the five groups necessary to be promoted to the highest level. And my goal is to be at the highest level; to run with the biggest dogs in this pack. What I have been teaching so far has created great results for me, but at the end of every month it's a scramble; kind of like dialing for dollars to make those last-minute sales before midnight. What I have been doing so far hasn't created the greatest reward, or a secure residual income stream or generational wealth for me or anyone on my team yet.

"That's why I want to do this. Honestly I don't think I have much to lose. The majority of my team is probably going to ignore all of this anyway and continue to do what they have always done. Thinking that this is some new ploy to try and find the silver bullet that would get everyone to do more, another feeble attempt to get everyone on the stage for recognition—even if that recognition is fake or contrived.

"If this works, it will launch my business to incredible success and many of the people who embrace it will also receive the greatest promises of the industry, and that's what excites me the most. *Hype* and *hopium* will be replaced with *promise* and *predictability*."

There was a moment of peace in the room as if they had just solved all the worlds' problems. Glenna asked what the next steps were. Gary told her to keep him informed on a regular basis how things were going and, if she wanted him to, he would attend the next monthly meeting.

Glenna agreed and thanked him for his time and energy. Walking to the door she gave him the time and date of the next monthly meeting and then got into her car.

On the way home a feeling of appreciation for such great friends in her life came over her and after a few minutes she reflected on what the ramifications or fall out would be if she actually implemented this plan in her group. How would her team react and respond? For that matter, how would her upline react and respond? She was alone with her thoughts for a few minutes and during that time the excitement of moving forward was beginning to well up in her. A tear came to her eye as she pondered the possibility of greater success. This is my time, she thought and then said, "This is my time," out loud, "and by golly I'm going to do it! This Tuesday I am going to roll this out to the team in the meeting after the meeting. When I get home I need to call everyone and let them know that they don't want to miss this week's meeting, that there will be a big announcement after the business presentation."

5

The Success Pattern

I answered the last question on the Personal Effectiveness Profile and clicked the submit button for the last time. My results of the assessment were immediately presented along with a way for me to print the one page report. When I saw the report I stared for what seemed like a long time. My heart sank—a fourteen! What kind of nonsense was this? The wind was totally taken out of me. I didn't even feel like going to the meeting. I was totally depressed. I thought everyone there would know what a bonehead I was and that I would be chastised or ridiculed for my score.

This was the first test of my resolve to do what I had promised Glenna I would do only a few days ago. So I decided to go despite my anxiety about the profile. I had promised Glenna that I would do what she said, even if I didn't want to do it, or even if I didn't understand why I was doing it.

I humbly sat in the back row so as not to be noticed. Doug and Cindy came in at the same time. Doug welcomed me and introduced me to his new guest. They sat toward the front of the room next to Cindy, who had two guests of her own. Susan, the woman who had carefully arranged the cookies last week, got everyone's attention and invited us all to sit down. She did a great job of introducing Glenna. The presentation was awesome and I got some additional insight as to what I needed to do to create a strong and profitable business. Glenna made a point to invite Doug to stand up and say a few words about the business and how it was going for him. He seemed to relish the opportunity to speak to the group. He then talked about how proud he was of Cindy, who had just enrolled a week earlier. She had already enrolled two people, and had introduced the business to five others. He even did something I don't think ever happens, Doug gave Cindy a few moments to talk to the group. She told them to make a decision to chase their dreams and take massive action to achieve them, that the results will come as fast as you want them to in this business. Doug looked as if he were a proud parent watching his child.

When the presentation was over, a few guests stayed to ask questions of Glenna and Doug and to congratulate Cindy. Within ten minutes the room was empty of guests and those who didn't care about the announcement that Glenna had promoted to the team. Doug was so excited about Cindy, his new trophy star to be, and his new guest, that he almost forgot completely about me. I was ready to enroll and was filling out the paperwork while Doug was talking to Cindy about qualifying for the Winners' Circle award.

I completed the application and tried to clarify a couple of things with Doug, but he was so engrossed in the conversation with Cindy that I couldn't get a word in. I noticed Glenna was busy preparing for the meeting after the meeting, so I asked Susan if she could help me, which she did without reservation. The meeting after the meeting was short and to the point. Glenna announced that she was starting a promotion called Operation Six Figures and anyone who was interested should stay to find out the details.

Glenna told Doug that I had enrolled, but Doug shrugged it off as interesting yet insignificant. He seemed to live for enrolling people who can do the business without much coaching or coaxing, and Cindy was his new superstar. I was obviously going in a different direction, so he didn't pay much attention to me. After all, my purposeful action was not enthusiasm on fire.

Glenna started by telling the group that above the money and the lifestyle, Operation Six Figures would qualify people to be able to go with her on an all expenses paid Seminar at Sea. Each person who wanted to participate needed to enroll in the promotion and follow the guidelines very specifically. Glenna concluded with the clarification that not only did the participants have to create specific results, but they had to engage in specific activities in a specific order to qualify. Then she did something very interesting; she told us what the promotion was designed to do! Jen, who was in a different group than I was, whispered, "It's rare that the underlying purpose of a promotion is out in the open. The reward and the activities are always very clear, but beyond the promotion itself, most team members are left to themselves to figure out why they are supposed to do certain things within the promotion," Jen continued.

Glenna said this was all about becoming professionals in the business. "It's about personal effectiveness and doing things on purpose, with purpose, and doing those things in their proper sequence aimed at creating specific results, including duplication and predictability, residual income, and generational wealth. This promotion is about getting people started out right instead of just getting them started," Glenna explained.

Jen asked, "So what do we do exactly?" Glenna spelled out the promotion by telling us that we must qualify each of the next four months. In each month you need to: (1) be on autoship, (2) have tickets to the next event, (3) attend every Saturday training, (4) take the PEProfile, (5) register for and engage in our education system, (6) gain and share our knowledge and testimony of either the company or products in at least one weekly meeting per month, (7) read at least one book, and (8) in the next two months you must listen to the audios in the Improve Yourself set of *Skills of the Million-Dollar Earners*, memorize and (9) demonstrate at least one cold and warm market contacting approach at a Saturday training, (10) make an effective list of at least 200 names that is segmented into hot, warm, and chicken categories, and sorted by PEPs and (11) have a personal improvement plan in place.

In the third and fourth month you must: (1) listen to the audios in the Build a Team set of *Skills of the Million-Dollar Earners*, (2) contact at least eight new prospects each and every week, (3) enroll at least four new associates in the third and fourth month, and (4) have a PEProfile score of at least forty by the end of the fourth month.

Jen was writing as fast as she could, and in a bit of frustration she said there are things that we don't even know what they are or how to do them! Of course Glenna replied, "That's why we are having this meeting so, we can get clear on what to do and how all this will work out." She expounded,

- "With regards to autoship and sharing knowledge and testimony of the company and products, this is based on the most basic concept of business. You can't talk effectively about something you know nothing about or haven't experienced for yourself. So these parts are meant to help you get this foundational information and experience.

- "The Saturday training, monthly event, book, and audio CD requirements are based on the importance of learning from and being inspired by experts in the business. Each of you may start by reading *Think and Grow Rich* by Napoleon Hill, *How to Win Friends and Influence People* by Dale Carnegie, *Three Feet From Gold* by Sharon Lechter, *7 Habits of Highly Effective People* by Stephen Covey, the *One Minute Millionaire* by Mark Victor Hansen, or the *Success Principles* by Jack Canfield.

- "The PEProfile and personal improvement plan are critical for you to progress at an accelerated rate. They help you focus on areas you need specific help in and teach you how you can strengthen them.

- "Making a names list that is categorized and sorted, along with learning and practicing how to contact them, prepares you to take effective action when you move to the Build a Team phase.

•"And if you are diligent in the first two months of the promotion, the contacting and enrolling part of the promotion shouldn't be much of a problem. But if you don't do the first two months, the last two will be very challenging."

Glenna continued by making sure everyone knew that the first two months of the promotion were not at all focused on contacting, presenting, or enrolling; that was the second part. "This is a special promotion to help those who want to participate to create an incredible foundation that will accelerate their business growth and develop long-term stability in recruiting, training, and retaining people on their teams.

"There is also going to be a new club called the High Peppers for people who have at least thirty, forty-five, and seventy PEPs along with special awards for people in the promotion group with the highest profile score, the least amount of areas with red in the Improve Yourself phase of the success pattern and the largest improvement in PEPs during the promotion, starting this Saturday," she stated.

I wondered but didn't ask where Doug was and why wasn't everyone in this meeting? There must be some good reason for his absence, however Cindy wasn't here either! Jen and I were the first of ten associates to sign up for the promotion. In some ways, a kind of friendly competition began when we rushed to be the first to enroll for the promotion; a new friendship was born. The meeting ended, I arranged a personal coaching session for Thursday with Glenna. I went home with renewed passion and a set of specific things that I could work on.

On the way home I remembered that somewhere I had a copy of some of those books. They had helped me develop some of the characteristics of leadership that had made me a championship baseball coach and teacher. I wonder if reading them again with a different purpose would make any difference?

Over the next few days I made a serious attempt at reading the whole book, setting some goals around the specifics of my deficiencies on the PEProfile, and gaining a testimony of the products. I still couldn't believe that I got a fourteen on the profile. I started gathering names of people I knew around town, from school, parents, past friends, and so forth. The idea of categorizing them into hot, warm, and chicken lists didn't make any sense at all, but at least I would have them so that I could follow Glenna's recommendations.

In my meeting with Glenna I asked her a lot of questions about the success pattern. I wanted details about it and about the three phases. She gave some vague answers in regard to the Build a Team and Become a Leader phases, then saying that she would give me the specifics as they became relevant as next steps or for planning purposes. For now she told me to focus on personal improvement and getting the basics down until I reached thirty or more PEPs. I told her that I was reading the books from her reading list and was listening to the Improve Yourself set of audios and was planning to attend the weekly Saturday training.

I asked about the names list she was talking about and she told me that the people on my hot list were people who I knew well that I could just knock on their door and walk right in, or, those people who I felt comfortable enough with to just open the refrigerator and take out something without asking. "Typically these people are your family and very closest friends. The warm list people are those who know you and you know them, the kind of people you can call and will know you by name or with a very brief reminder will remember you. The chicken list has people you might be apprehensive to talk to about the business. Once you have the categories," she continued, "you need to estimate how many PEPs they have and put the people with the highest PEPs at the top of each list and the people with the lowest at the bottom, sorting everyone in between from high to low. In the next few weeks I'll be teaching you how to contact them and will help you accomplish that. Also, I'll schedule time to work with you to do some presentations with the ones who make appointments with you," Glenna encouraged. "But for now let's not worry too much about that. I will help you when you are ready, but we need to get your PEPs up first. For now, you need to spend about 95 percent of your time working on personal improvement in the areas indicated by your PEProfile report. Do you have it with you by chance?"

I pulled it out of the folder I was keeping my notes in and she asked me what I thought of it. I was eager to tell her I was surprised and embarrassed at my score on the test. She told me it wasn't a test; there aren't right and wrong answers, it's just a snap shot of my current abilities in certain areas. She reminded me that the Operation Six Figures promotion was intended to help everyone increase their PEPs so that when we started contacting, presenting, answering questions, overcoming objections, asking for the business, following up with prospects, and getting them started as customers and associates, that we would be really good at those skills ourselves. By then we would be able to get new people started in the right place by doing the right things that would lead to real duplication and income stability in the business.

A giant weight had been lifted from my shoulders. Now I understood the assessment better. I had suddenly wished that all the professors of all the classes I had taken could have so easily been able to tell me what I didn't know. I probably could have completed the ten years of college I had in about two years, and would have saved tens of thousands of dollars in the process.

As I was listening to Glenna talk about the specifics of what I needed to work on, my mind wandered momentarily. I thought about Doug, Cindy, and Jen; how many PEPs do they have? I asked Glenna where they were in the success pattern, pointing to the Build a Team phase on the diagram she had written during last week's meeting. Glenna said, "That's where they think they are!" Neither Doug, Cindy nor Jen had ever taken the assessment.

I tried to reconcile this in my mind. I asked, probably inappropriately, why she was emphasizing the PEProfile to the point where she created a promotion around it. "Well, I am learning for myself what it takes to achieve the highest level in the business. And I have been counseling with others. They have told me that it's critical to teach those who want to be big leaders what they really need to know to build the business on purpose to create a strong and profitable organization. Therefore, I invented this promotion to give incentives to my team, or those who want to participate, to learn the predictable success pattern and the specific skills and knowledge that prepare a leader to build and prosper in this industry—instead of just going out and creating chaos and hoping for the best," she added.

"Security in this business is built on a foundation of critical skills, essential knowledge, and effective action taken in its proper sequence," Glenna said emphatically. "Residual income and generational wealth comes from developing a team of capable partners who can build the business with or without you. Success comes from calculated and consistent work applied toward meaningful goals. Simply faking it until you make it and throwing mud at the wall hoping some will stick are gimmicks intended to motivate people to get out and do things they don't want to do and aren't prepared for, especially when they have spent a lot of time repelling their family and friends with their shear enthusiasm and ignorance on fire. Long-term success just doesn't happen this way. It's like success in baseball. You don't just throw the ball and tell your boys to go get' em do you? Of course not. You teach and practice everyday, and then you evaluate your progress by playing other teams. Well, network marketing is no different. You need to learn, practice, and improve your skills in specific areas so that on game day you will be prepared to take effective action that creates intentional results. Only in this business, your games are business activities like contacting, presenting, asking for the business, and enrolling prospects as either customers or associates," she continued.

"A big problem with the traditional enroll, hope, and replace strategy is that there are only two ways of keeping score; one is by how much money you make, and the other is by how many people you enroll. Of course, making money is the very reason you started your business. And enrolling people is one of the principle ways that you get paid. But it's not the best way to keep score early on in your business journey. Your journey to being a professional schoolteacher started in college, not the first paid day of school as the teacher. When you were in college, did you measure your success in income, lessons taught, or graduating seniors? No way! So, keeping score in this business in the beginning by using enrollments and income as the measuring sticks is no different. Income and enrollments are a few of the ways you keep score when you get to the Build a Team phase. And rest assured, that if you have at least thirty or more PEPs when you transition from the Improve Yourself phase to the Build a Team phase, your success will be significant because you will be taking purposeful action and you will be extremely effective at the things you do each day in your business.

"The challenge right now for Doug, and soon will be for Cindy, is that the people they recruit aren't professional sales people. Most people simply don't have the knowledge, skill, or PEPs to be effective at building a successful business in the beginning. In fact, neither Doug nor Cindy has ever built an effective business organization. They have spent their professional lives talking to people and making single transactional sales. Therefore, they try to apply this philosophy to network marketing and usually they can make a big splash in the beginning, for a short time. They soon realize that no one else can do what they can. And because the commissions are not thousands of dollars on each sale, like they are in real estate, they soon get tired of the hundred dollar checks that come from enrolling people faster than they quit. Most people quit out of frustration that they couldn't duplicate the results of a professional like Doug or Cindy.

"The promotion I have started gives you multiple ways of keeping score. You have the traditional ways of keeping score for the people who are in the Build a Team phase. Also, you have added ways of telling where you are in relation to financial goals related to residual income; that comes not only from enrollments, but from retention as well. I know that enrollments are a critical element to business. But let me tell you that your goal in this business is not only to get customers and associates. True residual income comes from getting and keeping customers and associates. The glue in your business is your ability to teach others to create success so they can build and maintain their own businesses with or without you. The challenge is that very few people know how to do this effectively. And that is what this promotion is all about; starting right instead of just starting. Because starting right is always better than starting over. The only reason I tell you all of this isn't to cast a negative light on others, but to help you see the cause and effect of how residual income really works as opposed to income from transactional sales like enrollments. By the way, I noticed that you didn't say you already had tickets to the monthly event. What's keeping you from that?" Glenna asked.

"Well I got into this as a way to make money, not spend it." I blasted back! "I have already paid to enroll, ordered products, bought the PEProfile and purchased audio CDs. Thank goodness that the weekly business and training meetings you have are free. I can't see how if I do what you want me to do in the next few weeks, I will make any money to cover the cost of what I have already spent. I know it will come eventually, but right now I simply don't have the money to buy anything else!" I think I caught her by surprise. I am grateful that she had high PEPs because she could have easily blown me right out of the business right then and there. However she handled it beautifully.

She started by clarifying that I hadn't spent any money. That instead I had invested it in the most important asset I had: me. She went on to tell me that money is an interesting thing when you think about it. It either earns or it burns. Investing money in personal improvement, the business, and people was a way to put a few dollars in and get 20's, 50's, and 100's back in return. "When your father-in-law gave you the $1,000, did you immediately go on a shopping spree, or did you enroll in XL-8, take the PEProfile and buy the audio library? The money you think you spent on these things will be multiplied many times over. That's money earning. On the other hand money burning is like buying a bag of potato chips instead of a personal improvement book, or using your time to play in the city softball league instead of learning, practicing, and applying the critical skills in this business that will provide the life you want your family to have."

My respect for Glenna and how she explained this increased a hundred fold. No wonder she was making six figures and was at the business level she was. I asked her if she had tickets with her so I could buy them right then. She, of course, did and I got them. Before we ended our meeting, Glenna expanded my diagram of the success pattern.

3-STEP SUCCESS PATTERN™

IMPROVE YOURSELF	BUILD A TEAM	BECOME A LEADER
0-30 PEPS	31-45 PEPS	46-70 PEPS
14-30 Days	60-120 Days	10 Leaders
*20 Critical Initial Skills	*20 Critical Building Skills	*10 Critical Leadership Skills
Time Focus	Time Focus	Time Focus
95% on personal effectiveness		
5% on recruiting		
Action Items	Action Items	Action Items
1. Get associate#		
2. Enroll on product autoship or autopay		
3. Have tickets to next event		
4. Take the PEProfile		
5. Gain a firm knowledge and testimony of company and products		
6. Memorize contacting scripts		
7. Make an effective list of 200 names		Goals
8. Subscribe to education system		
9. Have personal improvement plan	Goals	
Goals		
1. Increase PEPs to 30+		
2. Score green or yellow in first 20 skills		
3. Enroll 1-5 customers/associates		
4. Receive products for FREE		

She reiterated that I was in the Improve Yourself phase of the success pattern with my current PEP score. She also told me if I really applied myself everyday that I could be ready to advance to the Build a Team phase in just a few weeks. She put 95 percent of my time focused on personal improvement and wrote almost the exact same list of items in the business characteristics section as she had included in the promotion she had begun. Lastly, she put down what my goals should be during this potentially brief time in the business.

When she finished writing, we ended the meeting, shook hands, and went our separate ways. I took the paper I had with the success pattern diagram and sat in my car for a long time studying it. I had in my hand what seemed like a treasure map, the road map for success in this business. It seemed like I should guard this with my life. Sounds kind of funny to think about it, guarding an old napkin with some scribbling on it. But I was serious; this was unlike anything that anyone had ever given me before. It was like the secret to success. And I sure wasn't going to share it with Doug, Cindy, or Jen. It felt like I was competing with them.

There were a lot of things I didn't understand about what Glenna had written, but what really intrigued me was what was missing from the diagram. What will she fill in the blanks with and how will that all work out? I was so excited to travel the journey that I couldn't wait to get started.

6

The Third Week

Glenna was sitting in her home office pouring over the numbers that Gary had asked her to collect and report to him each week. She had begun to meet weekly with each individual leader on her team. She was looking at amounts of contacts, presentations, follow-ups, and enrollments that her personal recruits had been doing. Then it occurred to her that her numbers didn't seem to be very good. The sheer amount of people an average associate needed to contact in order to enroll enough people to create a six-figure income seemed like it was really high. In the quiet of her office an idea came to her that Gary had alluded to in their meeting. "People will do what you reward them for, and you can teach people to do anything if you know the process of success and can effectively teach others how to do it."

Glenna's mind was full of questions. What if her people didn't have to talk to fifty people every month to make ten to fifteen presentations to enroll one or two people? What if associates could contact thirty people a month, show twenty presentations and enroll ten people per month? She knew the pattern of success, she thought, but she hadn't been rewarding people for some of the proper foundational things that would help them create the success they wanted and, in many cases, needed to create. The promotion and the new recognition programs should solve that. But what about teaching the team how to fully engage in learning and then doing the right things in the right order?

Glenna kept a close eye on her promotion group. She wanted to separate the numbers and results of those who were in the six figures promotion from those who weren't. Those who hadn't signed up for the promotion enrolled twenty-seven people this week, including Doug's one and Cindy's two. That's one enrollee for every fifty associates on the team! The people who are part of the promotion enrolled only three. Neither Steve nor Jen had enrolled anyone. Glenna didn't expect Steve to. She specifically told him not to contact anyone yet, but the others who have been in awhile could have enrolled at least a few. Perhaps that's why they are in the promotion. They want to become effective business builders and now they are increasing their PEPs. In the coming weeks they will be able to take effective action that has kept them from the success they have wanted. When Glenna looked at the enrollment *ratio* between those in the promotion group and all the others, she found they were very different. She created a tracking sheet for the people in her promotion group where they could report their statistics weekly concerning contacts, presentations, and follow-ups.

"By my second full week I already felt more confident," Steve told Sara in a short conversation before he left for the preview meeting. "The path to success in this business seems to follow the general rules of success in anything; gain competence and the confidence to take effective action comes as a natural result. If I were a philosopher, I would say confidence comes from competence. I think I am getting close to being able to start building a team—although I'm not sure what that even means or if I have enough PEPs right now to begin working in the business. A few things I am sure of are that my decision to enroll was a good one. The products work and they do exactly what we advertise. XL-8 as a company has done everything it promised, and Glenna is an awesome teacher and leader."

I stopped at the car dealer on my way to the meeting to look at new pickups. I allowed myself to actually think what it would be like someday to be able to drive one. Stopping made me a few minutes late to the meeting, but even as I had to climb over some people to find a seat in the back, I wasn't sorry. Doug was in the middle of introducing Glenna, and Cindy was toward the front. She had two more guests with her. During the dream-building part of the presentation, I sank into "what-if" land. What if this really does work like Glenna describes? I pictured Sara going to the grocery store and buying what ever she wanted without looking at the price tag. What if we could go out to eat at our favorite restaurant on date night without looking at the right-hand side of the menu to decide on what we would order? Yes, the things I had gone to bed longing for are dreams, I decided. No, they aren't the size or scale of what Glenna or Doug talk about. But they are my dreams and they are driving my every decision and action. They do help motivate me to read, listen, and improve as Glenna has instructed.

And at the end of the meeting, Doug brought Cindy up again and let her show the check she got from the company. "Only two weeks into the business," Doug explained, "and already she has made money." She was being put on a pedestal as the rising star—the poster child for following her dream and taking massive action to pursue it. Doug was sure to tell everyone not to hesitate to follow Cindy's example and enroll tonight so that "In a few weeks this could be you!" I realized I was jealous of Cindy and the preferential treatment she was getting. She already has people and money to show for her efforts. I wondered momentarily if I should be doing more of what Cindy was doing. But that's not what Glenna has told me to do. There must be a reason Glenna is telling me to build my PEPs first and then work on building a team. I have to keep my promise to Glenna and stay true to the promotion I signed up for. After all, Glenna seems to have the biggest business and most PEPs of anyone here; Doug only begins the meetings, Glenna actually conducts them. But it is annoying that Doug and Cindy are presented as the examples we ought to follow.

As I was driving home from the meeting, I decided to ask Glenna in our weekly coaching session if I was ready to graduate from the Improve Yourself phase to the Build a Team phase. Glenna had an appointment fall through, and so she agreed to meet with me earlier than usual. I was still a little anxious around Glenna. But she didn't give me any reason to feel nervous. Maybe it was her professionalism or high PEPs that made me feel like a schoolboy with his elementary schoolteacher. Whatever the reason, I felt a little small next to someone as successful as Glenna. She asked me how my week was and how I was feeling about the business and promotion? I told her I was feeling much more confident now than I had last week. I loved the Saturday trainings and our weekly meetings. I was finished with two of the books on Glenna's list and the *Skills of the Million-Dollar Earners* audio library. I asked her for recommendations on what I should read and listen to next. Once again her answer surprised me. She told me to read it again and to listen to the Improve Yourself set of CDs along with the first 5 CDs in the Build a Team set. Then she asked me what I could tell her about edification.

I hated it when she put me on the spot like this. I thought about what I had heard on the CD. I clumsily told her something about a boomerang and that people listen to and take the advice from people they trust. I also needed to learn to edify her so I could have her credibility with my family and friends when I talked to them. I finished this little exam by telling her if I edified her and then she edified me in return, her credibility could be passed to me. "That's awesome," she remarked. "You get full marks for that one. Your PEPs are increasing really fast. You are my prize student," she said. "And that boomerang thing you referred to is the process that enables you to get the high PEP person's credibility quickly. I want you to pay close attention to the edification CD when you get home, but here's how it works in a nutshell. There is a process that I use." She then explained the steps.

"Step 1. Get ready to throw your edification boomerang by telling your prospects you don't know everything yet. The beauty of the system is that you have help from coaches and mentors when you need it. This also helps your prospects to see that we will actually help them, and it also demonstrates that they don't need to know everything about everything to engage in the business.

"Step 2. Throw the boomerang by edifying Doug or me, or who ever is helping you. Make sure to say relevant things about the person you are edifying; you know the things your prospects will relate to. For example, if they say they don't have enough money to do the things they would like, then emphasize that your mentor has built a strong and profitable business, is making quite a bit of money, and is teaching people how to do the same. If the prospect dreams of vacations to exotic places, then emphasize that.

"You are not trying to sell, so just a short comment will do. Briefly talk about the fact that your mentor's success came as a result of engaging in this business, and that she has been an incredible help to you during your association with the company and this leadership team. Make sure to give a few details that have enabled her to be successful. Things like she is service-oriented, is a great teacher, or actually cares about your success."

"For example, I might say, 'Suzie, I met a woman who has built a million-dollar business by mastering a success process. She is teaching a few people what she knows about creating residual income through a strong and profitable business model and I would like to introduce you to her.' Or I might say, 'I have someone I would like you to speak with. This person is having great success in our company, and we have an opportunity to meet her.' In either case, complete the edification process through the actual introduction and then be quiet! Don't be fake or cheesy. Be sincere and share from your heart what your mentors mean to you and why," she instructed.

"It's important to remember that when you begin to edify, you have only one job; introduce the upline and edify her as an expert in the business, someone who knows what she is talking about because she is walking the walk, not just talking the talk, and she is having a lot of success with this business.

"Here are a couple of helpful hints in edification. First, never interrupt when the person you edified is talking! You have set them up as the expert. If you interrupt you take away from her credibility, so don't say another word unless your prospect either asks you a question directly or the upline turns the conversation back over to you. Second, make sure that you give some information about your prospect during the introduction. If you can tell your upline what the prospect does professionally and what their interest is so far in the business, that is extremely helpful. She will get to know your prospect and make a connection with them. Then she will return the boomerang to you.

"Step 3. The upline will return the boomerang by edifying you. She will say something like, 'You should listen to Steve because he is learning and tapping into a business and industry that includes leaders and a predictable pattern of success.' When she gets done edifying you, her credibility will transfer to you. Your prospect will then have much more confidence in both of you. As simple as all this sounds, *it works*! Something magical happens when you tap into the credibility, expertise, and experience of an upline mentor that would otherwise not happen if you tried to handle things by yourself.

"So your homework between now and Saturday is to listen carefully to the edification CD and practice what you learn there. This is going to be the training topic on Saturday, and I want to use you as the example of how to do it. When you feel like you have this down, I want you to start contacting the people on your hot list. Make sure to listen to the contacting CDs in *Skills of the Million-Dollar Earners*. Use a script you feel comfortable with and set up a few meetings. I will come and help you either on Saturday or on Monday night to do the presentations for you," she offered.

Glenna finished our meeting by talking about the goals of the

Improve Yourself phase of the success pattern, including increasing PEPs, signing up one to five customers or associates, and getting the products for free. She reminded me I was still in this phase until I had at least thirty PEPs. She consoled me a bit by anticipating that I might be a bit frustrated with all the personal improvement stuff I had been doing while Cindy and others in Doug's business were already contacting and enrolling people. The goals of enrolling customers and associates would begin to happen in the next few weeks because of the foundational work I had done to build my PEPs first. Because of this, she was sure I would be more effective at enrolling new people and getting them to take effective action.

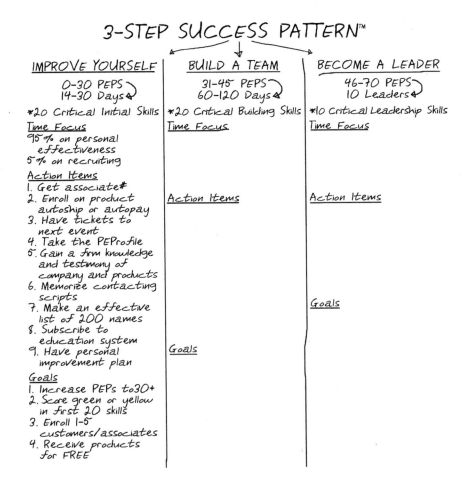

3-STEP SUCCESS PATTERN™

IMPROVE YOURSELF	BUILD A TEAM	BECOME A LEADER
0-30 PEPS 14-30 Days	31-45 PEPS 60-120 Days	46-70 PEPS 10 Leaders
*20 Critical Initial Skills	*20 Critical Building Skills	*10 Critical Leadership Skills

IMPROVE YOURSELF

Time Focus
95% on personal effectiveness
5% on recruiting

Action Items
1. Get associate#
2. Enroll on product autoship or autopay
3. Have tickets to next event
4. Take the PEProfile
5. Gain a firm knowledge and testimony of company and products
6. Memorize contacting scripts
7. Make an effective list of 200 names
8. Subscribe to education system
9. Have personal improvement plan

Goals
1. Increase PEPs to 30+
2. Score green or yellow in first 20 skills
3. Enroll 1-5 customers/associates
4. Receive products for FREE

BUILD A TEAM

Time Focus

Action Items

Goals

BECOME A LEADER

Time Focus

Action Items

Goals

When I got home I immediately listened to the edification CD and practiced on Sara and our kids. Later, when they had gone to bed, I even started talking to the stuffed bear one of our kids had left downstairs. The next morning while I was exercising, I listened to the contacting CDs and chose a script that I could relate to. When Sara got up, I practiced on her and then with each child as they came down for breakfast. My last practice before I went to work was with the same stuffed bear. I was so good that I was sure I heard the bear tell me he was excited to meet Glenna, and that Saturday at 5:00 PM was a great time for us to come by.

I practiced in my mind all day. I think the janitor at the school was a bit surprised that I was talking to the broom in my classroom. But it didn't matter. The end of the month was coming and I knew the $1,000 that Sara's dad had sent us was running out quickly and I had no way to replace it yet. That night when I got home I was almost too excited and too nervous to eat dinner. I went downstairs in the basement to be alone when I made my first calls. I heard Sara tell the kids to play upstairs because daddy was working for a while and he needed to be left alone. She was serious about supporting me in this; it was awesome. Right before I made my first call, Doug called me. He apologized for not paying much attention to me lately. He had been talking to Glenna and she had filled him in on how much progress I had made in the past few weeks. He offered to help me anytime I needed it. I thanked him, but I didn't have anything for him to help me with at the moment. I told him that I was about to make my first calls. He wished me luck and hung up.

After the call, I thought for a minute about how much courage it must have taken for him to call. It gave me some confidence that Glenna would have taken the time to call him and get him engaged with me. And so with the confidence I got from his call, Sara's support with keeping the kids away for a while, and the practice I had been doing, I picked up the phone. I never noticed that it weighed so much before; it was really hard to pick up. But I managed, and as I dialed my mind went blank. The phone rang on the other end and the only thing I could remember was that I should start the conversation by saying who I was and to make sure that I wasn't interrupting them. I had called Tony, my best friend and assistant coach from the baseball team. Words can't describe how much I was hoping he would say that now was not a good time. But he didn't. This was the most uncomfortable thing I had ever done. Even raising money for the baseball team was easier than this. But in that moment, the stuffed bear's face came into my mind and I relaxed enough to say, "I haven't seen you in a little while, and I was just thinking about you. What have you been up to?" He told me he had been busy getting ready for the summer break by making sure he had a job for the summer.

I asked him what he was going to be doing and he told me he thought he was going to be working at the hardware store around the corner from the mall, but nothing was promised just yet. He then asked me what I was doing and what I had been up to. I told him I had been exploring the idea of starting my own business and that I had met a successful woman who had been coaching me on how to get started. He asked me faster than I could answer how I met her and what the business was, and what it meant for the baseball program. I finally interrupted him by asking him if he had ever considered owning his own business? He told me he had, but that he didn't feel like he could be successful. I told him I thought I had found something for people like him and me. Because of our relationship, he asked me what I was up to and he tried hard to get me to tell him. However, I had listened to the *Skills of the Million-Dollar Earners* enough to know I couldn't tell him. I was only supposed to invite him to a meeting or to make an appointment with Glenna. I told him I didn't know enough about it to tell him over the phone, but that Glenna, the successful businesswoman, had consented to meet with a few people who I knew to teach them the same things she was teaching me. Tony said that Saturday at 5:00 PM would be a good time for him. I confirmed the appointment at his house, and then got off the phone.

I did a dance that I would never have wanted anyone else to see, right there in my little basement office. Afterward, I went upstairs to get that stuffed bear and put him on my desk for the next calls. That night I made three calls. I was able to make two appointments; one with Tony and one with Dan Jacobsen's parents. On the third call I got voicemail. I wasn't prepared for that so I ended up leaving a weird message and hung up. I was sure that Glenna would teach me how to do effective voicemails later. My heart was pounding, and I was easily as excited as the day I won my first game as a coach or my first state championship. I had worked hard and done what Glenna had told me to do and I had made appointments with both of the people I actually talked to. I remembered that Glenna told me to call only the people on my hot list. I certainly didn't want to go through that whole list in one night, so I stopped at those three names. I called Glenna to tell her the news. She was ecstatic and gladly scheduled time with me on Saturday evening for the presentations.

At the Saturday training meeting Glenna noticed that the only people who were there were those who had signed up for the promotion. So she threw out the idea that maybe this ragtag group should have a name. We all agreed and started thinking of ideas, but Glenna's idea was what we all agreed on: the Rhino Power Team. She told us the difference between rhinos and cows; rhinos had to go out and make their own way and cows depended on someone else to keep them safe and feed them. We agreed that cows were like people with jobs, depending on someone else for their income, and that we were like rhinos that made things happen, instead of waiting for things to happen.

Glenna used me as the demonstrator for edifying when we did our role-plays. Jen was getting into a friendly competition with me. She was a bit ticked off that she wasn't chosen as the demonstration person. However, when we took turns doing role-plays together, it was awesome. Jen was really good at this. I wondered why she didn't have a bigger business or why she was even in the promotion group. There must be something that was holding her back and it had to be in the Improve Yourself phase. Everything in the promotion was based on the things Glenna had written on my napkin diagram. What ever it was, it wasn't edification, because she was much better than I was at it. I learned a few things from her and my PEPs went up again. It was cool to have a language to be able to identify what was actually happening in my business and a road map to track my progress.

Glenna picked me up in her powder-blue Jaguar convertible for the two appointments I had scheduled. It was like a dream I had had when I was growing up. I used to have visions of a powder-blue Jaguar convertible with a supercharged engine, twenty-inch spoke wheels, and charcoal-colored leather seats with a premium surround system. For a block or two, I didn't hear anything Glenna said to me. I closed my eyes and returned to the dream. I was completely wrapped up in feeling what it was really like to sit in this car. I made sure to take a breath and smell the new car. I felt the leather seats and the wind in my hair as we drove to our appointment with Tony.

We arrived a few minutes early and Glenna explained what typically happens at a meeting like this. She told me to introduce her and then get caught up on a few things for a couple of minutes to get Tony talking. Then I needed to remind him of the conversation we had had when I set up the appointment (that he was talking about needing money for the summer and the possibility of starting a new business). She continued, "Next, edify me and I will take over. I will be going through some basic steps of a presentation so you can watch and learn what I am doing; soon enough you will be able to do it yourself. You may need to be ready with your testimony of the company, products, and mentorship from others and from me if I call on you. But other than that, it will go the way it's supposed to."

The meeting was awesome. Glenna had Tony eating right out of her hand and she didn't even seem to have to do any hard-core selling. She found out what he wanted his ideal life to be like, showed him exactly how XL-8 could provide that for him, asked him how he saw XL-8 meeting his needs, and then gave him three choices at the end of the meeting. She told him that (1) he could do nothing right now, which included taking a day or two to make a decision; or (2) he could take advantage of the features and benefits of the products as a customer; or (3) he could enroll as a partner with us, work to get those products for free and then make some money, possibly a lot of money. I had never seen anything like it! In about forty-five minutes Glenna was done and Tony enrolled as my first associate, complete with a commitment to come to the Tuesday business preview meeting. If I had tried to present to Tony, it would have been a disaster. I was thankful for Glenna's help.

We excused ourselves and repeated the process at the Jacobsen's house. When Glenna got to the three choices at the end of the presentation, Mr. Jacobsen told us he was too busy right now to do anything with the business side, but he was interested in trying the products. He enrolled as my first customer. In less than an hour we were out of there as well. It was only about 7:30, so Glenna reminded me that I had left a voicemail on someone's phone. She asked me where that person lived, and we drove over to the Barkley's. They were home but they said they were so confused by my message that they didn't think they would be interested. Glenna had a really good conversation with them, but still no luck. I am pretty sure Glenna was talking to them as some sort of teaching moment for me, so I was paying close attention.

As I watched her, I noticed that she almost never answered questions with answers. It seemed odd at first, but it seemed like her strategy was to keep them talking about their interests, goals, and circumstances. By the end of the conversation they had shared with Glenna that despite their dissatisfaction with their situation, they were more committed to complain about it than to take action to fix it. This was a very important lesson for me. For the first time in my life I was able to experience a professional conversation in real time. The kinds of questions Glenna asked, and the way that she asked them, seemed natural and inoffensive. They told her things I never would have been able to find out and didn't know, even as one of their closest friends for years. By the end they didn't do anything with us—at least not yet, Glenna told me.

On the way back to my house, Glenna asked me what I had learned. I told her that it seemed important to focus on what other people wanted and needed and then to highlight the things we offer to provide those wants and needs. I learned that I don't need to be a hard-core salesperson to get people to take action at the end of the presentation. In the conversation with the Barkley's I learned that questions showed you are curious about people and get them to talk to you more freely. Glenna asked if I thought my PEPs went up and I said I thought so, but it seems like there was a lot to learn to succeed at this. She reminded me how far I had come in the past few weeks and that was what the Rhino Power Team was all about. Yeah, but what about skill in asking questions, presenting, and all that stuff? She smiled and told me, "It will come as you learn and practice in the Saturday trainings and as you do more of the meetings you set up in the next weeks. I want you to spend the rest of the time between now and the Tuesday meeting listening to the high-yielding questions CD in the *Skills of the Million-Dollar Earners* and practice the six types of questions talked about. I will test you after the meeting on Tuesday."

She congratulated me on a very productive evening and then drove away. As I stood in my driveway watching the powder-blue Jag drive down my street, I said silently, "Thank you for helping me," and then I looked up to the sky and repeated the same words, "Thank you!"

7

The Fourth Week

It was only a few days until the monthly business-development conference. I sat in the back row of the business preview meeting and surveyed the crowd as they mingled and took their seats. Doug had a new guy with him, but none of those who had come with him before had returned. I also noticed that Cindy had two new people, but none of her previous guests or recruits had come back either. It could be that her recruits had all been customers. Mr. Jacobsen wasn't here and I didn't think he would show up either; he was a customer not a business builder, so it wouldn't necessarily make sense for him to be here. But it did strike me as interesting, following what Glenna had told me in our last meeting.

Tony arrived a few minutes late, as was his habit. I had saved a seat for him. Doug welcomed the guests and edified Glenna. I wondered if Doug ever had the edification lesson from Glenna that I received last week? Doug's edification was interesting and probably adequate, but either Jen or I could have done better. However, neither of us had any credibility to be standing up front just yet. Speaking of Jen, I wonder where she is? Glenna began the meeting just as Jen came in the door. She had two guests. Ugh, that meant she had more than I did. I secretly hoped that maybe they were a husband and wife couple and so combined, they would still count only as one associate number. I wondered if Doug would bring Cindy up to the front again at the end of the meeting and laud over her as the example of pursuing her dream with reckless abandon. Glenna finished and Doug got up. He turned some time over to Cindy and she told them that XL-8 was the best opportunity to make their dreams come true, that they really only needed to take action because everything else was in place to help them succeed.

Doug completed the meeting with an invitation to get some refreshments, meet Glenna, and fill out the enrollment forms. He ended with a reminder to get tickets to the business-development conference this coming Saturday at the Events Center. Tony had already met Glenna and was already enrolled. He asked about the Saturday conference and how to get tickets. Over Tony's shoulder I could see Jen introducing her people to Glenna. They were holding hands, so I was a bit relieved that they were a couple. I got Tony a pair of tickets and made an appointment with him for Thursday night. I didn't know how this was going to affect my usual meeting with Glenna, but it seemed like Tony should come first.

In the meeting after the meeting, Glenna asked everyone who was enrolled in the promotion group to begin sending her the number of contacts, presentations, follow-ups, and enrollments we did each week. Doug snickered at the requirement, not understanding how she might use the information to help us. She reminded us that we all needed to retake the Personal Effectiveness Profile before Saturday so she could give the recognition she had promised. Doug rolled his eyes about that requirement too. He whispered to Cindy, "I told you they would be doing all kinds of crazy things that don't help you really build the business." Cindy nodded as if she understood what he meant and whispered back in agreement that *they* were the top producers of the team, and smiling when she told him that we were all chasing imaginary success.

Glenna postponed our personal meeting this week. She told me that scheduling, logistics, agenda, and getting her final thoughts for her own presentations at the conference had put her behind schedule in many areas. If I wanted to meet for a few minutes right then, she would be happy to do it. I told her that I needed to know only if I should begin to change how I was applying my time to the Build a Team numbers, or if I should keep them the same as the last weeks. She told me to stay the course until I had at least thirty PEPs. She reminded me that I would be taking the assessment again in the next few days, so it shouldn't be too much of a problem. I agreed and then asked her how to invite people to the conference.

Glenna told me how important events were; when people learn how to promote them effectively, others can begin to build their business with or without you. She told me there was a perfect correlation between event attendance and residual income. Or in other words, her experience was that people who have the best event attendance, make the most money. She went on to tell me that if I wanted my team to grow by 50 to 100 percent every month, and if I wanted my income to grow by at least 50 percent each month, then I needed to increase my PEPs in event promotion.

She told me the good news was that I already had my tickets to the conference. I was almost afraid to tell her that I had sold mine to Tony. But I knew that I needed more, and the only way I was going to get them was to tell her and ask for more. She chuckled and complimented me on taking care of the situation in the best way possible.

She then gave me a simple script that she uses to invite new people to events like the business-development conference. She might say, "Bob, remember when you told me about wanting to be able to spend more time with your family? This Saturday I am going to an event to learn from a couple of people who have built multiple million-dollar businesses. They will be teaching exactly how to have more time. I have two extra tickets. Will you come with me?" Of course she reminded me to insert whatever *their* personal challenges are instead of more time.

I realized there was a lot I needed to learn about this business. But the more I learned, the more I also realized that the principles of success seemed pretty simple to understand. Glenna had a great way of teaching me just what I needed to know to get to the next step. I made a mental goal of inviting at least four more people to the conference. I had no idea what to expect, either from the experience of inviting people to a meeting that I had never attended, or from the event itself; but I was excited to try out my new knowledge and see what happened.

It was getting late and Glenna was looking at her weekly numbers before she sent them to Gary. She was trying to get a better feel for how things were going for her team and what they needed to improve upon as a group.

She was compiling the results of everyone on her team who had taken the PEProfile in the past month and saw that they had the greatest and most immediate need to improve in product knowledge, compensation plan, listening, contacting and presenting. The PEProfile report was one of the most important tools she had, and she relied on it often to help guide her on her team training needs.

Again she was captivated by the numbers her team was submitting to her. She looked at the total contacts, presentations, follow-ups, and enrollments that her team had from the week. Those who didn't sign up for the promotion enrolled twenty-four people, including another one for both Doug and Cindy. Overall, that was still only about one enrollee for every fifty associates on the team! The Rhino Power Team members had enrolled seven. Both Steve and Jen had enrolled two new team members, and the rest of the promotion group had enrolled three more. This group was starting to create a positive result. Seven enrollees came out to an average of one enrollee per three associates. Comparatively speaking, the Rhino Power Team was lapping the rest of the team. The very idea that Gary had given her to begin looking at these numbers every week and then examine the ratios was already proving to be very helpful. She was able to see trends and specific needs of her group rather than just training on the "generic basics" of the business on a regular basis. In the middle of this reflection an idea came to her.

The total numbers are not the most important things she told herself! The totals are what checks are calculated from, but then she reminded herself about the conversation she had had with herself last week. What if an associate didn't have to talk to one hundred prospects to enroll three new team members? What if they could contact fewer and get the same result, or what if the result they got from the same work was better? "It seems that conversion rates are more important than the overall total numbers. I already look at conversion rates of enrollees compared to associates," she told herself. Why not look deeper into what is creating that result? How many contacts will it take my team to make a presentation appointment? What percentage of business presentations result in follow-ups? And what will our percentage of enrollments from follow-ups be?

She didn't gather this information currently, and her overall team was probably not going to be willing or able give it to her. But she will start getting it from the Rhino Power Team beginning this week. This could be something that she and Gary could discuss in regard to some kind of recognition, maybe the most effective contactor, or the most effective presenter.

One thing was for sure, the Rhino Power Team was making great progress. One hundred percent of them had improved their score on the PEProfile, and their ratios were much better than the rest of the team. Maybe it's not fair to compare, but they had an average enrollment rate of 33 percent and the rest of the team is at 2 percent. That's fifteen times higher for the Rhino Power Team than the rest of the team. She was excited to see if this held true over the next weeks and months.

One other thing she noticed from the numbers was that most of Doug and Cindy's recruits seemed to be customers only. They made an initial order, but didn't come back to the weekly business preview a second time and they didn't seem to enroll anyone else either—not that there's anything wrong with customers, but they usually don't produce more revenue or sales beyond their own purchases. Glenna was interested in keeping track of this and seeing what happens. Just a quick click and the numbers would be on Gary's computer, along with an invitation to the monthly business-development conference.

Steve's heart was feeling a bit heavy as he realized that Wednesday flew by almost without his noticing that it was gone. "There was only one more week of school and I still hadn't told anyone that I was retiring as the baseball coach. I was dreading the meeting with the school and the phone calls I presumed I would get from parents of the kids on the team. I didn't want to explain to everyone why I was retiring. I wasn't even sure what to say to them. But I knew I had to do it. Maybe Glenna could help me with this in our next meeting," he thought.

I invited the custodian who had been cleaning my classroom for the past four years to the conference. He looked at me as if I had been speaking Greek. He told me he'd think about it and get back to me. I also invited Jerry, the vice principal of the school. He took me a lot more seriously. By the end of the school year a vice principal is exhausted and has the feeling of resolution like we all get on New Year's Day to do something else, anything else so that he doesn't have to go through this again. But he didn't buy tickets. Instead he made an appointment with me to see what I was talking about, before he spent a whole Saturday going to a meeting. We arranged to meet on Friday evening. And then I realized that this might be a great way to contact people. It seemed that event promotion was very close to edification in the contacting script I was already using.

I met with Tony and his wife and they had a few questions. We found the answers together on the website and I told him about the PEProfile, and the promotion group I had signed up for. I also showed him my napkin diagram and explained as much of it as I could. I think they got that there were three steps and that we needed to take them in sequence to succeed. I also committed him to take the profile before the conference on Saturday and he agreed. Our time was well spent. His wife was as outwardly excited as I was. Tony always kept his emotions to himself, but I could tell by his questions and the way he accepted my challenge to take the profile that he was excited, too.

When I got home I called Glenna to see if she could help me on Friday with the appointment I had with Jerry. She couldn't go because of a leadership meeting with her mentor that night. I reluctantly called Doug, but he didn't answer. What was I going to do? Jerry wanted to make sure he wasn't wasting his time and I had no idea what to say to him in a presentation. So I did something I probably wasn't supposed to do—I called Jen. Yes, I was turning to my rival for help. I figured she had at least done presentations by herself before, and anything she did would be better than anything I would do. She was so willing to help me that I felt like a knucklehead for hoping that her people in the meeting were a couple instead of two separate people.

We met at Jerry's house and on the way to the door I asked her for something I could say to edify her as the expert who was there to help me. She had not really had anyone do this to her before so it took her a minute to think of something to say. She gave me the last idea just as Jerry was opening the door. He welcomed us in and I repeated what I had done the week before with Glenna. I asked Jerry a few questions to get caught up and to see if he was open to exploring a way to end his frustration as the vice principle. He nodded and then I introduced Jen as a friend and a teacher. I told him that I didn't really know enough about the details of what I had talked about at school to tell him, so I brought her with me to make sure he got all the information he needed. Jen was very capable of answering his questions, so he wouldn't feel like he would be wasting his time on Saturday. I don't remember much of what he said, but I do remember that Jen did a great job. So much so that when she told him he had three choices—he could either do nothing with the information she had presented, he could enroll as a customer and take advantage of the products, or he could enroll as a partner with us and make some money—he jumped right in and said, "Sign me up on the money option!"

I was so surprised that I wasn't sure what to think or say. Jen asked me if I had an enrollment form and a couple of tickets to the event on Saturday. Fortunatelly I did. She also got him to buy tickets for Saturday! I was overcome with gratitude for Jen and the way she had helped me. She was awesome. I thanked her and then asked her why she was in the promotion if she could present like that? She shook her head and told me that presenting wasn't holding her back, contacting was. She was deathly afraid of contacting people about the business. "Put people in front of me in a meeting like that and I am fine," she told me. "But the thought of setting up the appointment paralyzes me—I'm hoping that the promotion will help me get through it." I thanked her again and went home wondering if I could ever repay her for what she had done for me. She had doubled my team and sold tickets to Jerry and his wife. I was going to have four people at the conference! Even though they represented just two associate numbers, I was on cloud nine.

Saturday was a beautiful day. Sara got up before I did and sometimes she liked to sit out on the back porch, drink juice, and watch the sun come over the mountain. She took my notepad out with her and glanced over it. "There are so many things that we have learned in the past few months," she thought flipping through the pages. "Steve is working so hard to make this work. I am so proud of him. Sacrificing baseball for our family takes real dedication. I am so glad that he found something that can bring him personal satisfaction, and an income that his work and commitment deserve. I hope this will bring him the success he so badly wants. You know, I think I will start leaving him little messages in his notepad every day. He needs to know how much we love him. Maybe I can contribute a little by talking to my friends when we are together. I am going to surprise Steve with a few prospects of my own." Tearing out a page from the back of the pad Sara started her own names list. "Maybe Maria would be interested. She's a single mom, and she told me a few weeks ago that her job is really demanding. Sometimes she has to take her two kids with her because she doesn't have anywhere for them to go when she works. Maybe she would be interested in starting her own business with us."

"A feeling of excitement came over me when I got up," Steve thought. And when I went downstairs I saw Sara on the porch writing in my notepad. I just watched her for a minute. When I went out she reminded me of the goal I had written in the pad. I was still basking in the achievement from the night before at Jerry's house. I was thinking of taking a break this morning and was trying to justify the time off by telling her I had had a good week and I thought I needed a rest. She gave me that look that reminded me of who I was and the work required to create success. Then she gently reminded me of the frustration and financial challenges we had. I instantly went back to what Jen told me last night. Contacting was her major fear and roadblock. She had worked for years to overcome the challenges that held her back and I didn't have the same challenge she did. Contacting seemed easy to me. I didn't feel particularly effective at it yet, but I wasn't afraid of it. So I figured the only way to pay Jen back for what she had done for me was to honor her by making some invitations—this part of the business I could do right now.

I made invitations to everyone on my hot list. Two people made appointments with me for the following week. One other accepted my offer to go to the weekly business preview at Glenna's. I was a little bummed that only about 60 percent of those I thought I knew best, and who had in the past claimed to be my friends, would make an appointment to let me present to them. Oh well, I sighed, it's time to take a couple of hours and go fly kites with the kids before the conference. What a day this was turning out to be. I gave Sara a kiss and off to the park we went with kites and a picnic lunch.

I found myself a bit nervous when we arrived at the Events Center. I don't know why, I have been there many times. I have even spoken there a few times for banquettes and church conferences. But I knew what those events were about and knew what to expect. I didn't have any idea what was going to happen today. All kinds of thoughts went through my mind. I saw Doug come in with three or four people. Cindy and some of the people I had seen at weekly business previews were with them. Doug waved and welcomed me with a hug and a handshake. I noticed he had a special pin on his lapel. He explained in great detail that it represented his promotion level in the business. It was brass colored with a sapphire ring around it, had two stars, and had the XL-8 logo in the middle. He told me the sapphire ring meant he was in the Winners' Circle. He had been recognized in the Silver Star group twice for personal enrollments and was at the second promotion level in the business. Doug said something really cool was going to happen tonight. He invited me to sit with them together as a group—his group. If I wanted him to, he would save me some seats. He asked how many seats I would need, and seeing only Sara and me, he assumed only two would be needed. I told him I would need six; he seemed a bit surprised, but he quickly agreed and told me he would save six up front on the right hand side.

A few minutes later Tony, Jerry, and their wives came and we all found our seats with Doug. The meeting started with a prayer and the singing of the national anthem. I was surprised but pleased the company would do this. As we sang I felt a sense of pride that I hadn't felt in a long time. The first speaker was a man who opened the meeting by inviting all those who had served in the military to stand up while everyone applauded. It was one of those moments when tears of gratitude uncontrollably flow. I actually had to wipe a tear from my cheek seeing many others who also had served. Then the host introduced the guest speaker for this session. Her name was Kim and she was a woman from another of Glenna's teams. The host did a masterful job of edifying her. I had my notepad out and was ready to absorb whatever she was going to say.

She talked for over an hour about effective presentations. I wrote in my notes "The Anatomy of a Presentation." She told us that sharing the business opportunity is what fuels the engine of our business; the presentation is where we get the business in front of fresh eyes, and possibility comes to life. She paused and said thankfully there is a science to presenting and presentation skills can be learned, because without what Glenna had taught her, she would never have been able to build the business with any predictability.

Kim took us through an effective four-step process of a presentation. Step one, she told us, consists of uncovering your prospects' discomfort and dissatisfaction with some aspect of their life. "Most people skip right over this step, and because they do, their prospects don't enroll either as customers or associates about 90 percent of the time. You must get them talking about what they have too much of or not enough of; then find out what they might be committed to doing something about. During the time they are talking, you should be making a mental checklist of the features and benefits of our products and the business opportunity that will solve their specific challenges. Fully equipped with some information about them and their circumstances, you move to step two, which is where most people begin their presentations.

"This is where you get to tell your prospects why XL-8 is the solution to their pain." Kim reiterated, "If you skip step one, you appear to be selling *hype* and *hopium* because your presentation will appear to be a one-size-fits-all deal. Your prospects will be left to connect the dots to see how XL-8 really solves anything that might be specific to them.

Then, step three is to determine their interest in what you just talked about. Summarize the main points you highlighted, recap why they should be important, given the information your prospect shared with you in step one, and then ask them how they see XL-8, our products, or the money-making opportunity you chose to highlight for them would serve to overcome their challenges." She again told us that without step one, there was little hope for us to do a good job in step two or three.

The purpose of step three was to make sure that we chose the right things to highlight in step two, and to see if we did a good job of explaining those things and ultimately see if they got it. "Step three is a kind of test for you as a presenter. You're taking their temperature, so to speak, to see how they are receiving your message and to see if they have any commitment to do anything about the circumstances they told you about in step one."

Finally, in step four, we needed a well-planned ending that must include what she called "a call to action." She told us that far too many associates presented information and then left it up to the prospect to ask if and how they could join or buy; instead "You must ask for the business if you ever intend to build a strong and profitable residual income stream." Kim concluded by sharing her appreciation for the business and for Glenna's leadership and encouraged us to come to the next meeting to learn more about why the business was so important.

I was mesmerized by Kim and what she had told us. In each step she gave us some incredible insight and specific language, techniques, and ways of thinking about that step. She referred us all to the *Skills of the Million-Dollar Earners* audio library for more details on each part. I looked at Sara's notes. She had written down the following:

- Keep your business presentation informative, yet simple. A simple plan elicits a simple response, but if your plan is complex, cumbersome, and detail oriented, your prospect's ability to make a decision will also be complex.

- Keep it simple enough for your prospect to believe that he or she could easily explain it themselves.

- Drop a little sunlight in their life; believe in what they can achieve and experience the excitement of them achieving their hopes and dreams. That alone brings something to the table most people aren't getting anywhere else.

- Fill the presentation with high-yielding questions. Questions will get your prospect to talk and they will expose what they want and need that they're not getting now. Great questions lead people to visualize and imagine what their life would be like with their dream. And when people really see and believe in the possibilities of a greater future through involvement with you and your business, they will act on it.

Sara's notes alone were worth the price of admission. It hadn't occurred to me before that two people could be sitting in the same event and hear such different things. When the first meeting was over I asked Tony and Jerry what they thought. They told me they were blown away by what she had shared. Jerry said he saw at least a dozen ways he could use this in his vice principal's job every day. Tony's wife said she was going to use this process when she was talking to her children about life and lessons of growing up.

We all agreed to meet in the same place that evening and then we went our separate ways. I was hoping neither of them would suggest that we go out to eat. I mortgaged my next three months of dates with Sara to enroll, buy the audio library, take the profile, and get tickets to this meeting. However, I was also pretty sure that neither of them was in much better financial shape than I was, so my anxiety quickly subsided.

The meeting that night began more as a party than a business meeting. There were at least twice as many people now as there were in the afternoon. There was music and those who had attended before seemed to know that they should be singing, clapping, and even dancing in the aisles. I wasn't sure what to think of all this celebrating. But order was restored when the host came out and welcomed us. When the lights went down and the music stopped, we followed the same routine as we had in the afternoon session: prayer, national anthem, veterans standing, and the crowd cheering their appreciation. That feeling of pride returned and for a moment I remembered all the reasons I had served in the military. The host announced that this was a very special evening and to get it started off properly, we all needed to show our excitement and recognition for the one person without whom none of this would be possible. He edified Glenna and then let her recognize those who had worked hard to achieve success during the month. Then she began the parade of people for various achievements.

There were awards for having people personally attend the conference. A lot of people qualified for this award. I got my first taste of recognition from XL-8 for this. I had four people at the conference, but Cindy got top honors in this area. Then there was recognition for doing at least fifteen presentations during the month. Fewer people got this award, but both Doug and Cindy did. There was an award for personal enrollments, and Cindy won again. XL-8 has five promotion levels and there was a time set aside for each level. Cindy advanced to the first level, which was called Copper. Doug advanced from Brass to Silver as a result of my enrolling two new people and Cindy enrolling seven new people and advancing to Copper. Cindy and two others earned the award called Winners' Circle, which requires personally enrolling six people in any one month. The Brass Ring was given to Cindy for having met the minimum requirements for personal production points. The Silver Star for team enrollments in a month went to Doug, due to Jen's helping me enroll Jerry, the vice principal, the night before the conference. Lastly, there was the Golden Eagle, which was awarded for team production points and was earned by Kim and her husband.

When this part of the meeting was over, Glenna took a moment to tell everyone this would normally be the end of the recognition. "However, we are adding a few new categories for recognition in the months to come. We will be giving recognition in areas that we have neglected to honor as important and very meaningful to business development, residual income, security, and possibly generational wealth." Then she introduced the new recognition areas and the promotion winners for the month and explained each one as they were announced. She called up all the people who had thirty PEPs, followed by those who had forty-five PEPs, and lastly those who had seventy PEPs. She had us all stand on the stage and called this group the High Peppers Club. Both Jen and I were part of that group. Doug probably had at least forty-five PEPs and Cindy probably had at least thirty PEPs but no profile to show it. This was the first time that Jen had ever been recognized on the stage at any event. She had been in the business for a few years, and month after month she had seen others go across the stage. Glenna then called the person with the highest profile score during the month up on stage. Jen had top honors in this also. She deserved the recognition. It was emotional for everyone who knew her. She had worked hard for a few years and now suddenly she got two awards in a row.

Glenna kept Jen on stage when she announced that she also had the least amount of red areas in the Improve Yourself phase of the success pattern. Then came the largest improvement in PEPs during the month, *I was the winner!* My PEPs had gone from fourteen to thirty-four in just three weeks. I never had realized how much I liked the spotlight before. As a coach and as a teacher I had it all the time by the nature of my job, but this felt different and it was awesome. Maybe this is how movie stars or celebrities feel. I think I would do just about anything to get up there again next month.

Lastly, Glenna talked about the Rhino Power Team and the Seminar at Sea promotion. This was the first time for this promotion and it would be running for the next five months. She listed all the things she had announced in our weekly training meetings that were required to earn the promotion. There was a great group of people who had signed up for the challenge and most of us were able to accomplish the requirements for the first month. I had in some ways forgotten about this. So when Glenna called Jen up, it was no surprise, but when she called my name, I was a bit shocked.

As the night went on, I was outwardly excited for what I had gone through the past month and for what I saw happening in my business. However, deep inside I was envious and maybe even jealous of Cindy because she was recognized for real results, not just doing stuff that may or may not lead to money. Cindy was enrolling new people every week and actually making money. In fact, she had already recouped her enrollment fee and was making enough to pay for her products every month. I wonder if Glenna was trying to play some kind of trick on me. Why was she telling me one thing and letting Doug tell Cindy another?

I reflected on the past month. What am I doing differently from Cindy? I have spent over $1,000 to enroll and buy some marketing materials, get tickets to the conference, take the PEProfile twice, get the *Skills of the Million-Dollar Earners*, and put gas in my car. I go to the Saturday trainings, read books, and listen to audio CDs, but I can't see that anyone in the promotion group is making much if any money. Maybe we are part of some test to see which business strategy works best. I don't know, but it seems like we are doing a lot of things that Doug and Cindy aren't doing.

One thing I do know, Cindy is making money! I have some serious questions for Glenna in our meeting this week. At that moment I realized I wasn't paying any attention to the event. I was lost in my own thoughts. I hadn't heard one thing the host or Kim had said. In fact it was when the host introduced Glenna that I was brought back to consciousness.

In just a minute or two Glenna was on a roll. The audience was captivated by her and what she was talking about. It seemed as if she had struck a nerve with everyone, and that these were ideas she had not talked about before. I watched Doug and even he was paying close attention. Glenna spoke as if she were a dignitary. She started her remarks by saying, "In contrast to many teachers and institutions today that tell us success is gained with knowledge alone or that it comes from massive action for the sake of massive action alone, the truth comes from the challenge of all who are truly successful, which is to learn, practice, and apply knowledge and skill to become something along the way.

"All high achievers, and those who further their success by teaching others to become successful, teach and show that we may attain the full measure of our potential through proven processes that create predictability. And that success processes require far more than acquiring knowledge or simply taking random action. It is not enough for us to be convinced that the industry works and that our company is the best. It isn't even enough to become converted to our products and services. We must act and think so that by our thinking, actions, and results, others are changed along with us.

"An evaluation of our everyday work is not a sum total of tasks we have done. It is an acknowledgment of the final effect of our acts and thoughts on others, in other words, what we have become and what we have helped others to become as well. It is not enough for anyone just to go through the motions, prospecting, presenting, following-up, getting people started in the business. It's not a list of deposits required to be made in some cosmic account. Success is achieved only when we become what we were intended to become."

Glenna gave us an example from a book she had recently read by George Clason called the *Richest Man in Babylon*. It's about a wealthy man who knew if he were to give his wealth to his children who had not yet developed the wisdom and stature needed, any inheritance he passed on would probably be wasted. "The father said to his children: I want to give you all that I have. I want you to be able to take full advantage of all my wealth, land, business, and money, including my social position and standing. The material things I have I can easily give you, but all that I am and have become, you must obtain for yourself. You will qualify for your inheritance by learning what I have learned and by living as I have lived. I will teach you and exemplify the principles by which I have acquired my wealth, wisdom, and stature. If you follow my example, master what I have mastered, you will become as I am, then you will have all that I have."

"You see," Glenna continued, "we qualify for success in life through a process of learning, practicing, and applying correct principles in their proper sequence. We must achieve the ability to influence others to see who they really are and who they could become, through our own personal journey of profound change and development of our own potential.

"Now is the time for each of us to work toward becoming what we have the potential to become. As we do so, we should remember that in the development of lasting relationships, even more than the relentless pursuit of material gain, is the setting in which the most important part of that development can occur. For some this may take years, and some will have to toil for months; a small percentage will come to the business like prepared dry mix, to which it is only necessary to add water.

"But remember this: success is not based on how long we have worked. We do not obtain success by punching a time clock. What is essential is that our time and efforts have caused us to learn, grow, develop, and become something. No matter how long it takes, no matter how challenging the work is, no matter how bitter the disappointments may be, the reward we gain will be in direct proportion to who we have become along the journey we walk. The easy way provides temporary trinkets, the path of personal effectiveness delivers treasures untold, treasures that transcend the monetary and last an eternity.

"Because of what I do, I meet new people and reunite with old friends everyday. I love to encourage people to be all they can be, to do all they can do, so they can have all they want, to live the uncommon lifestyle of high achievers. I am so excited to work in a business where anyone can choose to be free, where winners can choose to win, where anyone can choose to be a high achiever because everyone is born with a piece of deity inside. I believe that greatness comes as a gift from God in the form of talents and passions for us to discover, develop, and use. I believe that dreams come from God, and I believe that God will always provide a way and the ability to accomplish the goals and dreams he gives us—if we do our part by developing our gifts, talents and passions.

"I believe so much in the power of committed people to make a difference, that I have dedicated my life to teaching and encouraging people to become all they can be; to develop a vision and dream; to build the courage to struggle and the persistence to achieve greater causes and higher purposes. I believe that everyone can be an extraordinary performer, one who can build relationships, create duplication, and live their dreams, while lifting others at the same time.

"This kind of success begins with a commitment to self, family, dreams, and like-minded partners. Successful people are always committed and willing to do what the unsuccessful are unwilling to do. Once the price of victory is paid, you will have a credible claim on whatever success you desire, whether it's a dream car, dream house, incredible vacation, retiring from a job you don't enjoy, bringing a spouse home from work, paying off credit card debt, or simply having the peace of mind that comes from being debt free. It is my belief that because of who you are, and what you could become, that you should set goals that take your breath away. You should chase dreams with such passion and intensity that they drive you to your knees!

"The farthest distance you will ever have to travel in this business is the eighteen inches from your head to your heart. Once you have made the trip and the decision to pursue your passion instead of your pension, people can begin to count on you, follow you, learn from you, and duplicate you. Make a commitment to change someone's life each and every day," exclaimed Glenna.

Quoting Loren E. Eisley from his book *The Star Thrower* she went on to say, "There was a man who was walking along a sandy beach where thousands of starfish had washed up on the shore. He noticed a boy picking up the starfish one by one and throwing them back in the ocean. The man observed the boy for a few minutes and then asked what he was doing. The boy replied he was returning the starfish to the sea, otherwise they would die. The man then asked how saving a few, when so many were doomed, would make any difference whatsoever? The boy picked up a starfish and as he threw it back said: it's going to make a lot of difference to this one!"

Glenna challenged each one of us to chase our dreams with unrelenting determination until we reached them. She closed by saying, "I am excited to share this business with you along with the new recognition awards and promotion program. I believe it will help you to accelerate your success because it teaches principles that will help you accelerate your growth —to help you take positive steps toward your dreams, greater causes, and higher purposes." She thanked us all for coming and looked forward to meeting us in the weeks ahead, then she ended the meeting.

All of my feelings of jealousy toward Cindy and worry about what experiment that Glenna and Doug may have been conducting on me had vanished. I saw a bigger picture—one that was so much bigger than myself. Tomorrow was the first day of the rest of my life, and I was going to make the most of it. I met with Tony and Jerry briefly. They were just as amazed as I was. They also commented on Cindy and how impressive she seemed to be. Tony knew her in the same way I did, she had been his real estate agent when he moved to town. We agreed to meet after the weekly business preview to come up with a strategy on what to do next and to go over the details on the recognition areas and the promotion. We were excited about the possibilities but ready to go home. It had been a long day.

Gary came up to Glenna after the conference was over and they agreed to meet later when they wouldn't be interrupted. Gary had some important questions for and research to share with Glenna. And Glenna had some insight on things that she wanted to share with Gary.

When the crowds left, Glenna and Gary went to a coffee shop close to the freeway. She was dying to know what he had thought of the meeting. He was impressed with how she had implemented his ideas for new recognition, and he shared some of the positive comments he had heard while sitting in the crowd. A lot of people had been talking about enrolling in the promotion for next month, and almost everyone said they were going to take the PEProfile before their next business preview. "But I became so engrossed in your presentation," Gary said, "that I completely forgot I was in a crowd. I have a few questions and some research to share with you, but first, you said you had some insights to share, so let's start there."

"I have compiled the results from my team since our last meeting in your office," she said. "My first observation is that the PEProfile, coupled with the things we talked about, has become incredibly valuable. I can see exactly what my team needs and how the critical skills affect each area of the business. And I can do this in about two minutes instead of a few months. The group of people who didn't enroll for the promotion is enrolling about one new person for every fifty associates in that group. The people in the promotion group (who I call the Rhino Power Team) are enrolling about one person for every three associates on that team. Comparatively speaking, there is no comparison. The Rhino Power Team is blowing the others away. In fact, I wouldn't be surprised if the Rhino Power Team members didn't out recruit the rest of the team this coming month.

"One thing seems very interesting to me in the midst of all this. It seems that conversion ratios are much more important than the raw numbers being produced, like total contacts or total presentations. But I don't fully understand why that might be true. As a result of this line of thinking, I have been wondering if it would be possible to teach my team to enroll a higher percentage of prospects, say 30 percent or more instead of the traditional industry standard of 3 percent? What if the result they got from the same amount of work they are doing now was simply better?"

"These are excellent insights," Gary complemented, "And I think they fit into exactly what I wanted to ask you about. But before that, I want to share with you a couple of things I have noticed and some things I have discovered from interviewing six- and seven-figure earners in other teams and companies. First of all, I want to congratulate you on training your team in the first part of the success pattern. Everyone in the Rhino Power Team improved his or her score on the PEProfile. And the fact they are enrolling people at a rate of fifteen and a half times higher than everyone else makes me wonder why the others are not jumping on board faster? One other thing I noticed from most team members is that almost all of them recruit people to become product users or customers only.

"We can see from your numbers that these people seem to make an initial order, but don't do much else. And they don't seem to enroll anyone else either. For instance, Doug enrolled six new associates and Cindy enrolled seven. I can't see in your genealogy where any of them enrolled anyone else, or even reordered the products on a regular basis. And yet Steve and Jen both enrolled only one or two people, but they were almost all at the event tonight. I'm pretty excited from your talk—I know I asked you about five questions all at once. Let's take things in order."

"In regard to the fact that only a few people joined the promotion during the month after I initially announced it seems a bit perplexing to me as well," Glenna said with a sigh. "My only explanation is that people don't like to be in the new group until it is proven to work, or that possibly old habits are hard to break. There is significant industry propaganda that people will only stay in the business about sixty days, that you must get through those people to their family and friends before the sixty days are over, then through those people before their sixty days are up and so on. This paradigm seems to make people do and say interesting things to get people to engage in activities they are not ready for. I don't know for sure, but if what you were hearing from the audience was correct, I expect this to change in my group this next month. It will be interesting to see," she concluded.

"This month is going to be interesting because this is when those people who achieved the promotion will be under the microscope of the rest of the team," Gary observed. "Which leads me back to the idea of conversion rates. This is an important point you are making and I think I agree. I have interviewed several big earners in other companies, and taking the information from them and combining it with your numbers, I have concluded that there is an actual calculation or formula that creates success. The highest earners in this industry are able to get at least 60 percent of everyone they contact to let them do a presentation. At least 60 percent of those people let them do some kind of a follow-up. And 90 percent of the people they follow up with enroll either as a customer or as an associate. So the top and bottom line is 30 percent of everyone they contact enrolls in some way, either as a customer or as an associate. It doesn't seem that success is determined by how much a person does, but by how effective they are at doing what they do.

"Of course people do have to work at a minimal level, but the idea that a person must contact hundreds to enroll a few doesn't appear to be in harmony with long-term success. In fact, it seems there is a multiplying effect of those who have high conversion rates; the people they enroll become more effective at these same things. They aren't just doing things for the sake of being busy. Or as one leader told me, they don't throw mud at the wall to see if some sticks. They do things on purpose, with purpose. Then they review their progress and make adjustments. No one else seems to have a vocabulary to be able to describe this yet, or a way to show people the whole picture like you do with the success pattern. I think as we perfect our language and implementation of it through the Rhino Power Team, they will create job-dropping residual income at industry changing rates. So as a training designer and human performance engineer, I'm curious about how many contacts it takes the Rhino Power Team to make appointments, what percentage of those presentations result in follow-ups, and what is their percentage of enrollments from follow-ups?

"I'm also thinking that we need to add a few extra measures for recognition at our next event. Those measurements will require everyone on the team to start tracking their results in the key areas of contacts, presentations, follow-ups, and enrollments. Of course, enrollments are easy to track and report, but anyone who wants to participate in the recognition program would need to report their numbers in each category each week. I am excited to get and analyze this information. This is going to be a game changer for you, XL-8, and the industry generally. The information we will get from this project is going to allow us to create not only predictability in training programs, but also in the specific activities that create precise, purposeful action toward meaningful results," Gary finished.

Glenna sat up a little taller in her chair with excitement and told Gary she would consider how to implement new ways to recognize team members for their effectiveness. She expressed her concerns about how to train people who are in different phases in the success pattern in the Saturday training meetings. Gary said he needed to think about how to do that effectively. He assured Glenna that he would get back to her in a week or so with some kind of an answer, and maybe even a system to make this possible.

8

The Pity Party

Early Monday morning Cindy called Doug and they discussed their plan for her business this month. She told Doug she had been contacting like crazy and that she was almost out of the names she had on her list. They considered past real estate clients and other professional colleagues. She had already gone through almost 120 people and that didn't count those she cold contacted in various places. Doug asked, vaguely remembering a past conversation, "Didn't you know both Steve and Tony before they got in the business?" Cindy explained, "Yes, I was their agent when they bought their homes."

"Let's consider the people that they might be thinking of. It's obvious that they aren't talking to the people they know, and it's not right to keep the business from them just because Steve and Tony aren't going to contact them. All this Rhino Power Team and building PEPs before building the business stuff is keeping them from doing anything meaningful in the business. You could call the people you know in the school district and parents of the players on the local teams. Simply tell them you are expanding a business in this area. Leverage your acquaintance with Steve, Tony, and Jerry by telling them that they are involved, then set up appointments or invite them to the preview meetings. This should give you another large group of people to contact and a great way to help people who are probably never going to hear about the business from Steve, Tony, or Jerry," Doug continued. "This is a great idea," Cindy replied. "No wonder you are at the Silver level in the business."

At the end of the school day Mrs. Jones, the principal of the school I work at, called me into her office and asked what my plans were for next year's contract as the baseball coach. She was so confident that I was going to coach again that she already had my contract made out. I had been dreading this moment for weeks now. Winning the state championship for the third time in the last five years had certainly put me in high demand. I fidgeted for a few seconds as I searched for some way to tell her I wasn't coming back as the coach. The momentary silence made it seem like an uncomfortable amount of time. Finally, I just came out and told her that I would still be teaching my classes, but wouldn't be coaching. She was stunned for a moment, then she asked why I was quitting as coach and what I was going to do instead.

As I searched for what to tell her, I blurted out that I was starting my own business as a way to be able to continue to teach. "Business," she replied "what kind of business, and how will that affect your teaching responsibilities?"

"I don't think it should affect my duties here in any way. In fact it should free up some time each day to let me be better prepared." As I was talking, it appeared that she was troubled about having to find another baseball coach. She sarcastically asked if the business was what Jerry had started. I told her it was and she became a little more agitated. "How long have you known about this?" I told her only a week or so, but I wanted to be certain before I announced anything.

"When were you planning on telling me?" She asked curtly. "I was going to tell you," but before I could finish, she interrupted by asking me if I knew how hard it was to find coaches without a teaching position to go along with the job? And then she went for the kill when she said, "You have put me and the whole district in a difficult position. All for this pipe dream of yours to make money and live the dream lifestyle of the rich and famous. I appreciate your consideration to all involved. Thank you Steve, I'll pass on this new need to the district office so they can begin their search for a new coach. That will be all for now," she said, turning around to look at a stack of papers on the desk behind her. "Please shut the door on the way out."

I had imagined how difficult this was going to be, but I never thought it would be that bad. Not only did she fail to congratulate me on winning the state championship or for building a baseball program from nothing to a perennial powerhouse, but she was genuinely angry and put out. To add insult to injury, she mocked the business and ridiculed me for pursuing my dreams. The more I thought about this, the more it made me angry. On my way home I thought how I hated it when the right things to say came to my mind after it was too late to say them. I wanted to tell her that if the school paid enough, I wouldn't have to go into business anyway. And if there were a bonus for winning state championships and for being Teacher of the Year, I would be able to afford decent food, pay all of my bills each month, and take my wife on a date without worrying about the cost of a babysitter. I might even be able to afford a second car so I could drive to work every day. After the conversation with Mrs. Jones I was ready for summer vacation to begin, then I could dedicate all my efforts toward a permanent vacation from teaching.

By the time I made the twenty-minute walk home, the news was out and the phone had already been ringing. Parents, school board members, boosters, school district administrators, and the sports guy from the local newspaper had all somehow heard that I was quitting as the baseball coach. They wanted to know the same two things: why I was quitting and what I was going to do instead? I tried to figure out what to say to them all, and in the process I got several laughs and more disparaging comments from those who didn't support me. They were only interested in having a top-notch baseball program. I heard all kinds of negative things about the industry. One by one I was crossing people off my list of warm contacts. One good thing about all of this was that I got through my list faster this way and I did manage to set a few appointments from those who knew and trusted me. They said if I was interested in something, then they wanted to know more about it because they knew I wouldn't do anything really weird, risky, or bad. In all, I took about fifty phone calls and then I sat back for a minute and called Glenna. I needed to talk to her about this. Maybe she could give me some perspective. She agreed to meet with me before the business preview at her house. I ate an early dinner and headed to Glenna's about two hours before the weekly meeting.

With all that had happened that afternoon I felt pretty beat up and more than a little negative about the business. I had gone from king to clown in a matter of minutes and I was happy to unload on Glenna. I told her how I had been feeling at the event; how I had wondered if she was playing some kind of trick on me. And why had she been telling me one thing while Doug was telling Cindy another? I reminded her that I had spent over $1,000 to enroll, buy some marketing materials, get tickets to the conference, take the PEProfile—not once but twice—get the *Skills of the Million-Dollar Earners* audio library, put gas in my car, and a host of other things. The result was that I had made a whopping

$150. I also told her that I was ready to take effective action and start making money like Cindy was.

Glenna listened patiently and took a few notes while I was ranting and raving. When I was through, she asked me if there was anything else I wanted to get off my chest. I took a minute and realized I had just vented to one person (other than Sara) who was willing to encourage me to achieve my goals, dreams, and passions. I put my head down and apologized for my emotional eruption. She accepted my apology and then told me that after all that it was perfectly natural to be upset. Glenna sympathetically continued, "This is where many people get discouraged and quit. They quit because they can't see the results of their work yet. Stay the course, follow the 3-Step Success Pattern and the result will be there, I promise," she told me without blinking an eye. She also told me not to listen to anyone who isn't responsible for paying my bills and caring for my family. "None of them get to have a vote on your attitude or your action; they simply don't get a vote in your life."

Glenna then instructed me to make sure Tony and Jerry got plugged into the Rhino Power Team and took the Personal Effectiveness Profile as soon as possible. They also needed to enroll on the Rhino Power Team and in the Seminar at Sea promotion. She reminded me to do the things I had committed to do in the beginning. "I told you those things because I believe in you, and I don't want the things I taught you to stop with you. Teach them to the people on your team. Although right now there may not be many, you do have a great start," she said.

She also told me about her meeting with a guy named Gary who was serving as one of her mentors. They wanted all of us to keep and report the amount of contacts, presentations, follow-ups, and enrollments each Saturday night. She asked me for my napkin drawing of the success pattern and started drawing out the info for the second step, or Build a Team phase. Glenna then told me I was ready to advance. As a result, I needed to adjust the way I was allocating my time and the business activities I was doing each day. "You need to begin allocating your time like this: 15 percent should be spent on personal improvement, 50 percent on recruiting, 30 percent on training your new people, and 5 percent should be spent on retention work. Personal improvement you already understand. You need to listen again to the CDs in the Improve Yourself phase and then make sure to listen to the CDs in the Build a Team phase that match your red areas on your most recent PEProfile.

3-STEP·SUCCESS PATTERN™

IMPROVE YOURSELF	BUILD A TEAM	BECOME A LEADER
0-30 PEPS 14-30 Days	31-45 PEPS 60-120 Days	46-70 PEPS 10 Leaders
*20 Critical Initial Skills	*20 Critical Building Skills	*10 Critical Leadership Skills
Time Focus 95% on personal effectiveness 5% on recruiting	Time Focus 15% on personal improvement 50% on recruiting 30% on training new people 5% on retention	Time Focus
Action Items 1. Get associate# 2. Enroll on product autoship or autopay 3. Have tickets to next event 4. Take the PEProfile 5. Gain a firm knowledge and testimony of company and products 6. Memorize contacting scripts 7. Make an effective list of 200 names 8. Subscribe to education system 9. Have personal improvement plan	Action Items	Action Items
Goals 1. Increase PEPs to 30+ 2. Score green or yellow in first 20 skills 3. Enroll 1-5 customers/associates 4. Receive products for FREE	Goals	Goals

"Now the work you need to start becoming effective at is going through your warm list. Part of that work was done today as a result of your coaching announcement. But you still have many names on your warm and chicken lists; there are still more people who live right here in town who you haven't met yet. So you need to begin working to contact those you know and show presentations on your own.

"Of course I will help you for the first few times, but you have higher PEPs now and are learning quickly. You just need to master the twenty skills in the Build a Team phase of the success pattern. Practice them in our Saturday trainings and follow the steps of an effective presentation, just as Kim taught at the conference. I will also be available to help you with three-way calls at the end of your presentations to give you some credibility and to help answer any questions your prospects have. This will help get them enrolled and started properly at the beginning of the success pattern instead of the middle. Is everything clear so far?" Glenna asked.

"Here is what you need to focus on during the Build a Team phase." Glenna said, as she took the napkin and filled in more of that section.

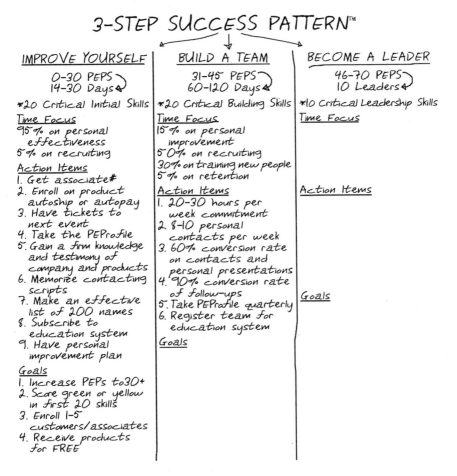

3-STEP SUCCESS PATTERN™

IMPROVE YOURSELF	BUILD A TEAM	BECOME A LEADER
0-30 PEPS 14-30 Days	31-45 PEPS 60-120 Days	46-70 PEPS 10 Leaders
*20 Critical Initial Skills	*20 Critical Building Skills	*10 Critical Leadership Skills
Time Focus 95% on personal effectiveness 5% on recruiting	**Time Focus** 15% on personal improvement 50% on recruiting 30% on training new people 5% on retention	**Time Focus**
Action Items 1. Get associate# 2. Enroll on product autoship or autopay 3. Have tickets to next event 4. Take the PEProfile 5. Gain a firm knowledge and testimony of company and products 6. Memorize contacting scripts 7. Make an effective list of 200 names 8. Subscribe to education system 9. Have personal improvement plan	**Action Items** 1. 20-30 hours per week commitment 2. 8-10 personal contacts per week 3. 60% conversion rate on contacts and personal presentations 4. 90% conversion rate of follow-ups 5. Take PEProfile quarterly 6. Register team for education system	**Action Items**
Goals 1. Increase PEPs to 30+ 2. Score green or yellow in first 20 skills 3. Enroll 1-5 customers/associates 4. Receive products for FREE	**Goals**	**Goals**

"I think you have a pretty good handle on the time commitment part and I have great faith that you will be able to allocate your time correctly. Do you think you can do eight to ten contacts each and every week?" After getting a commitment from me to do just that she continued, "When you master contacting, you will have an incredible advantage over many other network marketers. Because you know the difference between a real contact and just a conversation, you will have a great sense that you are doing things on purpose and not talking to prospects for the sake of talking to them. Your goal is to get 60 percent of those you invite to take action, to make an appointment with you or to do something that will help them move toward you and then with you, such as to come to the business preview on Tuesdays or watch a DVD. Then, your goal is to convert 60 percent of your presentations to follow-up meetings. It's important to know that if you do your presentations like Kim taught you, people will know why you are following up with them. You're not just there for a social visit; you're there to answer questions, give them any additional information they requested, and enroll them either as a customer or as an associate. Following this sequence will help you to convert at least 90 percent of your follow-ups to enrollments.

"If you are doing the math, contacting thirty-three prospects per month—that's just over eight per week—you should do twenty presentations per month, twelve follow-ups, and personally enroll ten to eleven new people on your team each month. As you teach your team to do the same thing, the multiplying effect that this has is unbelievable. That's why I have been so forceful in teaching you this. That's why I made you commit and promise to do what I told you to do, because of what can happen if you do this right. The temptation for everyone is to go out and start blabbing to his or her family and friends. When they don't enroll, the conclusion is that the business doesn't work and the people quit. It's not the business that fails. It's people's lack of skill and knowledge that fails. I don't want this to happen to you, Steve; I want you to go all the way to the top. So let me borrow the napkin one more time and then we will be finished for tonight.

"Our goal is to increase your PEPs to forty-five or more by mastering the next twenty critical skills. Look at your latest PEProfile report and focus on the skills that are red in the Build a Team section. Listen to the CDs in the Build a Team set from *Skills of the Million-Dollar Earners*. And make sure to practice what you need in our Saturday trainings. You won't be ready to move on to the Become a Leader phase until you add at least fifteen to twenty-five people on your team with at least three to five of them committed like you are to becoming a leader in this business. When you do this, you will be in the top 3 percent of all network marketers in the world. You will be able to create break-even income and then the beginnings of job-dropping residual income.

3-STEP SUCCESS PATTERN™

IMPROVE YOURSELF	BUILD A TEAM	BECOME A LEADER
0-30 PEPS 14-30 Days	31-45 PEPS 60-120 Days	46-70 PEPS 10 Leaders
*20 Critical Initial Skills	*20 Critical Building Skills	*10 Critical Leadership Skills

Time Focus
95% on personal
  effectiveness
5% on recruiting
	Time Focus
	15% on personal
	  improvement
	50% on recruiting
	30% on training new people
	5% on retention
		Time Focus

Action Items
1. Get associate#
2. Enroll on product
  autoship or autopay
3. Have tickets to
  next event
4. Take the PEProfile
5. Gain a firm knowledge
  and testimony of
  company and products
6. Memorize contacting
  scripts
7. Make an effective
  list of 200 names
8. Subscribe to
  education system
9. Have personal
  improvement plan
	Action Items
	1. 20-30 hours per
	  week commitment
	2. 8-10 personal
	  contacts per week
	3. 60% conversion rate
	  on contacts and
	  personal presentations
	4. 90% conversion rate
	  of follow-ups
	5. Take PEProfile quarterly
	6. Register team for
	  education system
		Action Items

Goals
1. Increase PEPs to 30+
2. Score green or yellow
  in first 20 skills
3. Enroll 1-5
  customers/associates
4. Receive products
  for FREE
	Goals
	1. Increase PEPs to 45+
	2. Score green/yellow in
	  team-building skills
	3. 15-25 associates
	  on team
	4. 3-5 committed to
	  leadership track
	5. Break even and then
	  earn at least $2,500
	  in residual income
		Goals

"Initially our goal is to get you to at least $2,500 while you are in this phase. My focus is going to shift from you to those people you enroll on the team for the next few weeks. Don't worry, I'm not going to ignore you. But as a leader, I need to make sure the people you enroll are getting started the right way so your promotion to leadership will be accelerated."

People were starting to arrive for the weekly business preview so we ended our meeting and began the preview. Glenna had asked me to welcome people to the preview meeting. I was eager to help out in this way until a couple of people came in who I knew. Two pairs of parents of kids from my baseball team had somehow been invited to the meeting. How could this have happened? Did Tony or Jerry invite them? Word of what I was doing and the location of any meeting that I would be affiliated with could never have circulated in the few hours since I talked to Mrs. Jones—could it?

I welcomed them and as I was shaking their hands Cindy came in and apologized for being a few minutes late. It was Cindy who had invited them! She saw who I had been talking to about the business and had obviously targeted the people who would have been in my circle of influence, baseball parents, school administrators, and so forth. Tony and Jerry came in right after Cindy. Doug invited us all to take our seats and introduced Glenna, who then started the meeting in earnest. I couldn't believe it! Maybe Cindy ran out of names, so she started talking to people who others on Glenna's team were connected with. It didn't take long for this situation to put me right back where I was emotionally after my visit with Mrs. Jones. My mind wandered and for a minute or two I seriously started considering doing what Doug and Cindy had been doing. After all, they were the ones on stage for creating tangible enrollment and income results on Saturday. And I couldn't really win a race with Doug and Cindy to contact all the people I knew before they did. I could see my future sitting on the front row with Cindy. They would certainly talk to the other parents and all the people I knew would be gone before I had enough PEPs to really make any headway.

My silent pity party was interrupted when Doug called Cindy up to the front to say a few words as the newest member of the Winners' Circle for business growth. She talked of making a decision to succeed tonight and to get to work on achieving it. She was pretty compelling. I was even inspired by her, and I had heard her before. But I still resented her for inviting my friends to the meeting. While Cindy was talking she didn't look at anyone else in the room except for the people she had stolen from me. She went to get them a cookie after the presentation, and they came over to talk to me. Luckily Jerry intercepted Cindy on the way back. While he was complementing her on her message, my friends asked me what my role in all this was. I quickly explained that I was in a training phase of the business so that I could take effective action and be a good mentor and teacher for those who joined my team. Tony and Jerry were the first members of my team, but I was going to be contacting each of them in the next few weeks, now that I was more prepared to provide great customer service and help to do what Glenna had just talked about. They both told me to give them a call this week to get the straight scoop on what this was all about.

Jerry was excited by what he saw. This was his first meeting. He commented positively on the people and noted the incredible energy everyone had. He told Cindy that everyone seemingly worked together to help each other succeed. How could this be a bad thing he wondered? He commented on Doug and Cindy and how they had been so inspirational and determined to succeed. Tony and Jerry both asked, "So now what do we do?" I asked them if they could stick around for a little while because Glenna usually had a brief training meeting after the business preview. Tony agreed, but Jerry told me he had to go. He shook my hand and said he would have at least two people here next week. Before I could make an appointment to help him learn the success pattern and take the PEProfile he rushed out. Glenna welcomed Tony to the team and she made an appointment with him to get him started right. She gave him the website for the PEProfile and asked him to take it before their meeting. He agreed, and I was relieved that he was going to be coached by Glenna. She was serious about taking care of those I enrolled.

I told Sara that the Browns and the Fords had been at the meeting, that Cindy had invited them, but that they wanted to talk to me about the business. I wasn't sure what that meant. I didn't want to spend time talking to them about the business and then have them enroll with Cindy. Sara reminded me about the help Jen had given me and then about the principle that what goes around comes around. "Do unto others," she taunted! I didn't want to think about it right now.

By the time I got to school the next day everyone knew I had resigned as the baseball coach. Consequently, I got to spend a lot of time hearing how it wasn't fair that I was quitting before the juniors graduated. Numerous questions were fired at me about what was going to happen now. I had never before been so glad to have a day of school be over. I got home and there were a bunch of messages on the answering machine with the same kind of comments and questions. Some of the messages pained me to listen to and others made me feel proud of what I had been doing the past five years. It was a little like being on a roller coaster, one message up and the next down. This was crazy, I finally realized. I was the one who needed support. If they were so upset with my quitting, then why didn't they pay teachers and coaches more? I remembered Glenna's advice, "If they're not responsible for raising my kids or paying my bills, then they don't get to vote in my life."

I took out the napkin and sat down at the kitchen table with Sara and tried to explain it to her. She examined it in the same way I did when I first saw it. She asked if all I had to do was follow this and I would be able to make the kind of money Glenna was making, live in the kind of house Glenna lived in, drive the kind of cars Glenna drove, buy the clothes and eat like she did? I answered as authoritatively as I had ever answered any question before, "Yes!" She told me to get a good night's sleep and start working for it as hard as I had worked for anything else, *ever*! I never expected her to be as definite and firm as she was. I think the voice messages had hurt her, too. She asked me what Glenna had told me to do next. I told her I was supposed to take my names list and begin contacting people on it. She wanted to see the list. "What about the Browns and the Fords? How do they fit into this? They are on your names list right here!"

"I don't know what exactly to do about them," I told her. "Glenna will know what to do, but I am in no frame of mind to call anyone tonight." On the way up the stairs I said I was going to start with the Browns and the Fords, to get them out of the way so that I could move on to others. "Too bad too; they could have been really great team members. Oh well, no use in worrying about it. There's nothing we can do about it now," I said wearily.

The next morning I called Ben Ford and Mark Brown and made appointments with them. The Browns asked if they could come over to the Fords and meet together. That seemed like a great idea to me so I agreed. They were friends with each other, so I didn't think the Fords would mind. Sara came with me to the meeting and we showed them what I could remember from the times I had seen Glenna and Jen present. I tried to follow the presentation steps I had learned from Kim at the event last Saturday. I asked them about Cindy and what they had been thinking since the business preview on Tuesday. They told me that they didn't get in because they didn't understand what to do or how they might do it. They told me all she had talked about was herself and how she was going to be able to quit her job soon and do this full time. It seemed like they were inspiring each other to tell me how much they liked the business, but that they didn't want to enroll with Cindy. Pam Ford told Sara that she didn't even find out what we wanted or why we might be interested in XL-8.

I breathed a silent sigh of relief when I realized I had made sure to include step one of the presentation as Kim had taught. I knew what their challenges were and I was able to help them see how XL-8 was the best solution for what they wanted. Before I gave them the three options at the end of the presentation, I felt like I should call Glenna to ask her what to do. I knew they were going to enroll, but I wondered who they should enroll with? I hadn't called Glenna beforehand to make sure she would be available, but it seemed like I should at least try to do a three-way call and ask the question. As I dialed, I was edifying Glenna and told them how much I had appreciated her mentorship and that she had offered to help me if I needed it. Fortunately, she answered the phone. I put them all on speaker mode so we could talk and hear her. She talked for a few minutes and then returned the boomerang of edification to me. Unexpectedly, we had to end the call before I had a chance to ask her what to do. I decided to give them the three options and see what their level of interest was. Both couples decided to enroll with me and I told them about the Saturday training meeting. I invited them to come and we would cover exactly what to do then. Glenna would be there and she would give us sound advice on the next steps.

I arrived a few minutes early to the training meeting to talk to Glenna about the Fords and the Browns. She asked me what would be best for the Fords and the Browns. Of course I told her it would be best for them to be in business with me. She smiled and inquired if she asked them what would they say? Then I told her about the meeting and conversation we had about Cindy and her approach to talking to them. I told her that they were both coming to the training and she agreed to talk to them when they got there. I got the sense that this wasn't the first time she had gone through this. I felt much better, at least for a few minutes. Then Cindy came to the training meeting. I think she somehow knew that the Fords and Browns would be there.

Glenna welcomed her and they disappeared for a few minutes. Glenna explained the situation and told her she was going to talk to the Fords and the Browns to see exactly what they wanted to do. She asked Cindy how she had come to know the Fords and the Browns. Cindy looked a little anxious as she searched for a logical answer, one that would also win Glenna to her side. She said she had run out of names and was thinking of people who knew people she knew. "I was going through the names of past clients and I noticed that I had sold some homes to a lot of school district employees. And so I called those who I thought would know teachers and other administrators."

"That sounds reasonable," Glenna responded. "So you just called people from the phone book—or how exactly did you find these particular couples?" Sensing that Glenna wasn't going to just let this go, she admitted that she and Doug had thought that since Steve, Tony, and Jerry weren't going to really talk to anyone, that this was the perfect opportunity to do so because they had just enrolled and had a strong relationship with them. "So you probably knew that both the Browns and the Fords were likely on Steve's names list?" Cindy replied, "Doug actually had a copy of his list from their first meeting. He told me that business was business. Since I was actually doing something, I should just go ahead and contact them because everyone deserved a chance at the business." Glenna sat back in her chair and sighed deeply a few times, pressed her lips together, and while squinting her eyes said as calmly as she could, "So Doug was in on this, huh?" In a last-ditch effort to save any chance she had at being able to enroll the two couples, Cindy quickly said it was his idea! Glenna thanked her for meeting and excused herself to make a phone call.

While they were in their meeting, Tony, Jerry, the Fords, and the Browns came in as if they had come together to the meeting. I took this as a sort of sign that they were going to be on the same team when Glenna got done with this. When Cindy came out of the meeting with Glenna she looked a little like I felt when I left Mrs. Jones' office after I told her I was resigning from coaching. She was plenty ticked off when she saw them all sitting together with me. Glenna came out a minute or two later to get the meeting started. The speed and directness of her walk and the fact that she immediately started the meeting sent a message that she was being purposeful but calm. There was something missing in her usual friendly demeanor.

Jen came in just as Glenna was getting started. The training meeting was awesome. We learned about commitment, how to set our expectations of results based on our willingness and ability to commit time, finances, personal improvement, and devotion to a team and to customer service. She taught us that commitment is measured by our willingness and determination to get the job done, no matter the circumstances. Commitment can be measured in many ways. It can be measured by how much it takes to make you discouraged and give up.

Some people become discouraged very easily and quickly, while others work harder and smarter when things aren't going as planned. She asked us all how much we would be willing to commit if what each one of us wanted from our business was guaranteed? "How much time and money would you invest to create that result, $10 per month? $50 per month? $100? $1000 or more? an hour a day? two hours a day? twenty hours per week? Would you be willing to give up hobbies temporarily or rearrange your busy schedule? Would you be willing to listen and learn a predictable pattern of success and then follow it religiously?" I had heard this before from Glenna. I looked around the room and I saw everyone nodding their head, including my team members. Glenna was so good at making things simple and then making you commit to doing those things that bring success, even if they don't always make sense when you are doing them. Her last request was to ask us to think of what's at stake. "It's your future we're talking about here. It's your children's future, it's your grandchildren's future." Then she excused us with this thought, "A wise man told me once that you can make excuses or you can make money; but you can't make both."

When the meeting was over I introduced the Fords and the Browns to Glenna. Cindy was right there to make sure they knew she was there to support them, as if to stake her claim to their allegiance. Glenna invited them to go with her into her office. I made an appointment with Tony and Jerry to meet with them this coming week to go over their game plan for the next few weeks. Tony and Jerry left and as they went out the front door I noticed that Cindy was standing just outside waiting for Glenna. She wouldn't even look at me, and I didn't think this was a good time to try to strike up a conversation. When they came out Glenna thanked them for coming and welcomed them to the team. She then invited Cindy and me to come in. Ben and Mark told me they would call me this afternoon to get started. This was my first real indication that they had chosen to be on my team and that Glenna had agreed.

Cindy and I sat across from Glenna and she told us how wonderful the Fords and Browns were. She went on to let us know that this kind of thing often causes some people to quit the business. Inevitably someone feels like the upline has chosen one side or the other, so they feel slighted. "But let me tell you that I counseled them to do what they felt was right in their own minds; to join with who they felt would give them the best chance to achieve their goals in the business, who they had the most trust in and whose counsel they would be most willing to take when things weren't going well. I didn't tell them what to do. I told them they're adults and that they should think about it and then call each of you to let you know their decision. I just want to make sure the two of you are going to be okay no matter what they choose, that you won't hold a grudge if they don't choose you. I want to remind you that they are just beginning in the business and they need to hear that you are going to support them even if they don't choose you. This business is about helping people whether or not you have a vested interest in them. Steve, I want to remind you that Jen helped you. And Cindy, I want to remind you that Kim helped you a few weeks ago. Neither of them had anything to gain by helping either of you, but they did it anyway. Of course I will find out who they have chosen by looking at my organization chart on the website, so you don't need to feel like you should call me to let me know how it turns out. One last thing I want to say before you go. I am not going to get in the middle of anything like this again for either of you. If this happens again, you get together and solve it yourselves, making sure you keep in mind whose welfare you are trying to take care of."

When I got home I had a message from Ben Ford. He told me he and Mark had talked and had decided to enroll with me because they knew me. Because of their experience with me as the baseball coach, they felt more comfortable with me and trusted me to always be straight with them about what to do and how to do it. They were free that evening if I wanted to meet with them both to get started. The message also told me that they had already called Cindy and apologized for the position they had put us all in. They thanked her for caring enough to call them in the first place. I sighed as I sat down to process what had just happened. I am not sure I realized how emotionally draining being in business was. I thought only kids on a baseball field or in a classroom could challenge your ability to stay in control emotionally. Obviously, this was not true. Tonight I will enroll my third and fourth associates in the business. Now how do I place them in the organization? Should I put them side-by-side, in separate groups, or one above the other? I didn't want to bother Glenna again as she had just spent a couple of hours with us. Then it occurred to me that she would be training me on how to handle this kind of thing for future reference—and besides this is why she makes all the big money, right?

9

Connecting the Dots

Glenna poured over the numbers for the past few weeks. She leaned back in her soft leather office chair, wondering why Doug's income numbers seemed low for someone who had been in the business a few years and why they fluctuated wildly from month to month in comparison to Kim's. Her income wasn't great either, but her numbers seemed to be pretty consistent. In a moment of inspiration she looked at the numbers through a different filter and almost immediately saw the difference. Doug was focused on recruiting new people and then dumping them into the company success system, leaving them to fend for themselves, that he was continuously having to out recruit attrition. Going back over his enrollment numbers and then looking at his organization structure, it was incredible to see what was happening to Doug. He seemed to have the idea that his job was to bring people into the business and it was the company's, uplines', and enrollee's personal job to succeed once they had enrolled. Looking at it in this way showed how huge this problem was. He had personally earned the Winners' Circle award five times. And several of his team members had earned it as well, including Cindy who earned it last month. But he had just advanced to the third promotion level, Silver. And Cindy achieved her first promotion to Copper in her first month just like Doug did. However, no one on Doug's team, including Doug, had ever been recognized for team production points.

Kim, on the other hand, seemed to have a different challenge. She was so focused on helping people succeed once they enrolled that she was not enrolling enough people. She appeared to feel like her job was to mother her team. And she did this to the point of smothering them. Kim had never earned the Winners' Circle award or achieved Silver Star for team enrollments. She had been slowly growing to Gold and that's why she was invited to speak at the last event. Kim was great at helping people to understand the business and to feel like they could succeed with her help.

Both of these wonderful people are excellent in their own way. The fact they are so singularly focused keeps them from seeing that they need to improve in the other areas and that a whole system is in place that could help them predictably progress to their greater causes and higher purposes. With this knowledge they would teach their team members to do the same. The problem is that these two strategies seem to be creating about an 85 percent fallout rate in both of their groups. Glenna had been going crazy searching for the answers until she started using the Personal Effectiveness Profile and tracking the items that Gary asked about. Now it was clear that few on her team understand how everything fits together.

People join Doug's team and they enroll others, but no one stays in for very long because everyone knows how to enroll, but not how to build a team or lead the group. People join Kim's team at a slow pace and they become focused on helping the few people they have; knowing and understanding *everything before they do anything* becomes a top priority, which results in no recruiting and causing them to quit early. In both cases they quit because no one is making any money. Leaning back again, Glenna looked up and asked the ceiling, "So what can I do about this, and if I had the answer, would they even want to be helped?" In the still night air she thought about how dedicated her team seemed to be to success. She reassured herself that most everyone would be open to learning how to increase his or her income from the business.

So how was Glenna going to implement Gary's lessons about things we focus on expanding, to get people doing what they get rewarded for and tap into their desire for recognition? "I think I have done this for the people on Steve's and Jen's teams in regard to the Improve Yourself phase. So what do I want to expand in the Build a Team phase, and how will I reward people for it?" Glenna wondered. "It's late, but I really need to get this under control," she says to herself as she starts dialing Gary's phone number. Just as she is about to hang up, Gary answers. "Hello, Gary. This is Glenna. I'm sorry to call so late. I have a problem I need to talk to you about. Do you have a minute to talk?" He agrees.

Quickly she explains her predicament with people only doing part of the success pattern, like recruiting but not training, or training but not recruiting effectively. She shares her idea that this comes from their not fully understanding the whole success pattern, and how everything fits together into the entire process. Gary asks, "Are there people on the team who don't experience this problem that we can use as examples of doing it right?" Glenna is surprised by the obvious nature of this question.

She described Steve's and Jen's teams. "Steve enrolled in the business in the past month or so and Jen has been around a few years. Jen has experienced the ebb and flow of associates and income doing the business in traditional ways. She and Steve both joined the promotion we started last month. You saw them earn almost every award we invented for the Improve Yourself phase at the business conference. Both Steve and Jen are converting more than 60 percent of their contacts to presentations, and over 60 percent of their presentations to follow-ups, and nearly 100 percent of their follow-ups enroll in the business. They are following the success pattern with precision and they are teaching their teams to do the same right from the start. I tried to figure out how to do the three things you talked about in your office by focusing on the things I wanted to expand, rewarding people for specific activities, and tapping into their need for recognition, but I just needed to discuss this with you," Glenna said apologetically.

"Don't worry about it; I love this kind of challenge. So what is it that you want to highlight to your team? Recruiting, training, retention, relationship building, communication skills, what?" Gary asked. Glenna was stuck momentarily trying to get at the most foundational concept she could. There was silence for a full thirty seconds. Gary interrupted the silence by interjecting the idea he got while she was describing her problem a moment ago. "It seems there are three problems: (1) most people don't know what the whole success pattern is; (2) they don't know where they are in the success pattern; and (3) they have no idea what they need individually to do next to move forward. The first problem is easy to solve. In your weekly training meetings make sure to explain it in detail to the associates who show up. For all the others who don't, you might hold a conference call or webinar to help them get it. You may have to do this multiple times to catch the majority of your team, but it will pay dividends in the end. Make sure to promote these meetings or trainings as something special that they can't miss or they will miss the secret of success. In every meeting you need to talk about the success pattern at a high level and then focus on one of the three phases or a specific skill within the success pattern. Make sure everyone knows how that skill relates to the overall process. You must connect the dots for people or they won't get it.

"Second, you must reward people for doing what you want them to do. As you were describing Steve and Jen you focused on their conversion rates. I wrote down 60 percent contacts to presentations, 60 percent presentations to follow-ups, and almost 100 percent of follow-ups to enrollments. Have you recognized anyone in any meeting for this?" Gary asked.

"Oh my gosh, we have never done this," Glenna exclaimed, "And I don't know anyone else who has either." Gary continued. "It seems you need to reward people for mastering the success pattern. We will know they have mastered it by measuring their effectiveness in the key indicators or their conversion rates in contacting, presenting, following-up, and enrolling. We will know if they are taking the right action in its proper sequence by the results they get in these key areas. I think we need to put Steve and Jen on the stage as examples of the success pattern working, and, of course, they must give credit for their progress to the process as the reason for their success.

"And last, off the top of my head I remember that you explained in our first meeting that you suggest, but don't demand or track, the idea that associates should do fifteen to twenty presentations every month, is that right?" Glenna realized that Gary was really paying attention to everything if he could remember this from a conversation he had had a month ago! "That's right," Glenna responded. "So how many contacts can a person reasonably make in a week?" Gary asked. "I teach my new people to make at least eight to ten per week. That usually gives them a way to do about fifteen presentations a month," Glenna replied.

"So using the results that Steve and Jen are getting, that would mean that at a minimum of eight contacts per week, a person could contact thirty-two to thirty-three people per month. If those with at least thirty PEPs could get the same 60 percent conversion rates that Steve and Jen have produced, then everyone on the team would do twenty presentations per month. At 60 percent they would do twelve follow-ups, and even at an 85 percent conversion of follow-ups to enrollments, they would enroll ten new people each month! Is this happening on your team right now?" Glenna laughed, "I wish it were."

"At our last leadership conference we learned that the industry averages are about a 15 to 20 percent conversion rate on contacts to presentations and about 3 percent on overall enrollments. I suspect my team is doing about that. But what I think you just said Gary is that if everyone on the team learns what Steve and Jen seem to understand, our conversion rates of contacts to enrollments will go from the industry average of 3 percent to about 30 percent! Did I hear you correctly?"

"That's what the math shows," said Gary. "Do the results of Steve and Jen's work reflect this? Are they enrolling 30 percent of the people they are contacting? And, if so, I would begin immediately to scream this from the rooftops."

Glenna looked through her numbers for the past few weeks and then, suddenly realizing the enormity of the moment and its possible effect on her team, income, and future, she gasped as she shouted out that it seems that both Jen and Steve are actually enrolling about 30 percent of their prospects! "So Gary, what is the best way for me to shout this from the rooftops?" Glenna asked.

"I think the way to begin the introduction to this new way of thinking is to ask who would like to personally enroll ten new associates each month *and* have everyone on their team enroll ten new members on their teams each month? And who would like to still have those people on their team and engaged in buying and building a year from now? Explain the 60 percent, 60 percent, and 90 percent concept. Show the concrete example of contacting thirty-three people, giving twenty presentations, doing twelve follow-ups, and enrolling ten people. That's right. You only need to contact eight to ten people per week to create a six-figure income in the next six months. But you can't get these kinds of results or conversion rates unless you have high PEPs. And high PEPs start in the Improve Yourself phase of the success pattern with foundational skills to build on. Then you can be effective in the Build a Team phase when you start contacting, presenting, answering questions, overcoming objections, asking for the business, and teaching others to do the same duplicate-able, predictable process of success."

The next morning when Glenna got up she remembered something Gary had said the night before. He talked about connecting the dots. She had been telling people for a long time now that they needed to help their prospects connect the dots between what they wanted to create in their lives and how XL-8 could help them. Now, out of the blue, Gary had essentially told her she needed to help her team members connect the dots between what they wanted out of their businesses and the results they could get if they just followed the success pattern. For a moment she contemplated how universally true this seemed to be. Connect the dots and the picture emerges. "Wow, what this really means is, it's our job to find out what people want their life to look like and then connect the dots to show how engaging with us makes what they want not only possible, but probable," Glenna said out loud.

"The business preview was great," Steve thought as it came to an end. Sara joined us as a support partner for Maria, our newest prospect that Sara had invited to the conference. Tony, Jerry, the Fords and the Browns all came as well. Even though Jerry had been in the business only about ten days and his PEProfile score put him in the Improve Yourself phase, he had actually jumped the gun following Doug and Cindy's example by inviting a friend of his to the meeting. It turned out that he invited nine of his friends and one actually came to the meeting. "He did nothing bad, but others seem to follow our example," I thought, and inviting nine to get one seemed pretty ineffective. I had nine people at the preview. Over half of all the people there were mine! It was a cool feeling. Cindy had a guest and Jen had two. The momentum of the room was beginning to shift. The Rhino Power Team was dominating the room. Doug started the meeting as usual introducing Glenna and then he again brought Cindy up at the end. But it was obvious she was a bit anxious in front of two rows of people from my team and Jen's people as well. In fact, it was kind of weird when Pam Ford asked me why I didn't get to speak when most of the people in the room were on my team? I told her I wasn't worried about it. It actually gave me more time to spend with them and help them. But it did make me think for a moment. Jerry would not be recruiting yet if he hadn't heard Cindy talk about taking immediate action last week. I made a mental note to ask Glenna about this.

Maria got pretty excited about what she saw. "Finally," she confided in Sara, "there's a way to work on my own schedule and make enough money to get my kids decent clothes, pay for lessons, camps, and the little things they have gone without for so long, and most importantly, to relieve the stress of having more month than money. Finally, there is a way to pay for school lunches and stop worrying about being invited to socials because I can't afford a bag of potato chips." Glenna took a minute to meet her and edified Sara and me. Having Sara there was critical in helping put Maria at ease. I made an appointment to follow up with Maria tomorrow; I told Sara I could catch a ride home from Doug so Sara took Maria home in our car. Sara instantly knew I was trying to make sure we got the babysitter home early because we simply couldn't afford the cost. Oh how I looked forward to the day when Sara could go with me everywhere. But all in good time I suppose. And I mentally added affording a babysitter to my grocery-shopping goal. Now I had two whopping financial goals to shoot for.

Seeing that there were more guests than usual, I figured the meeting after the meeting was going to start a bit late. So I took advantage of the time. I took the Fords and the Browns into the kitchen and Tony followed. Jerry was busy talking to Doug and Cindy. Ben and Pam Ford, and Mark and Robin Brown had all taken the PEProfile and had their reports with them. They were ready to learn what to do next after the main meeting was over. I took out my napkin drawing. I didn't have anything to write on so I used a napkin that Glenna had on her countertop to copy the part Glenna had given me in our first meeting. I explained the three underlying principles that made the success pattern work. Principle number one—start at the start. Starting right is always better than starting over. Principle number two—build personal effectiveness before building the team. I gave them the quote, "Higher PEPs equals higher checks." Principle number three—follow the proven pattern that creates predictability, the outline drawn on the napkin.

We looked at their profile reports and I explained the three areas, Improve Yourself, Build a Team, and Become a Leader. We looked at the items they had that were in green, then in yellow, and finally in red. It was easy to see what they needed to work on and in what order. I told them about the *Skills of the Million-Dollar Earners* audio library and how it mapped directly to the profile report. What an awesome and invaluable tool to help people to get what to do next. Even a new guy can understand how to actually help people using this report.

Glenna was still talking to guests and new people, so I pulled out my napkin drawing and started explaining as much of it as I knew from my discussions with her. I told them what they would have to do to create the success Glenna had and challenged them to achieve. They were the same things I had agreed to with Glenna—to follow the success pattern no matter what, to get on product autoship immediately, to purchase tickets to the next business conference, and to come to the weekly meetings and the Saturday training. Pam Ford said it seemed that if we follow the success pattern we won't start making money like Glenna showed in the compensation plan right away, "Is that right?" I answered her, "You will be able to make some money pretty quickly if you make sure to use me and Glenna to help you talk to and present to your family and friends until you have at least thirty PEPs. That's what I did while I was in the Improve Yourself phase. The worst-case scenario is that you might not make any money for the next few weeks. But if you commit to a personal improvement program using the audio library and focus on the specific things you need to improve on, you can increase your PEPs really fast. Then when you take action, it will be effective action and the money will begin to come faster," I explained. Everyone committed to follow the success pattern, even Tony who had already been through this with me a few weeks ago.

Glenna got everyone together to talk about his or her guests and made a few announcements about a new product that was coming out. Then she told us about a new recognition category she was adding to the mix. Her focus was shifting from a causal look at a few raw numbers to a more specific tracking of some key categories of business-building activities. "The new emphasis is going to be on effective business building instead of just going out and contacting and presenting, hoping that enough of that would be enough. The new award is going to be called the Effective Business Builder award. There will be three levels of this award with bronze, silver, and gold medals for effective business building. There will be actual medals to hang around your neck and a lapel pin for you to wear to events. Each medal will also carry with it $250 for the gold medal winner, $100 for the silver, and $50 for the bronze.

"You can earn medals by getting one point for converting contacts to presentations at 60 percent or higher rate; one point for converting those presentations to follow-ups at 60 percent or higher and for converting those follow-ups to enrollments, either as customers who enroll on autoship, or associates who enroll on the Rhino Power Team. You must have at least thirty PEPs to be eligible to enroll in this program. Once enrolled, you must contact at least thirty-two people during the month and personally enroll a minimum of four people to be eligible to receive any of the Effective Business Builder awards. The numbers will be collected each week by your upline Silver and passed on to me. They will all have the forms to take care of this. You simply need to report total contacts, presentations, follow-ups, and, of course, enrollments each week to them. It will be easy for us to see the enrollments so please emphasize to your teams to be honest. Your upline Silver will have a good idea about what you are doing because he or she will be working closely with you during the month, just like always—only now more effectively. Your thirty PEPs must be verified by a PEProfile score from the last ninety days. I want to make sure that you all know where you are in the success pattern so that you will know what skills you should personally be working on.

"The purpose of the program is to help you focus on more than just doing work for the sake of doing the work, but for doing it with great effectiveness. And this week's Saturday training will focus on the specifics of the success pattern and what particular activities you should be doing to become the most effective business builder you could possibly be. One reminder, anyone who is enrolled in the Rhino Power Team has already committed to be at the Saturday training. Those of you who want to accelerate your business growth and build your teams faster and with less frustration should be here promptly at 9:00 AM," Glenna finished.

I looked at Jen, then at Tony, and then at the Fords and Browns to see if they were as excited as I was about these new developments. First, there was a new program for recognizing personal improvement and now rewarding effectiveness in the work during the Build a Team phase. I wondered why the public school system couldn't put a program like this into place. Oh well, we have it here and my financial future is here, not there. I guess that's probably why this seems to get better and better each week I am in the business. I couldn't wait to see what Tony and the others thought. Right now the Fords and the Browns are working toward their thirty PEPs and the Improve Yourself awards. But considering where they are, they will be able to advance to the Build a Team phase before the next business conference in a couple of weeks. Tony will be taking his profile a second time this coming week, and from what I can tell, he is ready to advance. This next conference he could be eligible for a bronze, silver or gold Effective Business Builder award, and all the others directly related to income.

In our follow-up meeting with Maria, we answered her questions and talked about the predictability of the business. She asked the same questions I had asked about what made this possible. Sara jumped right in by explaining the underlying principles that made the success pattern work: starting at the start, building personal effectiveness before building a team, and following the proven pattern that creates predictability. Then she drew, as was becoming our custom, on a napkin the first part of the success pattern. When Maria saw the diagram and the fact that Sara knew it and could explain it, she was in.

As she was signing her enrollment application, Maria said that she had seen a lot of presentations, but until now no one had been able to actually explain how it really worked and how all the pieces fit together. She thanked Sara for being a student of the business and for caring enough about her to find out what she wanted and needed then taking the time to effectively explain how XL-8 met those needs. Sara told her she would be willing to work with her twice a week to build the business and volunteered to babysit two other nights while she went to work if she needed it. Maria got one of those "no-words-to-express-her gratitude" looks and gave Sara a big hug. Sara was one of my most important assets.

On the way home Sara interrupted the silence by telling me that she had been thinking about the business. "I've decided to rearrange my schedule with the kids to go with you a couple of nights a week," she told me. "And I also feel like I need to help Maria build her business as well. The babysitting is no real extra work for me. But I really feel like, with a little help, her life can be different. So I'm going to partner with her to build that leg of our business," exclaimed Sara. "Wow, two women on a mission," I said. "How would anyone stand a chance against that?" I responded.

Gary was in his home office compiling the numbers for the past months in Glenna's business and as he did, he thought to himself that she was right about the life cycle of an associate seeming to be awfully short. The same people appear to be earning the Winners' Circle and other personal point production awards, but they also seem to have the highest rate of fall out. Doug leads the team in recruiting *and* fallout month after month. He is losing team members at an alarming 85 percent every ninety days. Kim is not enrolling as many as Doug and she has a great retention rate with customers. But she is also losing about 85 percent of her associate enrollees as well. The fact this seems to be consistent with other leaders is shocking. This many people who enroll, seeking a better future in an industry with real opportunity, fallout of the business in as little as one quarter, three months, ninety days! But the members of Glenna's Rhino Power Team have numbers that are almost exactly the opposite of the others. They are enrolling a high percentage of people they contact, and they are retaining, instead of losing, over 85 percent of their new associates.

"Why does this happen?" Gary wondered out loud. "Is the problem on the company or industry side of the business? Are the products or the business model incapable of performing as described? Or is it on the associate side? Are people being promised more than the industry can deliver? Are people paralyzed by a lack of knowledge, confidence, ineffective action, or a combination of all of these things? One thing I am certain of as a professional trainer, people with higher PEPs make more money, enroll a higher percentage of people, and build stronger more effective teams than people with low PEPs."

"What else do I know about the industry?" Gary asked himself as he began to take some notes about what he had learned from his interviews and Glenna's reporting.

"First, most associates don't know or understand the 3-Step Success Pattern, so they skip over the Improve Yourself phase and jump right into trying to build a team. This appears to have the same effect of jumping into the deep end of a swimming pool without knowing how to swim. They seem to drown rather quickly just trying to learn how to tread water. That is to say, they quit soon after they enroll because they can't enroll anyone or can't enroll enough people to make any measurable progress. Most of those who last long enough to tread water never learn to do more than tread water. It seems that most everyone is trying to enroll new people faster than the ones they have on their team are falling out. It might take a few weeks longer to get up and running, starting in the Improve Yourself phase, but think of how many people could get started the right way; think of the untold millions of dollars that could be made just by teaching 80 percent of the new associates how to get their products for free!

"Second, people seem to have unrealistic expectations. For some reason new people seem to think they can succeed in this business without any specific skills or knowledge. Looking at these numbers it appears that overall, new people do not have the skill or knowledge to create basic business goals or results, such as getting their products for free or break-even income—let alone build a million-dollar business.

However, for some reason many expect to, or they wouldn't enroll and then drop out so quickly once they discover they needed to learn and grow as a business owner. And when success doesn't happen quickly, they think they cannot do this business, or that the business doesn't work. I'm afraid that it's not the business that doesn't work—it's the individual's lack of skill and knowledge applied in its proper sequence that breaks down.

"Third, most associates seem to lack the confidence that comes from mastering skill and knowledge to effectively do any of the skills in the Build a Team phase of the business. Mastery of the skills would result in getting their products for free, breaking even, and then creating residual income. Lacking are personal beliefs that support success; a basic understanding of their products, company and industry, how to listen and ask high-yielding questions, and the inability to contact, present, and offer appropriate options at the end of their presentations—keeping people from being able to create any business success at all.

"Looking at these things it seems there are some major problems that may need to be addressed. However, the remedy to two of these three, and the associated problems they cause, are simple to implement. The first problem indicates a lack of belief, that people will quit if they don't achieve some tangible reward in the first week or so in the business. This is short-term thinking, spread by short-term thinkers. If they understood the success pattern and taught people how to measure their progress through the Improve Yourself phase, building up to the Build a Team phase, they would get more people mastering more skills and better results not only in initial sales and enrollments, but in the long term as well.

"More associates would stay in longer and would achieve a much higher return on investment, leading to greater credibility for everyone in the long run. These two problems are easy to repair. The second problem could be remedied by simply telling associates that their products and opportunity don't need to be overstated or oversold. This is clearly the best industry of opportunity for anyone wanting to take control of every aspect of his or her life. The third question is the one that is keeping me awake at night. There is something missing in the transfer of skill and knowledge from those who have high PEPs in business building and new associates.

"My first observation about this situation is that all companies seem to be really good at creating systems. Most have great systems for ordering and distribution of products, for getting people together to teach product ordering and circulating information about those products and services, and what associates need to do to spread the good news about the features and benefits of those products. My second observation about the third problem is that those who are really good at building the business are generally professional business builders, not professional trainers. They have access to the PEProfile, which helps leaders and individuals gain awareness of exactly what skills and knowledge they are really good at, what they are adequate at, and what specifically they need to work on to be effective in developing themselves, their team and their income—but not everyone uses it.

"This is an opportunity missed, but simply teaching people that it exists and promoting it into organizations can address this. They have access to the *Skills of the Million-Dollar Earners* audio library that is directly linked or mapped to the PEProfile so they should be able to quickly learn what they don't know and strengthen what they do. But what about effective, appropriate practice? The closest thing I ever hear about are videos on the back office website and role-playing.

"Videos can fill part of the answer to problem number one in regard to seeing something done properly. But I certainly wouldn't get into an airplane with a pilot who had been trained exclusively by watching videos of how to fly. And there is no scientific or social evidence that role-playing is effective in any way at transferring skill and knowledge. In fact, the research says that the person facilitating the role play learns the most from the exercise—not the participants!

"So what about effective practice?" Gary asked, considering the possibilities. Practice, practice, hmm I need to really think about this one. Police, fire fighters, the military, and airline pilots all use simulators to get real-life practice without the nasty consequences of learning and practicing new skills and knowledge. So what would a simulation for network marketing look like? How would it work? How could a participant learn the success pattern and practice the critical skills in each phase and apply them in their proper order? And how could they learn their compensation plan and the importance of PEPs to the conversion process of prospects to customers and associates, all in the same simulator? This calls for some serious training analysis and problem solving. The more I learn about this industry, the more excited I get. I am grateful to Glenna for coming to me; I think I can actually provide a few real solutions not only to her, but to the whole industry. With the right kind of practice, the average person who knows nothing about network marketing could become an effective builder in a few months of hard work.

"What I think I will do is use a few weeks of my vacation time to concentrate on this project. I am going to need to interview my panel of experts again, including Glenna. I want to present this to her at her next business conference in a few weeks, and I need to check to see if what I am interpreting from Glenna's numbers, the Direct Selling Association numbers, and the information from my industry experts are real or if I am imagining that there is no realistic practice mechanism in this industry," Gary thought and then began to formulate a plan of action.

10

The Way Things Are

Gary analyzed the over one hundred pages of notes he had taken as a result of three straight days of interviews, surveys, and conversations with Glenna and other industry experts. They all seemed to be saying the same four things.

First, without a concrete structure or construct in which to put all the things they talked about in meetings, conference calls, and on the audio CDs, coupled with a way to really transfer critical skill and knowledge, new people were forced to go out and give it the old college try by practicing on their family and friends. There is the hope that they will learn what to do before they run out of family and friends. Essentially this is the only choice for anyone who wants to do something without knowing how to train his or her team members effectively.

Second, all the leaders told him they talk, talk, and talk some more, but no one seems to be understanding. The people congregate and listen, but they don't hear or understand in a way that they can go and do anything. A lot is being said, but there is no clarity. Leaders are ill equipped to transfer necessary knowledge and skills to the masses to create job-dropping residual income. Traditional methods don't work, and leaders are not taught enough about training to discern the difference between effective and ineffective methods. So the leaders are left with the status quo: *out recruit attrition*!

Third, if recruiting is your focus, retention will be your problem because you will always be looking for the next recruit, instead of training the ones you have, to be successful. This surely seems to be the case with Doug and Cindy in Glenna's organization. One six-figure earner said, "Those who retain the most, make the most," and she should know since she was making about $160,000 per month.

Fourth, people quit because they fail to *quickly* learn basic foundational skills that keep them from being able to contact, present, follow-up, ask for the business, build relationships, or help anyone to take advantage of the business.

One successful leader, who had been a home builder before his retirement, used a story of building a house out of bricks to help illustrate these four points. The story starts with a new man on the construction crew. The foreman would expect the new worker to learn about the job before putting him on the crew of actual brick layers. The new man must spend at least a few weeks mastering the most common parts of a new job. The new brick builder would learn about bricks, what they are made of, how they are built, and what they can be used for. Then he would learn how to make bricks, including the processes and mixing of brick elements, molds, and curing. Then he would learn how to construct buildings out of bricks as well as architecture and building principles for foundations and walls. Without this foundational training, any brick building built by a new worker would predictably fall down in a short period of time.

The former contractor went on to say that people who skipped the foundational learning phase in construction, as well as in this business, are trying to build houses made of bricks before they learn what bricks are, or how to build with them. Inevitably, their house falls down around them. People who don't have good foundational knowledge or skill don't have a chance to build a successful business. They lack personal effectiveness to do any of the steps required in the Build a Team phase. They soon give up the struggle because they can't see, nor is anyone showing them how, the way forward is predictable or do-able.

Some people hear, the former contractor continued, but they don't understand. If they did, they would be able to go out and do it! They hear the same message repeatedly, but do they really hear? Are they paying any meaningful attention? This leader put the responsibility to learn how to succeed totally on the associate. However, when 97 percent of the students fail, it's at least partly the teacher's fault.

Another leader explained to Gary that she often asks her people what they have learned lately. They usually tell her something trivial or out of context but it is clear they don't know the business at all. They have books, they attend seminars, and yet they still don't know the process for success or how to implement it.

A third leader told Gary, "There is an interesting contradiction in our company, and maybe even industrywide. We have a system that allegedly removes bottlenecks in business building. Everyone is supposed to be able to do it, right? We even teach that a person should spend some time learning about the products and industry, and when they have this information everyone should be able to do it. But if everyone can do it, why is retention such a big problem? The answer is that they are unable to get it, or leaders are simply unable to teach it. Giving out the information is not enough; people in the industry need something more, or different, but no one seems to know what the *more* or *different* is," he continued.

"It's probably rare that leaders are so candid," Gary thought. But as he explained that he was working on a solution to help them recruit, train, and retain more people onto their teams, they were intrigued enough to share openly with him. However, each one said he or she would only talk with him if he didn't give out their names or the company they belonged to. This information confirmed what Gary had been observing since Glenna first talked to him. So the summary of all this is that Gary went into these interviews thinking that:

- Most associates don't know or understand the 3-Step Success Pattern and how it creates predictability, so they unknowingly skip over the Improve Yourself phase and jump right into trying to build a team.

- Many people seem to have unrealistic expectations of the time and work required to succeed in this business.

- Most associates lack confidence in their ability to build a strong and profitable business.

And the leaders Gary talked to confided:

- Everyone needs some kind of concrete structure to help them put information into context.

- The traditional teaching method of a leader—talking, talking, and talking some more—is not effective.

- Recruiting is important but it's only the first step in the business process. It's what you do with your recruits after they enroll that makes the long-term difference.

• People quit because they fail to *quickly* learn basic, foundational skills that are prerequisites to theoretical money-making skills of contacting, presenting, following-up, and asking for the business.

The good news is that Glenna has the 3-Step Success Pattern that serves many functions. One, it has the structure associates lack. Two, it should keep people from skipping ahead to try business activities they aren't ready for. Three, it functions as a road map and a way to measure progress in real ways, in every phase of personal business ownership. And four, it should help set people's expectations correctly. The bad news is that there are still some challenges to deal with to increase the predictability of success for everyone who comes into this business. We still need to help people quickly acquire competence in the foundational skills that will enable them to convert more of their prospects to customers and associates. High PEPs will overcome the confidence problems, but the problem of teaching still needs to be addressed. Leaders need a way to transfer what they know and do to their teams much more effectively.

So back to the question that started Gary thinking of all of this: What kind of practice would really help people learn foundational skills, increase confidence, and help leaders effectively transfer what they know and do to their teams? Gary thought a moment and then said out loud, "A simulation is the only solution to all these problems! I need to create a simulation to help leaders teach, new associates learn, and veterans take the next steps in their journey to success. A simulation will help prospects get on the business jumbo jet with confidence that the pilot is well trained and that there is a flight plan. It will help the pilot have the confidence of what to do next in every situation and get them to their destination safely. A simulation will also help leaders to be able to create and maintain predictable income, all without the nasty consequences of accidents and crashes from the learning process." Drifting off into a vision of winning another international award for training design, Gary imagined that he could present a prototype at Glenna's event next week. He was brought back to reality by the "ding" of his my email alarm. It was a message from

Glenna with her weekly report of the numbers.

The message read: "I am excited to talk to you about what you are working on. I have what appears to be a serious problem. I don't want to alarm you, but I do need to talk. Here is my weekly report.

"Doug's team report: He has enrolled two new personal associates. Only one made an autoship order. Cindy enrolled one new person. None of her previous recruits are attending any meetings or conference calls and only two of them ordered the second month. Steve enrolled two personal associates, Maria and Sharon. They both took the PEProfile, enrolled on the Rhino Power Team, and have tickets to the event next week. Tony is starting to work with me. He has enrolled one new associate, his first. Jerry has enrolled one new associate. However, the new guy didn't attend the weekly business preview or make an autoship order. The Fords and the Browns are working specifically to increase their PEPs to over thirty.

"Jen's team report: She enrolled three new associates personally and two of her team members, who are on the Rhino Power Team, enrolled one new associate each. No one else enrolled anyone new.

"Kim's team report: Kim enrolled one new person. Her team enrolled nine new people.

"It seems like all of this attention to the Improve Yourself phase has slowed down my recruiting numbers. They are down about 30 percent over the past two weeks. I know you are working on something. But I am worried and need to talk to you about this! – Glenna."

"I have never heard Glenna sound nervous before, but this sounds pretty urgent," Gary thought. "I had better let her know that I have solved some major problems, including the recruiting challenge, *and* that there is fantastic news on the horizon."

Steve was lost in his own thoughts, "I'm beginning to love business-development conferences. I get excited to review my personal progress. For the first time I have a team of people who will be here with me. I actually have sixteen people plus Sara and me. Even though these numbers represent only eight associate numbers, it's great to have everyone here together." They sat near the front, where they had been last month. They had arrived a bit early, even Tony was early. His PEPs were increasing. Then Doug came in. He had three or four people with him. But Cindy was by herself. Doug waved and came down to where the group was and gave Steve a big welcoming hug and a handshake. He met all of the team and introduced his new people. His Winners' Circle pin had a third Silver Star for personal enrollments. He had his new Silver promotion pin as well, which meant he was at the third promotion level in the business. The group sat together and Doug made it clear this was the part of the auditorium set aside for his team. But as he talked about Dougville, Steve was boasting to himself as he remembered that last month he had six people here, and this month he had three times that amount. It looked like he had the most people of anyone in Doug's group.

The afternoon meeting started with the singing of the national anthem and a prayer. Steve looked around at his team to see their reaction to the meeting starting in this unique way. He was glad everyone seemed to be smiling. The same man who opened the last conference opened it again this month with a military recognition and then the introduction of the guest speaker for this session. His name was David McKay, and as the host introduced him it became obvious this was no ordinary man. In fact, he was Glenna's mentor and he had achieved the highest level in the business. This was a big deal that he had come to speak. Steve had his notepad out and made sure everyone else had a pen and paper. David talked for over an hour, mostly without any notes at all. He was amazing. His topic was what he called high-yielding questions.

"I had never heard of high-yielding questions," Steve thought. David shared some incredible insights about communicating and connecting with people. He told us that in this business you don't have to love people. In fact, you don't even have to like them. However, to create success, you must be curious about them. Curiosity is the foundation of your business. If you can be curious about other people, you will find something they are passionate about, and that thing is the key to helping them get an abundance of whatever they are passionate about. "I am going to talk today about the science of curiosity. Step one is asking high-yielding questions, step two is to listen, step three is to repeat the process," he began.

"Curiosity helps you see the world through other people's eyes, like walking in their shoes for a while and understanding how they view the world. If you are not curious, you won't take the time to learn about others and the way they think. The idea is to seek to understand and then to be understood. Curiosity forces you to ask questions. You can't learn what your prospects need, want, or care about if you're doing all the talking. Learn to ask questions that will get your prospect to talk about what is working and what is not working in his or her life. I call this a pain dialogue," he told us. "If you can find out what they want more or less of in their life, you can give them a specific prescription to solve their pain. If you learn to do this, the world will be at your feet."

He continued with a story of a visit to the doctor's office. He talked about going to his doctor with his wife a little while ago. While he was there he noticed an interesting process. First, the nurse asked a few general questions and then took some vital signs. She wrote her comments on the medical chart and she took them to the examination room. She put the file in the pocket on the door before excusing herself. When the doctor came in, he quickly reviewed the nurse's comments and then asked some very specific pointed questions about why his wife had come to see him.

While she explained, he poked and prodded a bit in some very specific places, then gave her his diagnosis and some exercises he wanted her to do along with a prescription for something he thought would help eliminate her pain. It was the perfect example of curiosity. "The doctor doesn't love my wife, he may not even like her. But because he was curious about her, he spent a few minutes asking questions that got my wife to talk about her circumstances. He listened for specific meaningful information that helped guide him to the appropriate diagnosis and treatment recommendation. What if he had come in without reading the chart, simply pulled out a bottle of pills, and told my wife to take two a day and then come back in two weeks to see him again? My wife wouldn't have taken any of those pills. She would also never go back to that doctor, nor would she ever refer anyone else to him; would you? But isn't that what we do when we rush in and tell people about what we have and why we think it's so great? We behave like a doctor who has the miracle cure for everything but don't take the time to find out what's ailing people before we tell them what the cure is!

"When my daughter takes her car to the mechanic, she tells him it's making a funny sound. The mechanic of course has no idea what this means, so he's forced to ask a lot of questions to get to the heart of the problem. However, when I go to the mechanic, I tell him what I think is wrong with the car because I think I know something about it. He doesn't ask nearly as many questions and invariably it takes longer to fix, because

I think I know what's wrong and he thinks I know what I am talking about. We both waste time and I spend a lot more money because we both think we know what the other is talking about. And, yes, we do this when we rush in telling people what is so great about XL-8 and they reject us because we both think we know what the other is talking about.

"High-yielding questions are the key to communicating clearly and effectively. When we rush in with nothing more than enthusiasm and our products to show off, we are acting just like the second doctor in my story and me in the mechanic story. What makes XL-8 great for you probably won't be what appeals to your prospects. For every person there is a need, a specific need they have that they can't meet doing what they are doing now. And some part of XL-8 is the solution. There are literally thousands of features and benefits to the company, our products and the business opportunity. But if you don't spend some time talking to your prospects, you'll never know which ones are the most relevant to them and their specific circumstances. You will be left to chance instead of choice. You'll only connect with the people who are in search of the specific things you highlight in your presentation. Everyone who has a different need will be left to wonder how XL-8 helps him or her in any meaningful way, and therefore these people won't enroll either as a customer or an associate.

"High-yielding questions are very powerful in determining your prospect's interest in learning more about your product, company, and the industry. Find out what is important to him. Find out what his pain is; it may be money, health, time, stress, debt or a myriad of other things. Find out what he loves. What does he want more of in life? What does he want less of? If you don't know him very well, you could start the conversation asking where he lives and what he likes best about it. Find out if he could live anywhere in the world, where that place would be? Ask about his work. How long has he been doing it? What does he like and dislike about it?

"High-yielding questions are also very important to use when you enroll new associates. These kinds of questions allow you to learn what they want out of the business and to establish their commitment level.

"This is a business of relationships. You will accelerate relationship building if you ask a few questions and let your prospects and associates talk about the one thing everyone loves to talk about, themselves, their family, and the things they are dissatisfied with.

"Learn to talk less by limiting your part of the conversation with high-yielding questions and listening carefully to their responses. Ask high-yielding questions about them. Don't spew all over them with your dazzle and sparkle. People like people who show interest in them. Ask questions and show interest in their responses. When the prospects are talking, listen carefully because they will tell you exactly what to say and do to help them take the next step during your presentations, follow-ups, and counseling sessions.

"Spend more time learning to listen and less time learning to talk, present, answer questions, and overcome objections. Prospects will feel that you care and that you are sharing something that could benefit them. Asking questions to ensure that you fully understand their circumstances and situation can help you provide the most accurate solutions. Don't worry too much about having exact memorized answers to all of the questions people could ask. Most people are more interested in the fact that there is an answer than the actual answer itself."

David said the goal in asking high-yielding questions was to get prospects to share what they really think. "No matter what they say to any of the six types of questions, your prospects will begin talking to you instead of excusing you."

He gave everyone a gift: a key chain with the six types of high-yielding questions and an example of each written on it. On one side it had the first three types, and on the other it had the other three. It read:

Have you ever considered questions
• Have you ever considered starting a home-based business?
• Have you ever considered bringing in extra income?
• Have you ever considered a different career?

What kept you from questions
• What kept you from doing it?
• What kept you from being successful?
• What kept you from being interested in it?

What caused you questions
• What caused you to look into the XL-8 opportunity in the first place?

Confirming questions

- So, if I understand you correctly, shifting your thinking from selling to sharing would help you feel more at ease?

Implication questions

- How does having too much debt affect you?
- How would you benefit if you increased your income by 20 percent this year?
- How would your life be different if you had whatever you wanted?

Diagnostic questions

- What are your expectations of a future working where you are working now?
- How serious are you about achieving whatever you want?

When David was finishing his presentation he gave an assignment to work on between the afternoon and the evening meeting. Everyone needed to have two conversations with people who were not in the room using the key chain and high-yielding questions. There would be a chance to report on the experience at the evening session.

Now Steve could see how David had become a Double Platinum in the business. Steve thought, "He must have had 100 PEPs! He was truly amazing. And when I looked at my team, I was grateful they had all come. This was probably the most important workshop I had ever been to, and I have a lot of money invested in college degrees. The information David shared with us coupled with what Glenna had taught us, including the success pattern, were strategies similar to a few I had used in my baseball program. I spent about ten thousand hours teaching the kids to think like I did, to act like I would, to make decisions like I would. I taught them a predictable, simple strategy for winning that I called the anatomy of baseball. Then I taught them specific skills and knowledge that would enable them to win using that strategy with or without my being there.

"I hadn't realized it at the time, but at the state tournament when I put it to the test, the kids could plan and execute with precision with or without me! This is what Glenna was trying to do with the Rhino Power Team. My confidence grew even more in what she was telling us each week and in each training. I looked at the activities of Doug and Cindy and somehow they seemed to be chaotic. They appeared to be doing things for the sake of doing them. But everyone on the Rhino Power Team was doing things on purpose, with purpose. We were part of a system that was creating measureable results toward specific goals and milestones. I folded my notepad back to the top page and there, circled from the very first meeting, was the word *predictable*. So I rephrased my thought. We were creating measurable results toward specific goals and milestones in a predictable manner.

"If this keeps working like it looks like it's working, I am going to be rich beyond my wildest imagination." And with a smile Steve told himself, "If it doesn't, I can always abandon it and easily begin to enroll, hope, and replace like Doug and Cindy. Anyone can do that. It doesn't require special skills, schools, or tools that I can see. But it doesn't seem to create much of a result either. It seems that Doug has been at this a while now and he doesn't seem much closer to the dream lifestyle he talks of from the front of the room at the business preview meetings. It seems like he has a glorified job. Yes he is in charge, but if he stops, so will the money. In a few months, with the dropout rate he seems to have, his group will be completely gone. True victory or residual income, can come only if there is a team of effective leaders helping to develop an even bigger team of effective leaders.

"Recruit, recruit, and recruit some more seem to create a few big-money earners. A person who implements this strategy, who already has high PEPs, might be successful in enrolling others. But if the people they enroll don't have high PEPs to begin with, or are inadequate at certain skills, they won't be successful. The *hopium* they bought into from the high PEP sponsor will soon wear off and they will quit.

"Now I have a different perspective of the time and money I used to think of as spending. It wasn't spent at all. It was really an investment in my future. I can see that the investment is paying dividends and not only can I build the business now, but those I have enrolled can build it with or without me—just like my baseball team. Once they had been properly trained they could plan, play, and win, with or without me. This is a striking difference between Cindy and me. Cindy has to be everywhere and in all actuality, she is the only one in her group that ever brings new people to events or weekly overviews. My people are following my lead, Glenna's lead. Each week my people are building a foundation of skill and knowledge. They are beginning to enroll one or two people per week and teaching them the three principles coupled with the 3-Step Success Pattern. They are teaching them to start at the start, build personal effectiveness before building the team, and to follow the proven pattern that creates predictability. Therefore, the action they take will be effective and purposeful, instead of the frenzied chaos I see Doug and Cindy engaged in—action that seems to lead to short-term gain but nothing in the long run," Steve mused.

After the session we decided to go out to eat at an inexpensive fast food restaurant. We invited Doug and Cindy, but they declined. Cindy wouldn't even look at me, and now that I think of it, she didn't even say hello this afternoon. I wonder if she might be feeling bad about the Fords and the Browns? As we drove to the burger house, I became a little more aware that there might be a bit of a competition brewing between Cindy and me. It's clear that our approaches are very different. And based on the attendance at the conference, our results were very different as well. The assignment that David McKay gave us was worthwhile. Each of us had at least two conversations and met some interesting people. The Browns, Jerry, and Maria all made appointments from the exercise.

The evening meeting was a party. It started with music, a prayer, and military recognition like last month. And then, probably because David had given us an assignment, which was unusual, Glenna began the recognition part of the session by calling on some people to share their experiences with the assignment. She chose five people, including Mark Brown and Maria from my team, and Jen—but not Cindy or Doug. The good news was that Cindy wasn't on stage. But then neither was I! In fact, I was a bit jealous that the others got to be on the stage with David. Sara sensed that I was a bit agitated and she grabbed my hand to settle me, somehow knowing it was better for our team members to be on the stage than for us to be up there. What they said was powerful; when Mark and Maria explained that they had made appointments, the audience went crazy!

I got so caught up in the stories of what each one went through during the moments of the conversations that I forgot all about wanting to be on the stage myself. It was rewarding to see people on my team sharing, growing, and progressing. When they were finished they came back to their seats and we all gave them high fives and hugs. It was like we were welcoming home the victors. It was at that moment that I realized what Glenna had done. She very carefully selected people to share. I already had my reward with people in the audience and on the stage. Mark and Maria needed to be on the stage to experience the excitement of having the spotlight, and Jen needed her new team to see her as the leader and hero. My slight jealousy turned into admiration when I understood Glenna's calculated predictability in building people so that they could build the business.

Since Glenna was already on the stage, she edified and welcomed David back on the stage so he could congratulate those who were going to be recognized. Then she began the recognition for various achievements.

I won the award for having the most people personally attend the conference. Doug, Cindy, and I were recognized for doing at least fifteen presentations during the month. Cindy won the personal enrollments award again. Cindy achieved the Winners' Circle again for personally enrolling six people in any one month, and she also earned the Brass Ring again for personal production points. The Silver Star for team enrollments in a month went to Doug, due to Cindy's and my personal and team enrollments. And Kim, the guest speaker from last month, earned the Golden Eagle for team production points. Glenna then called up all the people who had thirty PEPs, then those with forty-five, and those who had seventy. About one-third of the stage was covered with people being recognized as members of the High Peppers Club. A woman from Kim's team earned the highest profile score during the month. Robin Brown and Pam Ford were both recognized for the least amount of red areas in the Improve Yourself phase of the success pattern, and Tony had the largest improvement in PEPs during the month. Glenna invited everyone who had done 100 percent of the things required for the Rhino Power Team promotion to come on the stage. I was so excited to see all of the people on my team on the stage; it was also great to see Jen and her new people on the stage as well.

Glenna took a moment to tell everyone about a new area of recognition. She explained that she would be giving three levels of recognition for being effective business builders. "The three levels are gold, silver, and bronze and each will also carry with it a monetary reward; $250 for the gold medal winner, $100 for the silver, and $50 for the bronze. Medals are earned by accumulating points each week by earning one point for converting contacts to presentations at 60 percent or higher rate, one point for converting those presentations to follow-ups at 60 percent or higher, and for converting those follow-ups to enrollments, either as customers who enroll on autoship, or associates who enroll on the Rhino Power Team. You must have at least thirty PEPs, contact at least thirty-two people during the month, and personally enroll a minimum of four people to be eligible to participate in the Effective Business Builder award program." While Glenna was talking about this recognition, a couple of guys brought out a podium for the winners to stand on. Glenna brought out the bronze medal winner, who was Barry Jones from Kim's team. Jen earned the silver medal, and then the name of the gold medalist was announced—it was I! They played the Olympic music and the crowd cheered for all of us. It was amazing; not just for me, but for all of us to be there to be rewarded for *effective* work.

And last, came the promotion-level recognitions. There were a lot of new people who were promoted to Copper. Jen, who was already qualified as a Copper, which is the first promotion level, qualified again and so did Cindy. For Jen it was the first time in a year that she had actually qualified at this level. And as a surprise to me, I also advanced to Copper. This was important to me on a personal level because it made me feel like an equal to Cindy in the business. This sounds silly, but somehow I felt she was being propped up as the star of the business. Now we were at the same level. There were a few new promotions to the second level, or Brass. One new person advanced to the third level, or Silver, and no one was promoted to Gold or Platinum. When Glenna finished with the recognitions she edified David McKay again and turned the time back over to him. He began by edifying Glenna and telling us that she had one of the fastest growing teams in all of XL-8. She was his best student and the most dedicated leader in his group. And that is why he came to speak to us today, to make sure to support the leaders on his team who were making things happen. Then he spent the next half hour talking about why XL-8 was in a prime position to take advantage of market trends. He reassured us that we were all in a great position to make a lot of money in the next years because of that. It was obvious he was a leader in the company and industry. His PEPs must be off the chart.

When the meeting was over we congregated by the stage. Everyone on the team had been recognized. As we were all talking about the meeting and what David had taught us, I was thinking that if Glenna had not created the new awards, only one or two of us would have been on the stage tonight. Wow, what a difference a few months makes. Everyone was determined and they all verbally committed to being on the stage next month as well. It was an extraordinary feeling to listen to the excitement and hope we all had that there was a simple process to follow and a way to move predictably toward our goals.

On the way home I made a side trip. Sara asked me where we were going. I told her that dream and goal number one was about to be realized. I made her close her eyes and when we stopped, I had her open them. We were in front of the neighborhood grocery store, and we looked at it as if it were a shrine. "Sweetheart," I said, "you can now buy anything you want in there and not worry about how much it costs." Earlier I had made arrangements with Nick, the bag boy, to meet me inside the store with a cart for Sara. The kids and I made signs and the store gave us a discount card for anything Sara wanted to buy on this special occasion.

When we went in, Nick was waiting there with a fully decorated shopping cart and discount card for Sara and me. As Nick was handing Sara the card, a voice came over the intercom letting everyone know that their very special guest, Sara Thoms, was now in the store and how much they appreciated her business. We just walked around for a few minutes enjoying the moment, remembering what it was like only a few weeks ago not to be able to do this. I was a little embarrassed by all the attention, but there weren't many people in the store at this time of night. We stopped from time to time to take an item off the shelf and enjoyed the experience of putting anything into the cart that Sara wanted.

Sara beamed. When we got to the checkout stand to pay for all this I was nervous, out of habit, to see the final cost. The checker asked what the occasion was, and I told her we had just earned a promotion in our business. Unexpectedly, the checker asked what business we were in. Of course I couldn't resist telling her that we help people make money working from home. I told her we were expanding, and if she wanted to learn more about leadership positions, to write her name and phone number on the receipt and I would call her in a day or two to give her some details. She was happy to do it.

I hadn't noticed that there was a woman waiting in line behind us. She overheard the conversation I was having with the checker and saw me pull cash out of my wallet instead of a credit card. She asked me if I would call her as well. Sara suddenly realized that she still had the discount card from the store and felt like she needed to give it to her. We had been so richly blessed over the past few months that she wanted to share in what we had been given. Before tonight Sara hadn't realized how many women have the same pain she had, that is, until we started to take control of our circumstances and learn how to make a difference in people's lives. Two contacts from grocery shopping; who would have thought that was possible?

As we went back to the car, I thought to myself that as stupid as this may have looked, this was the reason I enrolled in the business. This was the reason I quit coaching the baseball team. This moment made all that worthwhile. We sat in front of the store for a few minutes basking in the realization that one of our dreams had come true. Our conversation turned to how important it was to have a level of success that the average person can relate to. Every workingman and woman trying to make ends meet can relate to this accomplishment. It's not like you come back from Hawaii with pictures of you swimming with the dolphins, but this real accomplishment means something in the way you live day to day. When I started the car and pulled out of the parking lot, it occurred to me that while we were in the store and just sitting there that I hadn't worried about how long the babysitter had been at our house. Maybe the babysitter goal was next on the list?

It was surprisingly quiet as Sara and I rode home. For the first time since I enrolled, I could actually tell I was winning. The momentum was kind of like a tidal wave that was forming in the middle of the ocean. I couldn't see it at first, but now it was becoming obvious. I broke the silence, blurting out that Sara needed to grab her surfboard because the wave of success was about to hit our shore. She looked at me and smiled, saying she already had it in the hallway closet for easy access. She could see the growth and was doing the calculating each week so she wasn't surpised. "I am the luckiest man on earth," I said as I knelt to pray that night before I went to bed. "Thank you God for those I have around me, for who I was, for who I am, and for who I am becoming," and I climbed into bed hoping I could sleep after all the excitement.

While we were celebrating, Glenna was meeting with Gary and David. Glenna introduced David to Gary and explained who Gary was and what they were working on. She explained the new recognition categories to David and put them into the context of the success pattern. When she started to report her weekly numbers to Gary, David interrupted and asked why she wasn't reporting those same numbers to him? Without trying to sound insubordinate, she asked him what he would do with them since he wasn't teaching the success pattern to the team or even talking about the Personal Effectiveness Profile anymore. He was surprised a bit by her push back, but the truth cut him to the core. Was it the numbers he wanted, or the allegiance to a chain of command he wanted to maintain? Either way, the fact that Gary was there made him measure his answer, "I'm just curious about what's going on in your group that's all," he replied. "I've noticed a big drop in your recruiting numbers" he added, "and I really wanted to talk to you about it."

Gary jumped in and said they had seen the same thing and assured David it was a temporary situation while they were transitioning from the enroll, hope, and replace strategy to the success pattern. "I think it's rather remarkable how the awards seem to bear this out. Let's take a look at the whole picture and then discuss what I propose we do about it," he added.

"Doug has enrolled his four new personals. Not one came to the conference. He earned an $880 check this month, which is only an increase of $150 from last month *and* almost the whole increase came from Steve's group. He has an 83 percent fallout rate for the whole year and his annualized income will be about $10,500 if the current trend continues. Cindy is personally enrolling about six or seven people each month and most have already quit or don't order consistently. Her strategy is to get people to take immediate action and run around enthusiastically talking to their family and friends, which they are apparently not prepared or capable of doing very effectively. Kim is able to retain people for the longest time; about ninety days, but her fall out rate is also above 80 percent for the year.

"There are a few teams that have shown real sustained growth, such as Jen and Steve and the others who are part of the Rhino Power Team. They are focused on following the success pattern. Being part of the team requires them to take the PEProfile and then invest a few weeks to get up to speed before they begin recruiting to any degree. These groups are all growing. That's why there is a bit of a lull in recruiting. Those people who would be enrolling one or two people in their first month or so are increasing their personal effectiveness before starting to recruit. Let's take the examples of Steve and Cindy. She was, and still is, personally recruiting more than Steve, or even Jen for that matter. But Steve did out recruit everyone else in Doug's, or Kim's, or Jen's teams *and* he had the most people at the conference, with every one of them on autoship. I predict that Steve, or someone on his team, is going to win nearly every award this next month. Tony has already begun recruiting. Jerry has a few people on his team. The Fords, Browns, Maria, and Sharon all have more than thirty PEPs now and are ready to begin recruiting this month. Jen will also make some serious progress this month as her people increase their PEPs and begin recruiting. How is Cindy going to keep up with that by herself, you might ask? This next month Steve will overshadow Doug as the leader of that whole leg, if we can support him," Gary declared. "Support him?" Glenna asked, surprised by the assertion. "Yes. We need a supersonic way to gain the foundational knowledge and skills of the business; to practice them in a real world way like policemen, firemen, astronauts, airline pilots, and soldiers in the military do," Gary confidently stated.

"The last few weeks I have interviewed six- and seven-figure earners in many different companies. I have put their feedback, along with your numbers, together. I could show you the three-hundred-page analysis of my findings, but I don't think you want to try and read it. The short version is that most associates don't know or understand what the predictable process for success is, nor do they know how to work their way through it. Most everyone has unrealistic expectations of the time and work required to succeed, and lastly, they lack confidence in their abilities to do the things necessary to build a strong and profitable business.

"Glenna has implemented the 3-Step Success Pattern that gives the structure associates lack. The process also appears to be keeping people from skipping ahead to try business activities they aren't ready for. It serves as a kind of road map or way to measure progress in every phase of the business, and it seems to help set expectations correctly. The XL-8 education system of videos and other training materials in their back office, coupled with the audio learning library *Skills of the*

Million-Dollar Earners, help associates learn the specific skills they need to acquire knowledge in.

"The missing link is a way to practice the critical skills that enable top performers to convert more of their prospects to customers and associates. Increasing their PEPs in knowledge and in real skill will help them overcome their confidence problems. An effective practice method will also serve as a way for leaders to actually transfer what they know and do to their teams much more quickly, reliably, and effectively. Having said all that, I developed a prototype of a simulation that will help associates learn, practice, and then be able to immediately apply the critical skills that are holding them back. Leaders and associates can use the simulation as a recruiting, training, or retention tool. And I think they could probably use it in all these functions at the same time. The simulation is called the *Residual Income*® game.

"Embedded in it is the success pattern. It forces players to not only make choices about what they need to do next, but to practice the skills as they play to get rewarded for their performance. Included are skills such as list building, contacting, event and product promotion, edification, presenting, asking for the business, overcoming objections, and the high-yielding questions you talked about today, David. There are literally hundreds of other skills they need to be successful in this business. They get rewarded for increasing their PEPs and are able to see how personal effectiveness increases their conversion rates of prospects to customers and associates. Which of course leads to increased residual income and promotion level advancements that are also embedded in the simulation.

"You might think I'm a little crazy for suggesting that you could learn how to build your business by playing a game, but decades of research prove that games are the absolute best environment to learn and practice skills, attitudes, knowledge, and beliefs that grow relationships and income.

"Setting people in a room with pencil and paper feverishly taking notes while some guru talks to them is monumentally ineffective. If your goal is to transfer skill, change behavior, and help your audience know more than what to do, simulations give the necessary practice of how to do it. We have all been students in this kind of arena. How well did it work for either of you? In the traditional system, within twenty-four to forty-eight hours learners forget or misrepresent 97 percent of what they hear the presenter say. After all it takes to design, develop, and promote a training event, the audience will accurately retain only 3 percent the day after tomorrow! That's why I started developing simulations decades ago and why I think we should use this game that is specific to the industry.

"Research tells us that games are also compelling and fun to play. They are so fun and engaging, that the average child spends as much time playing games as they are in school each week, and more time playing games than playing with their real-life friends. Combine the incredible realism of games with the fact that the mind cannot differentiate between fantasy and reality, and you have the recipe to shape the minds and values of anyone who plays, to transfer skill and knowledge from expert to beginner or novice.

"The feedback I got from the interviews I did the past few weeks tells me that the number one most important skill to acquire and teach is relationship building. Games are a powerful socializing force because they foster human interaction that matters. While playing a game, communication barriers are removed, so people are not on guard or defensive.

"Games contain many different practice opportunities that accelerate experience and create specific intentional results and lifetime lessons. Players are able to acquire, practice, perfect, and implement knowledge, skills, beliefs, attitudes, and processes at 'warp speed.' This game will help people connect the dots between what they already do and what they will get if they continue to do it. What got me so excited was the idea that associates will learn the cause-and-effect relationship between thought, action, and outcome. Because what you do in games determines what you get, and what you get usually is worth the effort.

"For example, in the *Residual Income*® game people quickly learn there is a predictable 3-Step Success Pattern. They also learn that if they skip steps or try to take shortcuts, their success will take longer and frustration will result, which will help properly set their expectations for work and compensation. Players also learn that they must master specific skills within each step. Ineffective effort or action taken out of sequence will diminish their results. For example, players with low PEPs will have low conversion rates of prospects to customers and associates. For the first time many people will be able to see why they aren't enrolling as many of their prospects as they want. It's usually not a matter of effort but a matter of effectiveness.

"Of course I'm not suggesting that the *Residual Income*® game is a replacement for what we are already doing, but rather it's an extension or augmentation to it. It will allow the team to experience the information talked about in the books, CDs, and from the stage.

"Players will be able to experience building a strong and profitable business with real residual income as a result of mastering the success pattern and implementing the education system of XL-8. The game will help us to create intolerance for things that don't pay off, to create clear links between what people are told to do and the rewards they get. We will be able to get associates to implement and do the things that actually lead to success. The game will also give them instant feedback because the payoff for any action is typically extremely clear in the game. And players will gain experience that transcends the game environment: create life-long lessons in a few short hours; facilitate the adoption of group values; motivate them to learn specific information processes to achieve success, provide experiences of the cause-and-effect of decisions, actions and results; and emotionally engage the team in planning, doing, and achieving goals. It will make the team active participants in the lesson, instead of passive partakers of information.

"Glenna and David, the research is clear. Professionals from all walks of life are using games right now. The use of games will only expand as the means that trainers, educators, and community leaders employ to teach and learn long-lasting knowledge, values, beliefs, and skills. Glenna, with your permission, I would like to use this at the next Rhino Power Team training meeting," Gary finished with a flourish.

Glenna was blown away by what she had just heard. First, from the detail of the report from leaders in other companies, and second, from the depth of thought and work to create the prototype of the *Residual Income*® business-building simulator, and third, from the commitment of Gary to have done all this. While Glenna was processing everything, David interjected first with congratulations on what must have been a herculean effort to do all this within a few weeks. Then David agreed on the report Gary gave, and asked a few questions.

He first asked where the content came from, and before Gary could answer, he asked how long it takes to play, and before he could answer that question, David asked the most important question of all, "Can we play right now?"

A little nervous that the maiden voyage of the game would be played with Glenna's mentor, Gary agreed. He said, "There wouldn't be any better people to test it on than the experts." So he set it up and they began to play. Fifteen minutes, then thirty, and before they knew it, they had been playing for over an hour and a half! Both David and Glenna agreed that they *had* to put this into their training program. In fact, they agreed it should be the cornerstone of their training meetings. David encouraged Glenna to introduce this at their training meeting this next Saturday. Then he proceeded to invite himself to the meeting. He wasn't about to miss seeing the team play the game.

11

Six Months in Two Hours

After the conference, Cindy made an appointment with Doug to get some counseling on her business. They met on Sunday afternoon at Doug's favorite restaurant. All the servers knew him. He had been going there after meetings now for a few years. When Cindy arrived she sat down and was taken back by the fact that the waitress knew Doug by name and asked him if he wanted the usual. She asked Cindy what she wanted to order and Cindy told her gruffly that all she wanted was a glass of water with a slice of lemon. Doug could tell that Cindy was pretty upset. He started the conversation by asking her how she felt about the conference after hearing David McKay. She was still excited, but pretty concerned about the business and without any tact at all she exclaimed, "Steve Thoms won five personal awards and his team won almost everything else. The fact that Glenna let him steal the Fords and Browns from me is really hard for me to deal with. And on top of all that Steve was promoted to Copper!"

"I'm doing the work," she pointed out. "I've been showing more than fifteen presentations each month, I'm enrolling more people than anyone else and I have one of the highest personal points. So why aren't I making any money? Why don't my team members stay in the business? I've been doing exactly what you told me to do now for two months and I must tell you that right now I wonder if the business works at all, if residual income can be created or if it's just a dream or fantasy. I'm out of people on my names list. I'm making five or six hundred dollars a month, but my people aren't re-ordering, no one is going to any meetings, no one is doing anything except me and I sold exactly zero conference tickets. I feel like I'm running myself ragged for a few hundred dollars!" Doug asked what her goals in the business were and then told her that it does take time to find the right people to do the business. He told her that every deck of cards holds four aces.

"Some people find their aces faster than others. But I assure you they are in there."

"You just need to keep doing what you're doing now and those aces will turn up. David didn't get to Platinum over night. Have some patience," he told her, "and keep working, it will come. The challenge is that we never know how close we are to the goal line. You might just be at the two-yard line, you never know. This month is the month I just know it."

"Why is Glenna working so hard with the other people, and why is she telling them to do things in a completely different way?" Cindy asked.

"Well," said Doug "because she is doing a test on them. Either the company is trying something new, or David is. That's probably why he was here this conference, to see how the test is going. They invented all kinds of new awards to keep people in the business longer. And not surprisingly, those people all won the awards that don't really mean anything. Did you notice that only one of them was promoted? Only Steve advanced promotion levels. I've seen this before. This Rhino Power Team stuff is only a gimmick to make people think they are doing something; but it's really no different from what we are doing, only we don't have to jump through all the hoops."

"Okay," she said, "I'm committing to thirty days of working like crazy to making a promotion level advancement to Brass this month. But this really needs to start working. My husband is beginning to question whether this is worthwhile," she concluded. "So I'll see you at the business preview on Tuesday, right?" asked Doug.

Cindy quickly drank the last of her water and left without responding. Doug was wondering himself if the business was ever going to work. But he wasn't willing to tell anyone that. He had way too much invested for it not to work.

When Steve arrived at the weekly business preview, he noticed that Jen was early, which was a little strange. She usually was exactly on time or a minute or two late. It seemed odd that she was welcoming people as they came in. Doug usually did this. And when the meeting started, it was Jen not Doug who introduced Glenna. Steve's team had a great showing of new guests. The meeting went well and at the end Glenna turned the meeting over to Jen to let the guests know what their next steps were and to invite them to stay around, eat cookies, and ask questions. When they were all gone Glenna sighed and asked Doug if she could talk to him before the meeting for a minute.

The door closed behind them. She invited him to sit in her chair behind her desk. Glenna sat where he normally would and asked if he was okay. "I noticed that both you and Cindy seemed kind of glum tonight." He hesitated to tell her, but his feelings had been a little bruised when Jen had been asked to be the host of the meeting. "Well, I decided it's time we let others have the chance to learn and lead. The organization is growing and I need to develop other leaders," she explained. "No one is replacing you. I'm just giving others a chance to learn how to do things as well. Is that all there is?" She continued, "I noticed that Cindy looked dejected as well." Doug replied, "Well, to tell you the truth, she is a bit discouraged and," pausing, "so am I."

"We're both working hard and enrolling new people every week, but they're not staying in the business very long. Cindy has won a lot of personal awards in the past few months at the business-development conference, but she isn't making much money and none of it seems residual. So we are both a bit down about that, but it will pass. We both had new guests here tonight and they seemed pretty excited. Maybe they're the ones," he said under his breath. There was a moment of silence as Glenna wanted to give him some time to continue if he desired it.

Then Glenna leaned forward as if the desk had suddenly turned around and she was on the other side again. She then began to tell him honestly, and in as soft a voice as she could muster that his method of building the business was not effective. "Doug, I will tell you that I have been tracking the numbers in a lot of areas in the past months. Everyone who is focused solely on recruiting is struggling with retention and autoship orders."

"You, Cindy, and some others, even Jerry, who's on Steve's team, are recruiting a lot of new people. But once they are in, they don't get the encouragement or support to learn the basic skills of the business. Without the help they need to succeed in the long term, they quickly quit. Recruiting is, of course, important and you're good at it, but most new people need some training to do it. You have two great people on your team now, and one of those groups is really powerful. But it's not the one you think it is. Cindy is great, but her results are similar to yours. Steve's team is now much larger than hers and they are engaged week after week. You have two teams that are growing, but you need three to make it to the next promotion level. Believe me, I know how you feel. I have experienced this myself. And that's why I am telling you all of this."

"The way I see it," Glenna warned, "if Cindy doesn't start seeing more lasting results soon, she will quit and you will be down to one leg that is actually producing. There's nothing wrong with that, but with a few changes you could solidify Cindy and her team, increase your ability to develop a third leg, and advance to the Gold promotion level. With all of that said, I would like to personally invite you to join the Rhino Power Team and promote it to everyone on your team. You're welcome to stay for the meeting now and come to the training on Saturday. You will be amazed at what we are going to do this Saturday. And bring your team—it will be fun and profitable, I promise," Glenna concluded. Doug stood up, told her he would think about it, shook her hand, and left. Glenna was a bit taken back by his response to her invitation, but she knew that all she could do was to encourage him. It was his job to follow her counsel or ignore it. She regained her composure and came out to the group waiting in the living room.

The meeting was short and sweet, Steve remembered. Glenna said, "The Saturday training meeting was going to rock our world." She talked for a minute about Gary, edifying him, and discussing the research and work he had been doing behind the scenes for the past few months. Then she told us to make sure to bring everyone on our teams, regardless of whether they were part of the Rhino Power Team. She told us this was the missing piece for many people and would accelerate our growth by months. Then she ended the meeting. Wow! With a build up like that, this was going to be awesome. Glenna never overstated or over sold things. Maybe her meeting with Doug got her fired up or maybe it was going to be spectacular. One thing I knew for sure, I went home with great anticipation and a new determination to get people to the training meeting.

When I arrived at Glenna's on Saturday morning, there were already twenty people there. I looked at my watch to see if I was late and, to my surprise, I was twenty minutes early! After the promotion Glenna did on Tuesday, no one was going to miss this. I parked next to a beautiful new Jaguar and wondered if it belonged to David McKay. I couldn't figure out why he would be here on a Saturday. The window was rolled down, so I checked it out thoroughly. For a moment I could feel myself driving down the coast highway with Sara riding next to me, the wind blowing through our hair. When I came back to reality Jen was standing next to me. I felt a little silly for drifting into dreamland. But a dream was born that day. Glenna had a powder-blue Jag, but this one was a deep sapphire blue with beautiful leather seats.

The meeting quickly became so packed that we were in three rooms: the living room, the dining room, and Glenna's office. There were more people at this one training than all the trainings in the past month combined. There had to be over forty people there. When we began Glenna introduced us to Gary. From Glenna's edification on Tuesday, he had some pretty tall boots to fill. David McKay tried to slip in unnoticed, but he was hard to ignore. Glenna welcomed him and asked if he wanted to say anything; he said he was just there to observe. When she turned over the meeting to Gary, he began by explaining this was the first time that this had been done anywhere in the industry and that Glenna and David were the pioneers to bring the most effective training method to the best industry of opportunity—more specifically to this group, the Rhino Power Team. Gary explained the success pattern in pretty good detail. Then he told us that the game in front of us was not a game at all, but a business-building simulator disguised as a game. Embedded in it were the success pattern and all the knowledge and skills necessary to build a strong and profitable business. He taught us how to get started, and he took us as a group through the first payday. He took a minute or two to answer a few questions and then he let us play.

In just minutes the whole room sounded like a beehive. It was crazy. People were talking and high-fiving each other. One woman in Jen's group got up and started dancing when she achieved a promotion level advancement. Before we knew it, we had been playing for almost two hours! Never had time passed so quickly. Gary was moving around the room helping people, and Glenna, it seemed, was learning how to do the same. Even David began helping people to make the proper choices concerning contacting scripts, product promotions, edifying, and asking for the business.

Glenna stopped us all and we did a final tally of our promotion levels, teams, residual incomes, and goals achieved. Glenna did a mini-recognition for people who had achieved the highest PEPs, the most associates, the highest residual income, the most goals achieved, and the highest net worth. This was awesome. Kim said it was like getting six months of field experience in two hours. How could we get this, and what was the best way to use it? That was enough incentive for David to decide to introduce this to his whole team.

Gary asked the group what their experience was in this kind of training simulation. I think the response was more than he had expected. One man said, "I love the vision that this will give new associates." The woman that was dancing said, "Wow! What a great idea! It's like a monthly business-development conference in a game!" Another said, "This rocks! Finally, a way for my prospects to really experience what the business is all about. This game hits it right on the head!" And then people started competing for a chance to comment. Instead of raising their hands to comment, people just stood and started talking—it was wild. "Who would have thought that a game would let me experience success and exactly how to achieve it," one woman spoke up and then another said, "I've never seen my group so energized. Everyone has been fully engaged for almost two hours. No one wanted to stop!" Another said, "In sixty minutes, I made over $50,000 and was making $7,500 per payday! I knew what to do, why, and how to do it!" And so it continued for over twenty minutes. Finally, David McKay stood up. As a twenty-five-plus-year veteran of the business he said, "Without a doubt that this is the best teaching tool I have ever seen! It teaches so many different skills in their proper context and in their proper sequence. I would say that this has been a great success. Thank you Gary and Glenna for putting this together." We all clapped and cheered as if we had been on the maiden space voyage to Mars.

Glenna encouraged us to think about the lessons we had learned in the game and to think about ways we could use the simulator to build our businesses. She also asked if we would like to play again next week. There was an overwhelmingly positive response. Glenna said she would be letting us know how she would implement it and how we might be able to get simulators for ourselves. There were some disappointed people when they found out they couldn't get them right then and there. Most everyone stayed around for another half hour talking and planning. A new member of Tony's team told me "I would love to have this to use at one-on-one meetings to show my family and friends the business." Mark Brown told me we should have a weekly event to recruit new people. By the time I got home, I had about ten messages in my voicemail. Most of them indicated they wanted to play the game on a weekly basis.

At the weekly business preview I took my turn as the host. It was exhilarating and yet nerve-racking at the same time. Glenna promoted the training meeting on Saturday and asked a woman from Jen's team to share her experience and a man from the Brown's team shared as well. They edified Glenna for her leadership, did a great product promotion for the simulator, and fantastic event promotion for the training as a revolutionary way to bring predictability to the business. Jen's person said, "The game was the most fun way to learn about what network marketing is all about. It debunked some silly myths and showed me how to grow personally to achieve my dreams." And the Brown's person told us, "I learned more in one hour from this game than in the whole time I have been in the business!"

The event promotion and edification must have worked because there were over sixty people at the Saturday training. There wasn't a place to put everyone, so some people sat on the patio next to the pool. I think people were coming out of hiding and were enrolling because of the buzz about the simulator and the notoriety of how predictably our teams were growing. Many people who had been disenchanted before or just didn't believe that the business worked were engaging with us. In fact, this was working so well that after Saturday's training we decided to start a new meeting just to play the game on Thursdays at my house. I wasn't sure how Sara was going to feel about it, but she had agreed to everything so far.

Of course, our home wasn't nearly as big or as beautiful as Glenna's, and it was our first scheduled meeting without her; she couldn't be there on a regular basis. I figured that it would be perceived as just another meeting to go to, so I didn't worry too much about a lot of people showing up. Based on what I know now about the industry, Glenna was pretty excited about this. Certainly she didn't do or say anything to challenge it.

Mark Brown conducted the business preview. It was a big one. There were about twenty guests. Doug had a few and so did Cindy. Glenna was beginning to gain a fair amount of notoriety in town. With all of us edifying her, a reporter from one of the local newspapers came by to see what all the excitement was about. By the end of the meeting Ben and Pam Ford enrolled him on their team.

Thirty people showed up at our first game play. I think Sara was a bit overwhelmed by it all. We ran out of everything, including cups to drink out of. There were new associates who were in the Improve Yourself phase from a lot of different teams. There were people who had been in for quite a while and some people brought prospects who knew nothing about networking or XL-8. But they came to check out what we were up to. I think it was easier for my team members to invite people to play a game than to go to a business meeting. Whatever the reasons were, there were a lot of people there. Well, we learned a few lessons on how to have a game play that would help it go more smoothly in the future, but two things I think went particularly well. At the end of the game we did a small accounting of who had the most PEPs, the most associates, the most residual income, the highest net worth as well as who had achieved the most financial goals. We gave prizes for these areas and we let people talk about what they had learned. To my surprise, almost everyone wanted to share!

The new associates talked about the importance of PEPs. The veterans talked about the power of duplication and teams. The prospects all talked about how, for the first time, they understood what the industry was about and how people actually made money through the compensation plan. It was an incredible event for me to watch and listen to people share their feelings of what they had experienced through the simulator. A woman who had been in the business for a while said that for the first time since she had been doing presentations, she didn't feel like she had to know everything to build her business. What a revelation! Each of the prospects enrolled. Everyone who needed a ticket to the next monthly business-development conference got one, and all the people left with a greater feeling of camaraderie and confidence. I took names of fifteen people who wanted to buy the game from Gary or Glenna so I could get this tool in the hands of my team as soon as possible.

Jen, Sara, and I arrived at the Saturday training at Glenna's at about the same time. Of course, Glenna had already heard about our game play and she congratulated us. Since she now had team members who had at least some experience doing game demonstrations, she decided to turn that part of the Saturday training over to one of us. It was a great idea for many reasons. Attendance at the weekly training at Glenna's grew to over eighty. She split them and let Jen run one group out on the patio while she did another team in her living room. I helped a group in the dining room, and Gary facilitated a group in Glenna's office. This meeting was starting to be like the meeting at my house. This was supposed to be a training meeting for the Rhino Power Team, but it was becoming much more than that. There were prospects coming to the meeting, playing the simulator, learning about the business, enrolling in XL-8, and joining the Rhino Power Team all in one meeting.

When the training meeting was over Glenna asked Jen, Sara, and me to stay for a minute to talk about what was happening. Gary was there, but mainly she talked to us. Glenna said she was going to move the Saturday training meeting to a larger meeting space in the Harmon Hotel to accommodate all the people. And then with a bit of a sigh, Glenna told us that she had never seen growth like this before in her business. She wanted to make sure that people were following the 3-Step Success Pattern and not just enrolling and then going out trying to enroll people without any real knowledge of the business. So she encouraged us to talk about the success pattern and the PEProfile at every meeting.

Glenna also told us that she had seen some teams in other organizations recruit like crazy and then have it quickly collapse because people didn't really know what to do and there was no structure like the success pattern to help them learn how to move ahead. The problem that resulted was that people were making all of their money on enrollments instead of product orders and re-orders. Pretty soon the fervor wore out, people stopped enrolling, and the whole thing fell apart. "I'm not telling either of you to slow down in any way. I just want to warn you that there are two sides to huge growth, to encourage both of you to keep growing personally so you will be the leaders that these fast-growing groups can look to for advice, counsel, and an example to follow for their own business development." Then she told us she needed to talk to Gary privately. On the way out I handed her the paper with the fifteen names of those who wanted to purchase the simulator. Gary was surprised at the amount who came from my game play, but he added it to the names he had collected at the end of the training today. He had over fifty orders for the simulator. He promised to have something the next week for us to be able to purchase.

She confided in him her fear that this was all going too fast. She loved the growth, but she didn't want to lose control of the team. They sat down, and Gary asked how convinced she was that the 3-Step Success Pattern was the road map for success in this industry? Glenna responded by saying, "Everyone I have ever met who knows and follows it creates job-dropping residual income." He then asked if she thought the PEProfile, *Skills of the Million-Dollar Earners* audio library, and the *Residual Income*® business-building simulator were all critical elements in the context of the 3-Step Success Pattern. "I have never seen so much positive, effective activity in all my days in the business. People are now doing things without my having to be everywhere all the time. Steve, Jen, and Kim are all having their own meetings—very successful meetings, I might add. Look at the enrollments in my report this week and the orders for *Residual Income*® games." "Then trust the system," Gary told her.

"Use the game as an extension of yourself and let it do the heavy lifting. I know you are used to having to hold all the meetings and do most of the work yourself, but now you have a complete system in place to support you in the specific things your team needs to build a strong and profitable business. The game teaches the 3-Step Success Pattern, it promotes PEPs, the PEProfile, events and training meetings, product promotion, upline edification, contacting, presenting, asking for the business, and all the other critical skills embedded in the success pattern—taught in their proper sequence." "I know I need to relax," she said. "I've been at this a long time now with some moderate success and I know that I told you I am ready to take the next step to the Platinum level, but I didn't expect the growth and response to be this dramatic."

"This is a good problem to have by the way, so let's continue what we are doing now and then re-evaluate the progress at the next business-development conference," Gary added as he stood up to leave. Glenna beat him to the door, gave him double high-fives, and thanked him for his help. She asked him how to repay him for all that he had done for her and her team. He shrugged his shoulders and told her that he wasn't sure, but he would come up with something—it was probably going to be expensive! They both laughed and Gary left.

The next two weeks passed quickly and with the same kinds of growth. The weekly business preview also had to be moved to the Harmon Hotel to accommodate all the people. The Thursday game play outgrew Steve's house and backyard, and had to be moved as well. The Harmon Hotel was grateful to have the business and the team began calling it the "XL-8 Business Center."

A storm rolled in on the day of the monthly business-development conference. It rained and the wind blew, but there was simply no stopping the enthusiasm of the team. Glenna had invited Stephanie to speak at the conference. She was the leader of one of Glenna's groups from the other side of the country. She was Glenna's expert on following up and asking for the business. Stephanie had an incredible conversion rate of enrolling people who met with her after the presentation, so she would be talking about that. But Glenna had another purpose as well; she wanted to introduce the *Residual Income®* simulator to Stephanie and help her to see the results in the other groups. There was nothing like an event like this to get her fully engaged in the 3-Step Success Pattern, the PEProfile, the audio library, and the simulator as the best way to practice the skills her team needed.

The afternoon session of the conference was always my favorite, but Sara liked the evening session better. I really liked the fact that these events were held every month because they gave me the opportunity to review my personal progress and now to track my team's progress as well. I personally enrolled five new associates this month, so I just missed the Winners' Circle. But Tony, the Fords, and the Browns all earned the Winners' Circle honors for enrolling at least six in a month. The team is growing fast. The whole team enrolled fifty-two new associates this month. And I am going to get my first four-figure check! This is so cool, I can't believe how blessed I am with Glenna, XL-8, and those who are willing to learn, practice, and then apply correct principles to create the success they dream of.

We all sat together in our usual section, which was now beginning to crowd out others who sat close to us. When Doug came in I think he was a bit surprised. I saved him a place in the front row of our section. I made sure to edify him as my sponsor and tried to put him in the proper place to be the leader of the team. But he didn't edify me back, which was kind of strange; maybe he was going to do that later. He had three or four people with him and Cindy had three people with her. One of them I recognized from the past few weeks at the business preview meetings. He seemed like a really sharp guy. Cindy wanted to sit by Doug, but there wasn't room for her and her new people so she sat behind us. I think she was a little upset with Doug for taking a place in the front row and not leaving room for her and her new people to sit beside him.

The usual host came out and introduced the guest speaker to start the session. He did an awesome job of edifying Stephanie. She wasted no time getting down to business. I had my notepad out and she talked for over an hour and a half about following up and asking for the business. She made this seem so simple. She warned us a few times that the simplicity of asking for the business didn't necessarily make it easy; it was just simple to learn and implement.

She started by sharing that her experience indicated that even if your offer is exactly what people are looking for, it's actually quite rare that someone will buy from you or sign up the very first time you present to them. She told us that only about 5 percent of the people you present to will say, "Yes" and only about 5 percent will say "No" during the first meeting. The remaining 90 percent will sway either way depending on your personal effectiveness in following up, which includes asking for the business. These statistics startled me a little. She paused for a moment and, when she did, it occurred to me that this would explain why we were being so successful over the past two months. The system portrayed success and predictability, and the game did the work of preparing prospects to take action to create the results they were experiencing in the game.

She brought me back to the meeting by helping us understand what the numbers actually meant. She said that to build a large and profitable business, you need to become a master at following-up. Because about 90 percent of the time, during the follow-up your prospects make the decision to become either customers or associates.

"If you don't have a systemized follow-up procedure in place for every single one of your prospects, and if you fail to increase your personal effectiveness in following-up, you're leaving untold amounts of money on the table. A good follow-up can easily quadruple your conversion rates of prospects to customers and associates."

"How would that affect your business?" Stephanie asked. "What would it mean to you and your income, if you could begin enrolling four times as many people as customers or associates as you are today?"

She pointed out that the fortune in this industry is in the follow-up. Effective follow-ups come from making a plan from previous meetings and having answers to common questions and to those unique or specific questions that your prospect has. Failing to prepare for your follow-ups or failing to follow-up at all is a leading cause of failure.

"Preparation is the key to a successful conversion of prospects. So take a minute to make some notes about their questions, concerns, dreams, and dissatisfactions, along with your prospect's current circumstances. These notes are crucial for your follow-up. They will help you prepare to meet your prospect's needs.

"When you prepare for the follow-up with real answers that pinpoint their personal situation, you demonstrate that you are there to solve their problems and are truly interested in them. Your credibility will soar and the 90 percent will either buy from you as a customer or sign up as an associate."

She went on to talk more specifically about asking for the business during the presentation or the follow-up. She told us that people seldom take action if they are not directly asked to do so. Asking for the business is a simple concept, yet it is challenging for many people. Some do not want to seem pushy, which is why most people struggle and fail. "Because most people who join your company are not salespeople by trade, some think asking for the business might seem pushy or will put their relationships at risk. Asking for someone's business is nothing more than a question that establishes whether your prospect is ready to buy, needs additional information, or simply is not interested in your product or business opportunity right now. If properly done, your relationship with family and friends should never be at risk, no matter what their response to your business offering. Remember that you are in business, and residual income in this industry is received in direct proportion to your ability to transact. So if you represent great value and effectively present that value, you won't have to convince your prospects; they will be able to see the value and, if asked, they will take the action they are most interested in."

Then one of those really important moments came as she shared that at the end of every presentation you must simply be clear about the fact that your prospects have only three choices and they are all good for you as a business owner. She said that when we transition from the second to the third step of the anatomy of a presentation, we should say something like: "Now that you know about our company, products, and different ways of making money, there are a few choices you can make, and I will support you in which ever you decide. First, you can do nothing and your life will go on pretty much as it is now.

This might mean that you want a day or so to get and review more information if you need it to make a decision. Second, you can enroll as a customer and take advantage of the benefits we talked about. And third, you can enroll as an associate and take advantage of not only the personal benefits of the products and services but begin earning income and take control of your future. Which of these interests you most?

"Of course there are many approaches like this one on the *Skills of the Million-Dollar Earners* audio library, and how to deal with each of the choices no matter which one they choose. So implement this topic into your personal improvement plan to increase your PEPs on this approach or others. By the way, which of these interests you most is a type of high-yielding question that you learned about last month."

She concluded by telling us that the greatest benefit of this approach is that you won't feel like you are selling to people and it helps your prospects feel like they don't have to be a master salesperson to build the business with you either. Essentially, it sets an example for those who choose to become associates, that they can do what you are doing and this approach is easily duplicated if they see you do it.

I was impressed that she spoke in terms our group could understand. She used PEPs and referred to the topic that David McKay had spoken about last month. This was yet another incredibly useful meeting that will help my team and I progress this next month. Then she invited some volunteers on the stage to practice this with her. Maria, Sharon, and Robin Brown practically ran to the stage. It was powerful to see them practice this with Stephanie and to increase their PEPs right there in front of everyone. Stephanie had us all recognize their achievement before dismissing them. When they came back to the group, they received a heroes welcome. I'm pretty sure that Stephanie didn't anticipate this, and she waited for us to settle down before she completed the session. Then she gave us the instructions for getting to the evening session on time and prepared us to listen to Glenna.

It was time for the evening session to begin. The lights went down and the host came out amid the great music and cheering from the audience. He also brought out Stephanie, who was dressed as if she were going to visit the President. They actually took turns announcing the recognition awards. This was probably part of Glenna's grand plan to get her involved in the recognition, like giving out awards that Stephanie didn't even know existed.

I won the award for having the most people personally attend the conference. There were about thirty people who were recognized for doing at least fifteen business presentations. We were able to count game plays that had a ten-minute XL-8 compensation plan explanation at the end as a presentation. Doug and Cindy also did fifteen presentations, but they did more traditional ones. Cindy won the personal enrollments award again. She achieved the Winners' Circle again, and four others from my team achieved this for personally enrolling six people. Cindy also earned the Brass Ring again for personal production points. The Silver Star for team enrollments in a month went to Doug, due to Cindy's personal and my team's enrollments. Jen earned the Golden Eagle for team production points. All the people who had thirty, forty-five, and seventy PEPs were recognized. About a half of the stage was covered with people being recognized as members of the High Peppers Club. A person from the Brown's team earned the highest profile score during the month. Maria was recognized for the least amount of red areas in the Improve Yourself phase of the success pattern, and Sharon had the largest improvement in PEPs during the month. Glenna invited everyone who had done 100 percent of the things required for the Rhino Power Team promotion. I was thrilled to be on the stage with a large portion of my team. Jen was there and this award was given to almost all her team and mine.

The Effective Business Builders gold, silver, and bronze awards were given out, and the winners stood on the podium as they played the Olympic theme music. Tony won the gold, Maria the silver, and a person from Jen's team earned the bronze medal.

And last came the promotion-level recognitions. There were about twenty new people who were promoted to Copper. Jen and I, along with five others from our teams, advanced to Brass. It was cool to have people advancing right along with us. I was now at a higher level than Cindy, which was evidence to me that the 3-Step Success Pattern was working exactly as Glenna had said it would. There were two people on Kim's team who advanced to the third level or Silver, which meant that Kim would be shooting for Gold or the same level as Glenna next month. When we were done applauding the promotion-level advancements, the host once again brought out Glenna. She began her remarks by telling us this was the most awards she had ever given out at one event.

Her gratitude overcame her for a moment. It was the first time I had ever seen her lose control of her composure. It was silent as we waited for her to tell us how she felt. For the next twenty minutes or so she talked about gratitude and what it really meant to her. I don't think this was what she had planned to talk about. But it was one of those unrehearsed moments that made a huge difference. Without any notice at all she invited me to come on the stage and share my goal achievement story from last month.

I was not prepared for this moment, so I brought Sara with me so she could share in my nervousness. She reluctantly came and I told about my big dream to have Sara be able to go grocery shopping for whatever she wanted. Then I explained how after the last business-development conference we drove to the store and parked out in front to take a good look at it. I had achieved my first goal in the business, and sitting in front of that store made me feel like king of the world. Then I had Sara tell about the decorated shopping cart and the loud speaker announcement and how it made her feel to be able to buy whatever she wanted without hesitation—and to be able to do this for the rest of her life. When she told how she was able to give the discount card to the woman standing in line behind us because she could relate to her circumstances, there wasn't a dry eye in the crowd.

I spent about two minutes talking about Glenna teaching me about the progressive realization of a worthwhile dream. "No achievement comes all at once, not even this little dream of mine," I told them. "I thought Glenna was crazy when she told me to take the PEProfile and devote 95 percent of my time to learning the skills of the business before I did anything without her direct help." Then I thanked Glenna because I knew what to do and how to do it before I started seriously recruiting. I thanked Jen for helping me recruit my second associate and for pushing me to increase my PEPs to keep up with her. "And besides Sara being there to support me, the thing I am most grateful for is the 3-Step Success Pattern as a road map to help me achieve my goals and to help others begin to achieve theirs."

Then Glenna brought Stephanie, Kim, and Doug on stage and told us how grateful she was for them. It was they who had created her success in the business and the reason she was at the Gold level. And it was they who had inspired her to stretch for Platinum in the next months. She needed a couple of leaders to stand up and take effective action, like these teams had, for her to reach this goal. The crowd began to chant, "Glenna, Glenna, Glenna." Then she asked Kim, Stephanie, and Doug to briefly share with us what XL-8 meant to them and what they were striving for in the next few months in the business.

Each shared an appreciation for Glenna and her leadership. In turn they spoke about integrity, persistence, love for others, leadership, focus, and a few other points they had learned from her. Before anyone was aware of the time, two and half hours had past. It was time to go, but I don't think anyone wanted this feeling to end. Glenna closed with a challenge for all of us to make this next month a record-breaking month, to double our results in PEPs, points, and advancements. To conclude, she called on me to give a closing prayer. It was an honor to do this, especially at the end of this meeting.

In her meeting with Gary, Glenna discussed an unanticipated difference between those on the Rhino Power Team and the others. The quality and depth of the relationships was remarkable. "Teams like Doug's and Cindy's seem to be distant friends," Glenna explained. "Team unity is built around random social gatherings that don't seem to have any purpose besides getting people together. They are meeting solely to meet together and have fun for the sake of having fun. Not that there is anything wrong with this. Conversely, the Rhino Power Team meets and has fun too, but they have purposeful fun."

"They have treasure hunts with the money in the *Residual Income*® game. They go around town experiencing what they want to achieve in teams of people who like the same or similar things, spending the money they are allotted based on the cash they earn in the game each week. Their meetings are purposeful. They are building relationships of trust and respect. Their fun is in achievement and the things achievement can provide them and their families. They don't limit themselves to socializing. They learn how to pursue their greater causes and higher purposes, like eradicating cancer and giving to perpetual education funds, homeless challenges, and missionary programs. They are learning to go beyond donating money to causes by creating the resources necessary to organize and participate in their passions. I never would have guessed this would be a benefit of using the system to bring people together and help them succeed together," she shared.

Gary reminded her of their meeting a few weeks earlier when she had been worried about things getting out of hand. He jokingly asked her if she would like to go back to the way it was before. "Let's compare the teams who are using different methods briefly and see if we want to continue what we are doing now."

"Doug is personally enrolling four to six people every month and Cindy is achieving Winners' Circle status every month. The problem with these people is that historically they also have the highest dropout rate. And this month is no different, about 85 percent of their people were for all intents and purposes inactive. Cindy enrolled a new guy this month and he seems capable. I noticed that he sat with Steve's people during the evening session and he didn't seem out of place at all. I also noticed that Jerry's people haven't been very productive. He seems to be doing what Doug and Cindy are doing. I noticed that he seemed to be a little depressed when Tony was being recognized on the stage. So I would encourage you to have a counseling session with him this week. It should be pretty easy to show him what is going on in Cindy's team compared to Tony's and higher up, Steve's other associates.

"Doug's team is growing slowly, but it is growing. He doesn't come to the Saturday trainings or the weekly game plays at Steve's does he? And it seems like he must be discouraging Cindy and others from going as well. It would probably be a good idea to meet privately with Doug also.

"Steve's team is growing well. He has over fifty people now! He probably needs to take the PEProfile again. As I look at the success pattern, he seems to have all the qualifications for advancing to the Become a Leader phase. Many of his team members advanced promotion levels and their PEPs are increasing quickly. It seems like his team and Jen's team are in fact using the 3-Step Success Pattern themselves and duplicating it in their teams. There is no way they could have done all this by themselves. So what do you think, should we stay the course or should we make changes to what we are doing?" Gary asked.

Glenna hit him on the arm as a reward for his sarcasm and then gave him a big smile as she told him she had never been happier with her business. "We aren't going to change a thing," she said as she handed him a glass of water and toasted their success.

12

Surprise, Surprise

After all that was happening, Glenna could now realistically see herself as a Platinum. The system was in place, the people were in place, and she felt invigorated. She didn't want to waste even one minute getting to the highest level in XL-8. She woke up early, like a schoolgirl before her first date. She had to come up with things to do before she felt like she could call Doug and Jerry to arrange a time to meet with them. She did something she hadn't done in a long time; she went outside for an early morning swim in her pool. She was usually sleeping at this time of the morning, because she had been out late the night before working with someone in her group. She had forgotten to take the time to live the life she was working for, as she was working for it. As she was sitting by the pool watching the sunrise, she decided to swim at least two times per week as a reminder of the Platinum lifestyle.

She called Doug and then Jerry as soon as the sun was completely over the mountain. Maybe the metaphor of a new day is just what they need. She woke them both up, of course, but her excitement overcame their disapproval over being awakened early on a Sunday morning. Each agreed to meet on Monday, Doug for breakfast and Jerry for lunch. As she drank a cool glass of grape juice by the pool, Glenna lay back and realized that this was the beginning of a new day and life as a big leader in the business. With the sun shining on her face she got the idea that she should have her leadership meetings at her house right here by the pool. She called Kim, then Stephanie, Susan, and Doug again. Doug was more noticeably agitated on the second call, but in her excitement she just passed it off as the early hour and went right on thinking of others that should be part of this new growth leadership team—Steve, Jen, and probably even Gary. They all thought she was a little crazy for calling on Sunday morning, but each got excited because she was excited. This was not really Glenna's style to be calling early in the morning with plans of taking the business to the next level and everyone accomplishing greatness. She was nearly delirious, but it was great to have a leader who was as excited as the newest person on the team.

Glenna met Doug at his favorite restaurant. The hostess welcomed them and talked to Doug as if they were life-long friends. The server came to take their orders and asked Doug if he wanted his usual breakfast. It seemed fitting that Doug would feel comfortable for this meeting. She was glad they weren't sitting in her office. But Doug's comfort didn't work to her benefit as she thought it might. When she asked Doug how he felt about the conference, she thought he would tell her about a renewed determination to keep working toward his dreams. Instead, he told her he had decided to quit the business. He thanked her again for all that she had done for him, but he had decided to put his energy toward other endeavors. He explained that he was tired of the never-ending cycle of contacting and enrolling new people, only to see them quit in a month or two. He was quite emotional about this. Glenna asked him about his remarks of devotion and gratitude a few hours earlier at the conference. She tried to tell him he had a great foundation for a six-figure income. Steve and Cindy were both working hard and both had achieved promotions in the past two months! She pointed out that six figures is as close as one more group that can get to Silver. "One more group, do you know how many people would love to be in your shoes? You would be crazy after all the work you have put toward this to quit now," she encouraged. But he was undeterred.

The server brought their food and it was quiet for a few moments as they ate. Glenna used the time to think of how to help him realize the mistake he was making. In those moments the thought came to her to invite him to a game play at her house. This was a way to get him and a few others to engage more seriously in the 3-Step Success Pattern, to understand PEPs and how to build the business in a more predictable manner. She made the offer and told him that he should invite Cindy and Jerry as well. For the second time in ten minutes he surprised her.

He declined this invitation also. He told her that he appreciated her efforts in trying to keep him in. But he had been on her side of the table before and he was simply emotionally bankrupt from trying to keep people engaged in the business. "First, you begin recognizing people on stage for things that don't result in anything real. Then you chastise me for helping Cindy find people to contact. Furthermore, I can't support you as a leader or mentor when you position fictitious achievers as heroes, putting them in charge of serious business meetings. This is incredibly offensive," he said. "And I can't see how any of this helps anyone."

"Steve and Jen are not serious business builders or leaders for that matter. They are serious game players! So I would like you to call the company and have my name removed from the system all together."

The silent pause in the conversation was incredibly uncomfortable. Doug quickly finished eating and then excused himself. Glenna was bewildered by what had just happened. But she drank her orange juice and reconciled herself to the fact that no matter what she would have done, it wouldn't have changed anything.

The server came back to check on Glenna to see if she needed anything else. Her question switched Glenna's attention from Doug to the future of her own business. Glenna asked if she could refill her juice and as she did, Glenna noticed her nametag; it had the name Amy engraved on it and was upside down. Glenna asked her about why her tag was upside down and, embarrassed, she responded that she didn't even look anymore when she put it on. While she was putting it on the right way Glenna asked her what she knew about Doug. "Well, he is in some kind of business is all that I know," she responded. "Has he ever told you anything about it?" "Hmm, no I don't think so," she added.

Glenna continued, "Well it just so happens that Doug and I are partners and we are expanding the business Doug is associated with in a big way. I have been impressed with you and the service that you have given me today. Do you know anyone who I could talk to about filling a leadership role and learning how to make a significant income in the next few months?" Glenna told her that if she would write her name and phone number on the receipt, that she would call her in the next few days to set up an appointment to talk about it. Amy told her that afternoons and early evenings were best. Glenna left feeling somewhat better about the meeting from what was a huge downer in regard to Doug's announcement.

When she got home she called Cindy and rescheduled with Jerry to play the *Residual Income*® game at her house on Wednesday in the afternoon. Glenna's goal was to build a better relationship with them and secondarily, make sure that these two learned the 3-Step Success Pattern and hopefully engaged in it. The good news about her meeting with Doug was that she knew his intentions. Of course Cindy was now at major risk because Doug, her upline and mentor, had just quit. Glenna wasn't sure how this would affect Cindy and her commitment going forward. The game play with just a few people should help Glenna connect to them both.

The weekly business preview was unusual. For the first time since I had been in the business Doug wasn't at this meeting. Pam Ford was the host and she did a fantastic job at introducing Glenna. There were over forty people at the preview. It was a good thing we had the hotel meeting room. Things were changing pretty fast: new recognitions, new training systems, new meeting space, a new host every week at the preview, and now no Doug. Glenna took a moment at the meeting after the meeting to explain that Doug had decided to take a break from the business. I wasn't sure what that meant exactly, but it sounded like the same kind of thing married people say when they decide to get divorced—except they call the initial time away from each other "a break." Glenna asked Cindy and me to stay for a moment afterword just to see how we were doing and if we had any additional questions. Cindy asked who could help her do support calls with prospects when she did presentations. Glenna gave Cindy her cell phone number and told her that she would be available anytime she needed someone. Glenna reminded Cindy of the game play the next day and told me that Jerry was coming with them. Glenna also invited me to take the PEProfile again in the next week or so and to schedule some time to meet to discuss the report. She told Cindy not to worry about that right now, they would be talking about it tomorrow.

When Cindy and Jerry got to Glenna's she was in a great conversation with Amy, the waitress from the restaurant. Glenna welcomed Cindy and Jerry and introduced everyone. She explained that she thought it would be okay to invite Amy since it was already scheduled for the best time for her to meet. Glenna said this was the first time she had used the *Residual Income*® business-building simulator to introduce people to the business, but she was sure it would work out great. She explained the game and in a few minutes they were playing. They all had some incredible learning moments.

The group played for about an hour, and Cindy said she finally understood why her business wasn't growing: she had missed the fact that she wasn't helping others learn how to build their own business after they enrolled. She had come to the business with some skill and knowledge, but the people she recruited didn't have that same skill level, so they weren't able to jump right in to prospecting. She also discovered that she thought when she had a few people on her team that she was the leader, but she realized there were many areas of the business in which she lacked skill and knowledge and asked Glenna how to take the Personal Effectiveness Profile.

Cindy committed to take it in the next couple of days and to come to the Saturday training. Jerry almost echoed Cindy's remarks. He added that now he could see why Steve and Jen's groups were exploding. Everyone on their teams start at the start and build personal effectiveness before building a team, learning what they need to do before they try to go out and do it, or get others to try to do what they didn't have the skill to do. Then they religiously follow what is called the 3-Step Success Pattern, which creates predictability in the business.

Amy had so many great moments that she couldn't describe them all. But she did ask if this was exactly how XL-8 worked. Glenna took a minute to talk more in depth about the products and services and then she asked Cindy if she would explain the compensation structure. She did a great job at helping Amy understand how they made the kind of money she had just made in the simulator. Before Cindy and Jerry left, Amy asked why Doug had never told her about this.

"Well, there are many reasons people don't share, but the good news is that you know now," and then Amy asked the million-dollar question, "How do I sign up and what do I do next?" Cindy and Jerry took this as their cue to leave them alone to finish the meeting. They got up, gave Glenna a hug, and confirmed that they would be at the Saturday training.

Glenna entered the enrollment information for Amy into the computer and processed her first order. She wrote their first meeting in her schedule and then began to look over the numbers for the week.

It hadn't occurred to her before now that with Doug gone, Steve and Cindy would become her personally sponsored team members. When Glenna looked at her team genealogy, it had increased by two legs today: one more for Amy, minus one for Doug, and one more each for Steve and Cindy.

Glenna's goal at the beginning of the year to go Platinum required her to have five total legs to achieve the Gold level. Kim, Stephanie, and Susan, the cookie arranger from Steve's very first meeting, were already at the Gold level and Doug only needed one more of his legs to achieve Silver so he could achieve the Gold level. Jen was at the Brass level and would probably achieve Silver this month; she was on track to be Glenna's fourth Gold in the next month. But now with Doug gone, Cindy and Steve became new teams who were at the Brass level and Steve was ahead of schedule for achieving Silver this month. In some ways, Doug quitting was a blessing in disguise. Now Glenna had legs five and six lined up for Gold.

"I am really going to miss him," Glenna thought. He added great energy and work ethic to the team. On the bright side however, he wouldn't be here any more to teach the ineffective "enroll, hope, and replace" business strategy either. Now if Cindy would embrace the 3-Step Success Pattern, she could be Gold in the next six months as well. The huge growth her team was experiencing could be managed only if she used the tools and duplication systems that were already in place.

"What I need to do first is to put the local leaders in charge of the weekly preview and training meetings, shifting my focus to work with the leaders in my group to help them create leaders in their teams. This is the only way I'm going to ever create the security and generational wealth David talks about while he sits by his swimming pool," Glenna thought.

Steve was thinking about the business and how it was growing for everyone who was part of the Rhino Power Team. "My skills and patience are really paying off," he thought more specifically. "It's not big time yet, but Sara is able to go to the grocery store now without reticence about the price of milk. She has even started to build a reserve of the supplies we use regularly. She had found that food was significantly cheaper when bought in bulk and together we had came to the realization that it was so much more expensive to be poor than it was to be rich. If this applied to the grocery store, what other areas of our lives could be improved if we could pay ahead or pay with cash instead of using credit?" Steve asked himself.

While Steve was doing some errands he stopped at the flower shop and bought a bouquet for Sara. When he got home he called the normal babysitter and made an agreement with her to take care of the kids on consistent days of the week. This was going to be a great surprise for Sara. Now she wouldn't have to worry about the money to pay for a babysitter and it would give her more time to help Maria. He hung up the phone and took the flowers and a little note to Sara, who was making dinner. When she read the note telling her that dream number two was accomplished and that she would have a babysitter at her disposal three nights per week, she looked at Steve with a smile and a tear in her eye. She was torn between leaving the kids that much and having the opportunity to help the business grow. She hugged him and told him how proud she was of all that he had done to make their life better. In that moment he realized his goals didn't seem to be the huge kind that were broadcasted from the stage at a conference. But in these moments, it sure felt great to set and then accomplish them.

Steve took the profile again and he got a seventy-one! About a half hour after he finished, the phone rang. It was Glenna. (He had put her email address on the report so that she would get a copy.) She congratulated him on the score and then scheduled a meeting to go over it and complete the napkin drawing.

Glenna and Steve met at the restaurant inside the Harmon Hotel after the Saturday training meeting. She congratulated him on his personal growth and how he had been building his team. He told her that he had been studying what she had been doing. Steve figured that she had been developing six or seven teams to achieve the Platinum level, and so he had copied that by building six or seven teams so he would be set up to be Platinum right along with her someday.

Glenna gave Steve that fox-guarding-the-hen-house grin and told him to keep copying, starting with developing a new dream or goal that he could be as passionate about as grocery shopping. The next step to master was the Become a Leader phase. Then she asked for the napkin drawing of the 3-Step Success Pattern so she could complete it. She started by telling him that he needed to begin reallocating the way he invested his time, that he needed to shift from 50 percent recruiting to 15 percent. And she pointed out that another major focus for him needed to become training new people how to successfully build a team and then advance to the Become a Leader phase, just as she had done with him.

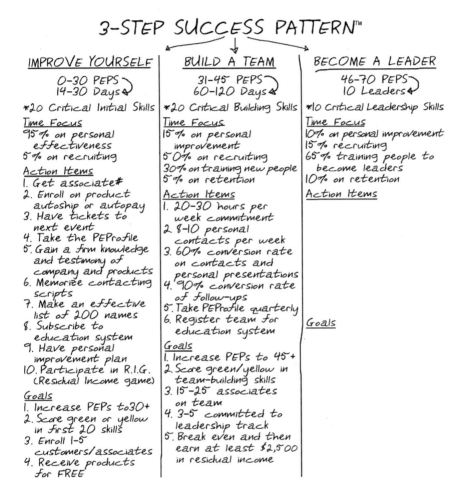

3-STEP SUCCESS PATTERN™

IMPROVE YOURSELF	BUILD A TEAM	BECOME A LEADER
0-30 PEPS 14-30 Days	31-45 PEPS 60-120 Days	46-70 PEPS 10 Leaders
*20 Critical Initial Skills	*20 Critical Building Skills	*10 Critical Leadership Skills
Time Focus 95% on personal effectiveness 5% on recruiting	**Time Focus** 15% on personal improvement 50% on recruiting 30% on training new people 5% on retention	**Time Focus** 10% on personal improvement 15% recruiting 65% training people to become leaders 10% on retention
Action Items 1. Get associate# 2. Enroll on product autoship or autopay 3. Have tickets to next event 4. Take the PEProfile 5. Gain a firm knowledge and testimony of company and products 6. Memorize contacting scripts 7. Make an effective list of 200 names 8. Subscribe to education system 9. Have personal improvement plan 10. Participate in R.I.G. (Residual Income game)	**Action Items** 1. 20-30 hours per week commitment 2. 8-10 personal contacts per week 3. 60% conversion rate on contacts and personal presentations 4. 90% conversion rate of follow-ups 5. Take PEProfile quarterly 6. Register team for education system	**Action Items**
Goals 1. Increase PEPs to 30+ 2. Score green or yellow in first 20 skills 3. Enroll 1-5 customers/associates 4. Receive products for FREE	**Goals** 1. Increase PEPs to 45+ 2. Score green/yellow in team-building skills 3. 15-25 associates on team 4. 3-5 committed to leadership track 5. Break even and then earn at least $2,500 in residual income	**Goals**

Glenna then wrote down five business characteristics he needed to be paying serious attention to. Three of the things really caught his eye: professional commitment, training using team PEProfile results, and the promotion of one new leader per month.

3-STEP SUCCESS PATTERN™

IMPROVE YOURSELF	BUILD A TEAM	BECOME A LEADER
0-30 PEPS	31-45 PEPS	46-70 PEPS
14-30 Days	60-120 Days	10 Leaders
*20 Critical Initial Skills	*20 Critical Building Skills	*10 Critical Leadership Skills
Time Focus	**Time Focus**	**Time Focus**
95% on personal effectiveness	15% on personal improvement	10% on personal improvement
5% on recruiting	50% on recruiting	15% recruiting
Action Items	30% on training new people	65% training people to become leaders
1. Get associate#	5% on retention	10% on retention
2. Enroll on product autoship or autopay	**Action Items**	**Action Items**
3. Have tickets to next event	1. 20-30 hours per week commitment	1. Full time/professional commitment
4. Take the PEProfile	2. 8-10 personal contacts per week	2. Training using team PEProfile results
5. Gain a firm knowledge and testimony of company and products	3. 60% conversion rate on contacts and personal presentations	3. Enroll 2 new personals each month
6. Memorize contacting scripts	4. 90% conversion rate of follow-ups	4. Promote 1 new leader per month
7. Make an effective list of 200 names	5. Take PEProfile quarterly	5. Training system using R.I.G.
8. Subscribe to education system	6. Register team for education system	**Goals**
9. Have personal improvement plan	**Goals**	
10. Participate in R.I.G. (Residual Income game)	1. Increase PEPs to 45+	
Goals	2. Score green/yellow in team-building skills	
1. Increase PEPs to 30+	3. 15-25 associates on team	
2. Score green or yellow in first 20 skills	4. 3-5 committed to leadership track	
3. Enroll 1-5 customers/associates	5. Break even and then earn at least $2,500 in residual income	
4. Receive products for FREE		

Steve told her he was already using the *Residual Income*® game to train his people and he was already enrolling more than two new personals each month. She congratulated him on using the game to train and then cautioned him to make it a point to continue to recruit new people each month. She shared a couple of stories of people who had achieved leadership and then stopped recruiting. "They lost touch with people and what gets you to the top. Eventually you lose credibility with your team and they stop listening to you and start doing exactly what you are doing. Pretty soon no one is recruiting; the team stops growing and then it begins to shrink until someday it disappears."

Steve asked her about the commitment part, and Glenna quickly taught him about five different areas of commitment. Commitment was measured by his willingness and determination to get the job done, no matter the circumstances. However, commitment could be measured in many ways. It could be measured by how much it took to make him discouraged and give up; some people become discouraged very easily and quickly, while others work harder and smarter when things aren't going as planned.

She went on by saying, "It's your commitment to personal goals, values, dreams, and family, as well as that of your business associates, that determine how you will react to adversity." Then she gave Steve the details about the five areas. She said commitment was also measured by the time you spend on yourself and in working on your business. "There are essentially four different levels of time commitment that people make or progress through on their way to phenomenal success. The sometime level that is measured with four to six hours per week in the business. The second level is spare time; this is when a person invests six to twelve hours of business-building activity each week. Then there is the part-time level, which is twelve to twenty-five hours per week. And lastly, there is the full-time commitment level that requires a twenty-five to fifty hour per week commitment."

Glenna continued, "Help people understand that no matter what level they choose, their immediate results will be reflected in their willingness to commit to a consistent effort each week during their available time. That is to say, nothing can get in the way or take priority over the specific hours they commit to consistently spend in their business."

She went on to the second area of commitment, which was the amount of financial investment a person was willing to make in their business. How much money were they willing to invest in personal improvement, business development, marketing materials, and relationships? She said that David once asked her, if her goal was to create job-dropping residual income in the next two to three years, and that outcome was certain, how much time and money would she invest to create that result, $10 per month, $50, $100, $1,000, or more? "He went on to help me think of what was at stake! He told me, 'I will tell you and the people you will now be the mentor to—it's your future we're talking about here; it's your children's future, it's your grandchildren's future.' David also shared with me what a wise man told him: you can make excuses or you can make money, but you can't make both," she revealed passionately.

"There are four levels of financial commitment," she explained. "The beginner level, which consists of many people who see the money they invest as an expense, hoping they will get the money back if the gamble to enroll works. Then there is the hobbyist who is willing to commit to larger amounts of financial resources, but probably won't fully engage in the training system of the company, or enroll on autoship until he or she is making enough to cover these items. Third there is the amateur; usually they like to pick and choose the parts of the business they are committed to invest in. And just like the beginner and hobbyist, they will invest some money, but they will be very selective. And lastly, there is the professional level. This is the level you must choose if you are going to be a successful leader of a great and growing group. Professionals who are fully engaged in the training system are enrolled in autoship, attend every event, have an ample supply of marketing materials, and invest in any program that is promoted by their successful upline mentors."

Glenna abbreviated the last three items and referred Steve to the *Skills of the Million-Dollar Earners* audio library for the details of each. But she did say that personal improvement was critical to success as he had already experienced. Devotion to the team was the fourth area, and lastly, he needed to learn about being fully committed to customer service. "When David told me these things I was a bit overwhelmed by it all. But I agreed from that day on to be committed to learning, practicing, and applying what we now call PEPs to these areas," she said.

Steve thought about the other insights Glenna had discussed with him. "She taught me that I needed to make sure to get the profile reports of my team members and use those to help them improve individually. In addition, I needed to put them together to make sure that when I was training my team, I used the team results to train on things that matter to the whole team instead of just one or two individuals.

"All of a sudden I realized why leadership came as a process instead of just through enrolling a few people on a team and then supposing by default that I was the leader. I realized the importance of helping my team members fully embrace the 3-Step Success Pattern, to advance when they were ready to advance based on what Glenna had written on my napkin. It seemed to be the only way to promote one new leader per month. Without it, the business would be based on chance and luck instead of predictability. How blessed I was to have met Glenna and to be her student," he thought.

Lastly, Glenna wrote down the eight goals that I needed to accomplish if I wanted to achieve my greater causes and higher purposes. These would help me advance to what she called "freetirement." "Freetirement," I asked, "What is that?" She explained, "It is when you reach a level in the business where you have developed enough leaders who are all making so much money that they could never afford to quit. It's when you can do whatever you want just because you want."

Glenna continued, "The nine goals are lofty and challenging to achieve, but if we work hard, stay focused, and consistently use and teach the success pattern we can do it. Okay. That's the whole success pattern. Your treasure map, as you call it, is complete.

3-STEP SUCCESS PATTERN™

IMPROVE YOURSELF	BUILD A TEAM	BECOME A LEADER
0-30 PEPS 14-30 Days	31-45 PEPS 60-120 Days	46-70 PEPS 10 Leaders
*20 Critical Initial Skills	*20 Critical Building Skills	*10 Critical Leadership Skills
Time Focus 95% on personal effectiveness 5% on recruiting	Time Focus 15% on personal improvement 50% on recruiting 30% on training new people 5% on retention	Time Focus 10% on personal improvement 15% recruiting 65% training people to become leaders 10% on retention
Action Items 1. Get associate# 2. Enroll on product autoship or autopay 3. Have tickets to next event 4. Take the PEProfile 5. Gain a firm knowledge and testimony of company and products 6. Memorize contacting scripts 7. Make an effective list of 200 names 8. Subscribe to education system 9. Have personal improvement plan 10. Participate in R.I.G. (Residual Income game)	Action Items 1. 20-30 hours per week commitment 2. 8-10 personal contacts per week 3. 60% conversion rate on contacts and personal presentations 4. 90% conversion rate of follow-ups 5. Take PEProfile quarterly 6. Register team for education system	Action Items 1. Full time/professional commitment 2. Training using team PEProfile results 3. Enroll 2 new personals each month 4. Promote 1 new leader per month 5. Training system using R.I.G.
Goals 1. Increase PEPs to 30+ 2. Score green or yellow in first 20 skills 3. Enroll 1-5 customers/associates 4. Receive products for FREE	Goals 1. Increase PEPs to 45+ 2. Score green/yellow in team-building skills 3. 15-25 associates on team 4. 3-5 committed to leadership track 5. Break even and then earn at least $2,500 in residual income	Goals 1. Increase PEPs to 70+ 2. Score green or yellow in leadership skills 3. Increase team PEPs average to over 30 4. 250+ team members 5. 15 or more leaders 6. 20+ serious builders 7. 100 people on autoship or autopay 8. 100 in education system and events 9. 50 recognized on stage

"I also want to invite you to start attending my monthly leadership meetings and weekly conference calls. You have certainly earned it. I have invited Jen and Cindy to be part of the leadership team as well. Our first conference call is next Wednesday night at 9:00 PM. You can come over to the house to participate if you want or I'll send you the dial-in information. The monthly meetings are held two hours before the business-development conferences." I gratefully accepted her offer as we stood up to leave. What an extraordinary opportunity I had. I couldn't wait to get home to tell Sara.

13

Accelerated Growth

On the way home I thought about what Glenna had said about a new dream or goal that I could be passionate about. I thought about the Jaguar that Gary drove to the training meeting a while ago and how incredible it was riding in Glenna's powder-blue Jag when we went to Tony's and the Jacobsen's a few months ago. I was lost in my recollection of these experiences when out of the corner of my eye I saw the Jaguar logo on a sign in the next block.

"There's the dealership," I thought. I stopped for a moment to look around to see if I could see one like Gary's or Glenna's. I did see one, but it was in the showroom. If I wanted to touch and feel it, I would have to come back when they were open.

When I got home I told Sara I had been invited to join the leadership team and that Glenna had encouraged me to start developing a new goal that I could be passionate about. Sara told me she could give me all kinds of ideas, but they would be her goals not mine. "What do you want?" I asked. She was quick to say a housekeeper would free her up to spend more time with the kids. Then she said a college fund for the kids would be awesome. She hadn't even stopped to take a breath when she told me that it would be great to be able to donate to and volunteer at the humanitarian group at the church.

Sara's list was growing by the minute. She talked about a clothes budget so that she could get whatever she wanted, about what an annual membership to the spa downtown would be like, and about how she would like to be able to get her hair and nails done regularly. She continued by telling me the bathroom needed to be remodeled and then maybe the kitchen. She stopped for a moment, took a breath, and then started to describe a four-thousand-square-foot contemporary home with five bedrooms, four bathrooms, and an office on the main floor, windows revealing a mountain view on twenty acres of land with a river flowing through one side, and a county maintained road on the other. She took me on a mental walk around the house. We stood on the porch off the master bedroom and she described the deer running on the side of the mountain. Her picture was so clear that I could hear the river flowing in the background. "Okay, I get it you have a lot of things you would like to do. Why didn't you tell me any of these things before?"

"Because there was nothing we could do about any of it so why bother bringing it up," she said. Then she asked, "So what have you been thinking about?" I thought for a moment, "Well, in the beginning of the business I rode in Glenna's Jaguar and a month or so ago I saw Gary's Jaguar at the Saturday training. The window was open and I gave it a pretty good inspection. In each case I fell in love with their cars. On the way home last night I stopped at the dealership and looked at cars for a minute. They were closed so I couldn't see the one like Gary's or Glenna's." Encouragingly Sara said, "Why don't you go down there this morning and check it out?" It didn't take much more than that for me to get into motion.

About fifteen minutes later I pulled up to the dealership in my iconic, success-indicating, twenty-five-year-old car. It hadn't ever occurred to me what my car was going to say to the salesperson. Thinking back now, they probably saw me drive up and drew straws to see who was going to get to waste their time on me. A man named Javier came out and greeted me with a smile and asked how he could help me. I told him I had been by last night to look at the car in the showroom. His smile grew even bigger. I don't know if it was because he could hear the cash register ringing in his head, or if he was deeply amused at my wanting to look at a car that I was obviously not going to be able to afford based on what I drove up in.

We looked at the car and he asked me if I wanted to drive one. Of course I did, if that was possible. "We have one in the detail shop, let me go get it and we'll go for a drive," offered Javier. That experience was the most awesome ten minutes I had ever spent driving. If I had the money, I would have bought it right then and there. When we got back to the dealership Javier asked, "Well, what do you think?" "I think I want it," I said. "I'm not really crazy about the color, but the car is just what I want." He said they could order a car made to my specifications if I wanted to. Timidly I asked what it cost, remembering stories my dad used to tell about people who had to ask the price on luxury items obviously didn't have the money to actually buy them. But Javier was patient. He told me the cost of this particular model, however if I wanted other things, the price would be somewhat different. Surprisingly the price didn't shock me. Then he asked if I was ready to buy or order? This guy was good. I'll bet he was pretty successful at selling. He let me experience having what I wanted, checked my interest level, and his presentation ended with a call to action. Maybe he had been at Kim's presentations seminar a few months ago.

I told him I would order the car only if I could pay cash for it and with the pace I was on at that time, that might not be for eight to ten months. He looked at me in disbelief. "What do you do that can create that kind of cash that fast?" I told him I had recently partnered with a company called XL-8 and that business was booming. My newly found instinct told me to contact this guy. I told him I was in a serious expansion mode and was looking for driven professionals who would be willing to learn how to make that kind of money—the kind of money that lets you pay cash for cars and live in houses on the hill with swimming pools in the backyard. When I asked him if he knew anyone like that, he had already written his cell phone number on the back of his card and was handing it to me. I told him I would call in a day or two to sit down with him and go over some details when he wasn't working. He told me evenings were best for him. I thanked him for his time and I drove away in my success magnet.

On the way home I imagined myself behind the wheel of that Jag. While I was in dreamland I thought of all the things Sara had talked about: housekeepers, college funds, shopping and massage budgets, remodeled bathrooms and kitchens, and that beautiful home in the country. I felt like a loser for not realizing she had dreams too. Because I had chosen to work at a job that didn't pay anything, her dreams were being sacrificed. So I stopped at the bank on the way home and I set up a college fund. I transferred the first hundred dollars into that account from our savings account, which a few months ago didn't even have one hundred dollars in it to transfer to anything—especially not to a college fund. And right then I made my first passion goal: to put

$1,000 each and every month into that account. When I got home, Sara had an interesting look on her face, the kind that always notified me that she had something to say, but she wasn't quite sure how to say it.

So I asked, "Okay, what is it, what are you up to?" She told me that her mother had invited us to come to visit for a week or so. The problem she said was that she knew I couldn't be gone for that long. I immediately began to create a plan. If Sara was gone for a week or more, I could hire a bathroom-remodeling contractor and get the job done before she got back. It would be awesome. So I suggested that she and the kids go and have fun while I slaved away here at home. She was pretty excited to get away for a while. I had to remind her I had been in the military and had lived in housing projects as a missionary, so I would be okay on my own for a while.

I made her promise not to tell them that we were in the business or that I had resigned as baseball coach. I wanted the opportunity to show up one day and write her dad a thousand dollar check to repay him for what he had done a few months ago. She called her mom and in a matter of minutes Sara received an email with the confirmation numbers and boarding passes to fly there. They were packed and ready to go before lunch. I took them to the airport and on the way home I started calling contractors about remodeling the bathroom and the kitchen. Three came to the house that afternoon and gave me bids. The kitchen was considerably more than the bathroom, so I could afford to do only the bathroom with the cash I had on hand. I chose a contractor and the work began the next day.

I took Glenna's advice very seriously and continued to recruit for myself. But I made sure as a leader to call every person who had enrolled over the past two weeks and welcome them to the team. I set up appointments to meet with some of them and essentially repeated what Glenna had done with me. As I drew out the first part of the success pattern and challenged them to take the PEProfile and join the Rhino Power Team I explained the three underlying principles that made the diagram work. I told them to start at the start. To build personal effectiveness before building the team and to follow the proven success pattern if they were really serious about accomplishing their goals in a predictable way. In fact, I even used a napkin to draw the first part for each of them as a sort of tribute to Glenna.

3-STEP SUCCESS PATTERN™

IMPROVE YOURSELF	BUILD A TEAM	BECOME A LEADER
0-30 PEPS 14-30 Days	31-45 PEPS 60-120 Days	46-70 PEPS 10 Leaders
*20 Critical Initial Skills	*20 Critical Building Skills	*10 Critical Leadership Skills
Time Focus 95% on personal effectiveness 5% on recruiting	Time Focus	Time Focus
Action Items 1. Get associate# 2. Enroll on product autoship or autopay 3. Have tickets to next event 4. Take the PEProfile 5. Gain a firm knowledge and testimony of company and products 6. Memorize contacting scripts 7. Make an effective list of 200 names 8. Subscribe to education system 9. Have personal improvement plan 10. Participate in R.I.G. (Residual Income game)	Action Items	Action Items
Goals 1. Increase PEPs to 30+ 2. Score green or yellow in first 20 skills 3. Enroll 1-5 customers/associates 4. Receive products for FREE	Goals	Goals

I got several calls from Tony, the Browns, the Fords, and Maria thanking me for helping them get their people started right. I told each of them that his or her turn was coming to help others learn the success pattern and implement correct choices in their proper sequence. I thought to myself, this is what Glenna must feel like all day long as she helps people achieve their goals and dreams and then receives thanks for it. What a great business.

The business preview was awesome. Glenna changed things up a bit. She started the meeting by welcoming everyone and she did the introduction. She began by saying that she had achieved great success in the business we were about to see. But the greatest achievement of all is to be able to see others who she had mentored become leaders themselves. Then she edified Jen and turned the time over to her to do the presentation. All this time Glenna had been waiting for a leader to step up and embrace the 3-Step Success Pattern so she could turn the meeting over to him or her.

Jen had a talent of relating with people and the meeting was great. It also seemed like more people than usual stayed afterward to get more information. In the meeting after the meeting, Glenna told me that next week was my turn. She also advised the others to get ready because everyone was going to get a chance to participate.

Jen, Cindy, and I all went to Glenna's for the leadership call. It was really cool because there were even more people on the call. Kim, Stephanie, and Susan all welcomed us to the team. We spent a minute or two talking and introducing ourselves, then we discussed the upcoming business-development conference. Glenna pulled out her team PEProfile and looked at it for a minute. She told us that based on the results in the past few months, the whole team needed to learn about personality types and focusing on others. Glenna wanted to make sure that we started each afternoon session with an overview of the success pattern and then address the specific topic for that month.

Stephanie suggested that different people do each part. For instance, Steve would do the success pattern, then Susan would talk about personality types. Glenna agreed, "And since those people are all here and very capable, I will put their names down as you have indicated Stephanie. Steve will take eight to ten minutes to talk about the success pattern and Susan will take fifty to sixty minutes to talk about personality types. I want to make sure Susan that you refer everyone to the CD in *Skills of the Million-Dollar Earners* in your presentation. Then in the evening session after we do recognition, I will talk about focusing on others." Efficiently, Glenna said that our time had been well spent for this week, she thanked us all for being on the call and for what we did each day to help people achieve their dreams and goals, then the call was over. I never knew so much went into the business-development conference, but now I was getting an insider's look. It was pretty amazing, all except the part where I got volunteered to present the success pattern. My problem was going to be keeping my part down to ten minutes.

I called Javier from the Jaguar dealership and invited him to the weekly game play. The meeting was excellent and because I had a guest of my own, I asked if Tony would host the game play. About fifty people showed up to play. I think some guests were beginning to show up because they didn't have anything else to do, sort of like Friday night bingo or something. But it was all right. Everyone made great contributions to the meeting. I played the game with Javier, Maria, and a guest she had invited. It was really fun. I hadn't played personally for a few weeks. During the game I had plenty of opportunities to talk about XL-8 and our products. I also talked about the Jaguar I wanted to get and the bathroom I was remodeling.

In fact, during the game I was able to achieve both goals. Afterward, Tony called me up to do the debrief and to describe how we make the kind of money in XL-8 that they made in the game that night. Javier and Maria's prospects both enrolled that night. They were impressed with the company and the unique way we conducted business; they had never seen anything like it. It seemed easy to invite their family and friends to play a game. When I got home there was that distinct smell of construction in the house. I was becoming familiar with it. As I passed the phone I saw the message light flashing. There was a message from my contractor.

He said the bathroom was completed and that I shouldn't use the shower or the sink for a day to let everything dry completely. He planned to drop by in the morning to make sure everything was all right and to settle the payment. I ran upstairs to see what it looked like. It was wonderful. I stood there admiring the new marble tub and shower surround, the marble double bowl vanity with four electrical outlets, full width four-foot-tall mirror with two swing-arm adjustable mirrors, and the beautiful heated tile floor. As I was taking it all in the phone rang—it was Sara. We talked for a while and it was all I could do not to tell her that I had a surprise waiting for her. But I wanted her to see it for herself when she came in the house. She told me they would be home that weekend. I was even more excited for her to come home now that the bathroom was done. She obviously sensed my excitement, but I think she thought I wasn't getting along well without her.

The Saturday training was growing even bigger. We actually had to change to a bigger room. We were excited and so was the Harmon Hotel. They had pretty much a guarantee of the room reservation every Saturday morning for the foreseeable future. Glenna continued her transition of power to the team by starting the training meeting like she had the weekly preview. She welcomed everyone, edified the guest trainer, then turned the time over to Kim to do the training. Kim was great, and it was no surprise that she was at the Gold level. I think she had about 90 PEPs. It was a sure thing that if I was going to be a Gold or a Platinum someday, that I had my work cut out for me. The good news was that my team was getting the very best training anywhere in the world. I stayed for a while after the training meeting answering questions for the new people and getting to know Kim a little better. We asked where we should go for lunch and Amy recommended the restaurant where she worked. A bunch of us went out and by the time I got home, Sara and the kids were already there—they *had* been busy.

The smell led her to the surprise and she had enlisted the kids in making signs and decorations welcoming me home as the conquering hero. I was planning the surprise for her and she was the one who surprised me! For the first time in our married life I actually felt like a winner, like I was the kind of person she deserved to marry and the kind of dad our kids needed—not only because we had a small amount of money now, but because of the personal growth I had been making through the business. I was a better dad and husband, and I had Glenna to thank for it. She saw that I could be something if I just had the chance to grow and be rewarded according to the value of service rendered. This industry made that possible.

Maria was the host of the weekly business preview, and Pam Ford did the presentation. Glenna came in a few minutes late and stood in the back with a huge smile on her face. Everything was going great and she didn't have to do anything to set it up or make it happen.

At the leadership call Glenna made a special point to make assignments for the different kinds of recognition awards. The Improve Yourself awards were going to be announced by Susan, the Build a Team awards by Kim, and the Become a Leader awards by Stephanie. Glenna also wanted everyone on the leadership team to be on the stage to shake the achievers hands as they walked by after receiving their award. She wanted to do the Rhino Power Team awards and the Effective Business Builders gold, silver, and bronze medals herself. She told us we needed to have the numbers of how many people on each of our teams would qualify for each award by next week. And that included how many we thought could qualify for a specific award, even if they hadn't achieved it yet.

We made a few changes to the weekly game play. We decided to put the newest people in the front of the room and walk them through the first payday, as we had in the past with everyone in the room. We moved the experienced players to the back on their own tables so they could sit down and begin without waiting for the new people to get past the first payday. This worked really well. No one was drumming their fingers or sighing while they were waiting to get past the first payday.

The second week we did this, the experienced players' game turned into what Ben and Pam Ford called a live table, where players at the experienced tables had to do in the real world what the cards in the game told them to do. When the practice cards said to contact someone, they had to do it for real. When they had to do product promotion, edification, event promotion, follow-up, or ask for the business, they had to talk to someone outside the room to get credit in the game for doing it. This was beginning to have a life of its own—I loved it! More and more people were participating as hosts, presenters, game play facilitators, and trainers in the Saturday meetings.

As I was preparing to report on my team members who had qualified for different recognition awards at the conference, I was amazed at what I saw. My heart soared like it had when I got that letter from Coach Curtis of State University telling me I was going to get a full baseball scholarship. I just looked at the computer screen, not able to fully comprehend what I was looking at. I had over 150 people on my team now, and almost all of them were eligible to receive some kind of recognition; many were qualified in more than one area.

I was pretty confident that my team could sweep the Effective Business Builders medals and dominate in the PEProfile related awards. Maria, Sharon, and Jerry all qualified as new Coppers. Tony, the Browns, and the Fords were going to advance to the second level, or Brass. And because I had at least two Brass legs, I was going to be promoted to Silver and was perfectly set up to achieve Gold next month. The good news about achieving Gold was that the average person at this level made at least $10,000 per month, which would be an annualized $120,000 six-figure income. That would only be a 300 percent raise over my teaching salary, including my coaching stipends!

It seemed that the momentum was starting to kick in. What excited me more was that the people I had enrolled were also making awesome progress. The things Glenna had told me about predictability in that first meeting and the success pattern being like a road map that made it possible were true. That's it; a light bulb in my head came on. I have it! I know exactly what I am going to teach in my ten minutes at the conference. I don't need to include all the details—the success pattern has that. I just need to talk about predictability and fill in the blanks like Glenna did for me.

The morning of the business-development conference came and I was eager to get the afternoon session started. It was like my first day of teaching or my first game as a coach. The time came for the leadership meeting before the conference and essentially we went through the afternoon session. I think Glenna was a bit nervous because there were so many new people involved. Then we went through the evening session. Mostly we practiced the recognition awards. Glenna asked if there was anyone who should get some kind of recognition that wasn't on her list, just to make sure that everyone received what he or she had earned. There's nothing like working for an award, earning it, and then not receiving it. We practiced taking turns introducing the next presenter. All too soon it was time to get the show started. I finally met the man who hosted the events every month. He was in Stephanie's group. He is a radio talk show host in the city she lives in, so he was quite good at announcing.

The session started. I was backstage waiting to do my presentation. Sara made sure everyone was gathered. It was kind of weird because there was no Doug in Dougville. But everyone seemed to know this was our spot anyway. The challenge was that the group was growing to the point where we took up almost the whole side of the auditorium. Cindy took her group and moved to the center section and sat right up front. Jen's group was on the other side, and they took up at least as much space as we did. Everyone else just kind of filled in the center behind Cindy.

The host announced me and when I came out on stage my whole group cheered and clapped. It was an emotional rush. I started by sharing my experience with the concept of predictability in this business. I showed them my notepad with the word predictability circled in it. As I drew the 3-Step Success Pattern on the overhead projector slide, I shared that most people will say this business is not predictable, that it's a matter of luck and chance. Well, I used to believe that before Glenna drew this diagram on a napkin one night at a restaurant. She explained that this is what made the business predictable, because an associate always knew where he was on the journey to whatever level of success he imagined.

3-STEP SUCCESS PATTERN™

IMPROVE YOURSELF	BUILD A TEAM	BECOME A LEADER
0-30 PEPS 14-30 Days	31-45 PEPS 60-120 Days	46-70 PEPS 10 Leaders
*20 Critical Initial Skills	*20 Critical Building Skills	*10 Critical Leadership Skills
Time Focus 95% on personal effectiveness 5% on recruiting	Time Focus 15% on personal improvement 50% on recruiting 30% on training new people 5% on retention	Time Focus 10% on personal improvement 15% recruiting 65% training people to become leaders 10% on retention
Action Items 1. Get associate# 2. Enroll on product autoship or autopay 3. Have tickets to next event 4. Take the PEProfile 5. Gain a firm knowledge and testimony of company and products 6. Memorize contacting scripts 7. Make an effective list of 200 names 8. Subscribe to education system 9. Have personal improvement plan 10. Participate in R.I.G. (Residual Income game)	Action Items 1. 20-30 hours per week commitment 2. 8-10 personal contacts per week 3. 60% conversion rate on contacts and personal presentations 4. 90% conversion rate of follow-ups 5. Take PEProfile quarterly 6. Register team for education system	Action Items 1. Full time/professional commitment 2. Training using team PEProfile results 3. Enroll 2 new personals each month 4. Promote 1 new leader per month 5. Training system using R.I.G.
Goals 1. Increase PEPs to 30+ 2. Score green or yellow in first 20 skills 3. Enroll 1-5 customers/associates 4. Receive products for FREE	Goals 1. Increase PEPs to 45+ 2. Score green/yellow in team-building skills 3. 15-25 associates on team 4. 3-5 committed to leadership track 5. Break even and then earn at least $2,500 in residual income	Goals 1. Increase PEPs to 70+ 2. Score green or yellow in leadership skills 3. Increase team PEPs average to over 30 4. 250+ team members 5. 15 or more leaders 6. 20+ serious builders 7. 100 people on autoship or autopay 8. 100 in education system and events 9. 50 recognized on stage

I quickly explained each section of the diagram, PEPs, and the idea of focused time. I ended by saying that the PEProfile, the *Skills of the Million-Dollar Earners* audio library, and the *Residual Income*® game, and my own personal success were all based around this business model. I explained that there were three underlying principles that made the 3-Step Success Pattern work. Principle number one: start at the start, because starting right is always better than starting over.

Principle number two: build personal effectiveness before building the team—higher PEPs equaled higher checks. And principle number three: follow the proven success pattern that creates predictability. I closed by inviting anyone who wanted more information about this to listen to the *Skills of the Million-Dollar Earners* or to come and see me, or at least to talk to their own leader. When I was through my team erupted again.

The host came back on stage, thanked me, and said the success pattern was the foundation that makes everything else possible. Then he introduced Susan. I was interested in her topic, so I wanted to go out and listen in the audience. However, there wasn't a place next to Sara, so I went around the building and sat in the very back of the auditorium. Susan spent a minute or two endorsing what I had just taught. The time that she spent doing that gave me a moment to get to a seat so I didn't miss anything she was saying about personality types.

She started by explaining, "If you can understand what drives and motivates people, you can help fulfill their needs and they will take the action you suggest. Generally speaking, the need to know the personality of your prospects and associates can be boiled down to the need to communicate in a way that is appropriate for them.

"Identifying the personality of your prospects and team members helps you adapt your language and presentation style to allow for the differences in personality types. This skill greatly increases the chances you will be heard. Speaking to people in the way they like to communicate and using terms they know and understand gives you credibility and builds trust quickly. If you were to speak in German to a person who understood only Spanish, your message would not be understood, and that person probably would not do what you want.

"Most personality experts break the concept of personalities into four general categories—dominating or controlling, friendly and outgoing, detail oriented, and a get-things-done-worker-bee category. Most people are some combination of the four, instead of being all one or another. You will have greater results as you adapt your approach and language to provide details to the detail prospect; the bottom line, to the dominant personality person; the fun and exciting things about the business to the friendly outgoing person; and explaining that once the work is done it will stay done to the worker-bee person. Using this knowledge will help you sell more, enroll more, and keep more people in your business pursuing their greater causes and higher purposes.

"If you contact, present, invite, follow up, promote products and events, and edify as if everyone thinks, talks and acts the same, you will resonate with only one personality type, probably the personality you are most comfortable with—yours! This of course will exclude about 75 percent of the people you talk to, and that will make your business growth slow and arduous," Susan concluded.

She told us some funny stories about times when she used approaches that were not appropriate for the person she was talking to and she told a couple of stories about how she was able to connect with people in life-changing ways when she did this correctly. If we wanted to master this skill, she told us we all could get the nitty-gritty details about personalities by listening to the audio CD in the *Skills of the Million-Dollar Earners*. She ended her presentation by telling the story of when Glenna talked to her about XL-8. Immediately they had formed a trust and a relationship, although Glenna is not the same personality that she was. "Glenna adapted her presentation, her examples, and her language to match my own personality type. That day she enrolled me in more than the business. She enrolled me in a life-long relationship with her as the leader of this team and personal guide to the achievement of my dreams."

When the meeting was over I felt great about what had happened. My team was taught well and I hoped they took all of it to heart. I learned a lot about personalities and in some ways I was emotionally drained from the experience of presenting and imagining how to implement what Susan had taught about personalities. I knew my team would want to talk afterward, and I wanted to thank them for their support. When I got up there I wanted to make sure they brought their walking shoes tonight because a lot of the team was getting recognized on the stage, and they didn't want to miss any of that or what Glenna was going to talk about. We spent about a half hour of the two hours we had in between meetings just standing there talking. It was great that so many people wanted to spend that kind of time with each other. Sara and I decided to be on the stage together as a team, not only when we got recognized, but when we did recognition as well.

The evening session started in typical party fashion. Sara and I sat together to start the meeting. We wanted to be able to either have a place to sit together when the recognition was over or be together backstage. When the host came out, we went backstage to make sure we were ready when the recognition began. We were on stage for the entire recognition portion of the program. We got to see the faces of the people who earned awards and got to shake their hands. What an honor—it was exciting. The host introduced Susan and she had the honor of announcing the awards for the Improve Yourself phase.

There was a long line of people who all got to come onto and stay on stage for being part of the High Peppers Club, those with at least thirty, forty-five, and seventy or more PEPs. Susan wisely had us hold our applause until they all got on stage for one big round of applause. Then Javier from the car dealership was called up on stage as the person with the highest profile score during the month. Two people tied with the least amount of red areas in the Improve Yourself phase of the success pattern; a woman in Maria's group and a man in Tony's group each eliminated all their red. And Ben Ford earned the award for largest improvement in PEPs during the month. Susan introduced Kim, and she did this part of the recognition awards.

Because there were now over five hundred people at this meeting, there was a huge amount of people who were recognized for personally bringing people to the conference. But Mark and Robin Brown earned the grand prize from my team. There was a great parade of those who did at least fifteen presentations. It was rewarding to see how many people were actually taking action to build their business. Personal Enrollments was won by one of Jen's people, with nine. Winners' Circle was earned by six people on my team and another five or six from Jen's, and a few others. Someone in Susan's group earned the Brass Ring for the most personal production points. Kim turned the meeting over to Stephanie with a tremendously edifying introduction.

Stephanie awarded Sara and me with the Silver Star for team enrollments this month with over one hundred. She then welcomed Kim back into the spotlight as the winner of the Golden Eagle for team production points. Stephanie talked briefly about promotion levels and that they were a measuring stick of great achievement. She started with the Copper achievers, the first promotion level. There were over fifteen people who qualified as new Coppers including Maria, Sharon, and Jerry from my team. Jen, Susan, and Kim all had new people as well. There were eight people who advanced to the second level or Brass, including Tony, the Browns, and the Fords from my team. Jen, Sara, and I were promoted to Silver. What a great day this had been. We were on the stage for almost an hour with the recognition awards. Next, Stephanie, who had been the afternoon speaker, introduced Glenna who recognized the Rhino Power Team promotion winners.

Again the stage was flooded with people who all got to stay on when she announced the winners for the most Effective Business Builder gold, silver, and bronze awards. Ben and Pam Ford earned the bronze award, Maria earned silver, and Cindy earned gold. Cindy had started doing things the effective way. She had about ten people at the event for the first time and she was not only enrolling people at a high rate, they also were learning what to do. I expected she would be advancing promotion levels next month as well. What a great moment this must be for her as they played the Olympic theme with her standing on the top step of the platform.

When everyone went back to their seats, Glenna took the remaining time to talk about a couple of things. She began by asking if we were measuring ourselves by the minimum standard or the legendary standard. "How often do we ask ourselves what would the legend do now? Would he go home, miss the event, be late to the appointment, show the minimum amount of presentations, contact the minimum amount of people, listen to the minimum amount of CDs, read the minimum amount of books? If we want a superior lifestyle, we all have to become superior performers. If we want to leave a legacy for our children and grandchildren then we need to become legends, and to be a legend we need to raise the standard to the level of a legend."

While she was talking I looked back on my month and decided it was a great month, but it wasn't legendary. My PEPs were in the Become a Leader phase of the success pattern. But I didn't win the most improved PEPs award. I had over 150 people in my business and I earned the Silver Star for team enrollments, but I didn't win the Golden Eagle for team production points. My personal income had tripled, but I didn't help anyone skip a promotion level this month. So I made a decision that my goals and effective work this month were going to be legendary. I was going to earn the Winners' Circle award and help ten people on my team achieve the Copper level, five new people get to Brass, and three people to Silver. I was going to be a Gold next month and double my income.

As I was plotting to do legendary things, Glenna changed the subject to learning to persuade people to make decisions and take action. She told us persuasion was not an art, but a science and when we mastered it, we could greatly increase the amount of people we could effectively serve. "To be effective in persuasion," she continued, "you must have the mindset that your persuasion is based on helping your prospect solve some challenge she has identified. With the right mindset, and high personal effectiveness in product, company, and industry knowledge—coupled with listening, relationship building, and personality recognition skills—we are able to convert more prospects to customers and associates. This is because we know precisely what problem we are solving that is specific to our prospects.

"Unlike influence, which is an important, intangible facet of your business, persuasion is the ability to present reasons that indicate that your solution will actually solve your prospects' problems. For some people your influence, posture, social, or professional status may be enough. But many require social proof and research statistics. The most persuasive arguments for your product, company, and the industry should be largely based on facts and figures. When you have indisputable evidence that our products, upline mentor, or company will perform exactly as you have promised, your prospects will have more confidence than relying on your personal testimony alone. The fact that many others have experienced positive results is a powerful motivator for people to take action, either as a customer or an associate.

"Persuasion is often misunderstood. For many, it conjures up images and feelings of making someone do something they might not want to do. This is very far from the truth of how persuasion really works. Persuasion is not manipulation or coercion. Those two things are necessary ways to get people to do things they don't want to do. Manipulation, for instance, is contrary to persuasion because it starts with the paradigm that you are going to get someone to do something she doesn't want to do. Somehow you are going to trick, overstate, or use hyperbole to control her decisions or actions.

"Persuasion involves the opportunity to help people do what they already want to do, even before you came along and presented XL-8 to them. In all reality, you can't get anyone to do anything that she doesn't want to do using tools of persuasion. That is to say if you have high PEPs in persuasion and a person makes a decision and takes action, she is doing only what she really wanted to do in the first place. You simply gave her the encouragement, inspiration, reason, data, or confidence to rationally take the action that would create the result she was already motivated to create.

"Persuasion happens when you discover a person's challenges and then present a solution or a set of solutions that are in complete alignment with your prospect's needs. Persuasion is providing choices and presenting the outcomes of making those choices. It's evidence that people can see, feel, or experience that creates trust and credibility that appeals to their logic or emotions. In short, high PEPs in persuasion allows you to take some form of research, data, logic, or social proof and put your prospects into the story. In this way they see themselves having the same challenges as others and overcoming them as a result of taking the specific action you recommend," said Glenna.

Recognizing the time had long since gone by when we were supposed to end, Glenna closed by letting us know we could always get more information about this subject by listening to the *Skills of the Million-Dollar Earners* audio library. She concluded by expressing how much she appreciated us and that until we were on the stage with a group like this, we would never completely understand how much she cared and thought about us.

Afterward I sat in my seat for a few minutes trying to digest what I had just experienced. It was beyond words. I was exhausted and exhilarated at the same time. Tony, Maria, Jerry, the Browns, the Fords, Sharon, and Javier all came up to let me know that they had written down what they considered to be legendary level goals and that they were counting on me to help them get there. I told them I had also done that and that I wanted to talk with each of them individually about their goals. We all agreed, and then for some strange reason we decided to go have an ice cream at Amy's restaurant. Of course Amy wouldn't be working there and she probably didn't even want to go there, but we all went, about twenty of us anyway. We talked until it was very early in the morning and the last employee there locked the doors as we left.

14

Legendary Rhinos

Right when I got up on Monday morning I sent everyone on my team a message titled The Month of Legendary Rhinos. I wanted the team to catch the vision of stampeding rhinos chasing and catching their dreams. I asked everyone to make an appointment with their upline leader to discuss his or her legendary goals for the month. I made an appointment with Glenna for that night to review my progress and to counsel with her on my legendary-level goals. I told her I had planned to earn the Gold promotion level this month. She smiled as she realized how serious I was about this. She said, "I know I talked about legendary goals, but if you achieve this, it would truly be legendary." "If?" I said surprised. "It's not a matter of if I make it; it's a matter of what day this month I achieve it—that's what's in question!" She was taken back by my rebuke. For a moment I think she wondered if she truly believed that legendary goals could really be achieved in everyday life. Sure, saying it from the stage to a crowd in an emotional moment was nice and easy, but she had someone sitting in her office actually believing it and acting on it.

She leaned back in her chair and seemed to gaze off into the distance for a moment remembering a fishing trip she had taken with her dad and uncle when she was a little girl. They had told her stories of all the fun they had at the lake and catching the big one. She fondly remembered getting up before the first light of day that first morning and her uncle telling her to go back to sleep for a while because the fish don't bite before sunrise. Her dad, not caring if they caught anything, helped her get ready and they started off for the lake. In her excitement, Glenna decided she couldn't wait for her dad, so she ran ahead, eager to catch that first trout and too naive to realize her uncle might be right. She beat her father to the lake by about five minutes and on her first cast the pole bent. Suddenly she realized the day's biggest catch got up early, too. In that moment Glenna realized that she wanted her response to me to be more like her father's instead of her uncle's. She wanted to support and encourage me instead of stifling my enthusiasm.

"Steve," she responded, "no one has ever reached the Gold level in five months like you are planning. That doesn't mean you can't do it," she said as honestly as she could. "It just means no one ever *has* done it. But no one has ever learned and adopted the 3-Step Success Pattern like you have either. In fact, I don't remember anyone ever teaching the success pattern to his or her team so fully as you have. It's been amazing to watch the power of the system work within an entire organization. I feel like I should tell you that most people on XL-8's leadership counsel are watching you and your success. And many of them have commented that you have made unbelievable progress for being in the business just three months."

"Three months," I interrupted, "I've been in for four months." "Yes I know," Glenna continued, "but many think you wasted the first month when you were increasing your PEPs and preparing for this amazing growth. Just think of it, in the past 120 days you have created a group of over 150 people. Over two-thirds of them have received recognition, many in more than one area. Your retention rates are much better than the industry averages, and any one in XL-8 for that matter. Because people in your group know how to take effective appropriate action, they are already making money with over 50 percent of all your personal recruits qualifying as Coppers in their second month. Ninety percent of your Coppers advanced to the second level, or Brass, in their third month. No one else has this kind of success record outside your team, well, except Jen lately, that is. And you personally advanced to Silver in your fourth month. Considering that you are perfectly set up to achieve Gold this month is nothing short of miraculous.

"There are a couple of challenges I want to point out, however; school has started again, which is sure to create some distractions for you and others. Jerry now lives three states away as the principal at a high school, and Sharon also lives across the country with her husband who relocated. So we need to put together a plan to keep up this momentum and help Jerry and Sharon, even though they aren't right here with us. I am willing to help you all I can—just be aware that there will be many distractions now that you didn't have during the summer."

She walked to her whiteboard and said, "Here is what we have to do to make it. First of all, you really do need to earn the Winners' Circle award as an example to your team members who are in the Build a Team phase. I know that this might be a bit difficult because you are in the Become a Leader phase, but this will make a huge difference to Tony, Maria, Sharon, Jerry, the Browns, and the Fords. It also will show the new people, like Javier, what is possible when they have high PEPs and follow their leader.

"Second, you need to start your own leadership team. I would make sure to invite everyone who is at the Brass level or has a goal to become a Brass this month. Remember that this is not like my leadership team. You aren't planning your own monthly conference events yet, but you will be soon, and these people will be like Kim, Stephanie, Susan, Jen, and you on my team. They will be critical to the training and game play events you have now. Being on a leadership team will also help them to grow their leadership skills so they will be able to duplicate you when their teams will support them as the leader of their own teams.

"Third, you need at least three qualifying Silvers to advance to Gold. I will tell you that Maria, Sharon, and Jerry all need to advance to the Brass level to help with the Gold sales points requirement and Tony, the Browns, and the Fords are our candidates to advance to Silver. To do that you will have to focus on helping each of them advance two people to the Brass level within their own organizations."

I suddenly realized that my goal of five new people at the Brass level wasn't going to be enough. I needed to help two people in three legs get to Brass plus helping Maria, Sharon, and Jerry get to Brass as well. I needed to help nine people, not five. "I guess this is what legends are made of," I thought. I need to turn possibility into probability by tipping the scale of predictability in my favor.

Glenna continued, "Fourth, for all of that to happen, your team needs to go from 150 people to over 300. Most of them need to be on autoship and the new people need to be diligently working on raising their PEPs to at least thirty this month. The people who enrolled last month need to be effective enough to get their products for free and at least ten of them must reach Copper this month. If your numbers are as consistent as they have been, you can make it. But again, this can be a challenging time in your business because of the circumstances you have to deal with. You are going to have to work smarter and harder than you have ever worked before. I repeat not just harder, but smarter. And I don't mean just harder and smarter than you have worked in this business; I mean smarter and harder than you have ever worked in your life. The good news is that you can do it. So organize your schedule and track your results every week to make sure you don't lose even one working day this month."

The phone rang and she excused herself for a moment. It was Gary. While she was on the phone I took a minute to glance at the huge monthly calendar on her desk. I wanted to see how she organized her life to get everything done. It seemed like she was making a big push to get Jen and me to Gold by the end of next month. If she could do that, I reminded myself, then she would achieve Platinum and be recognized on stage at the annual corporate super convention. It would be great, I thought, to be part of making that happen after all she had done for me. When she came back in, she told me Gary was working on a very special tool that they were going to announce at this month's business-development conference. "What is it?" I asked. "Well you will have to make sure to come to the conference to find out," she teased.

When I got home from school I gathered Sara and the kids into the living room. I explained to the kids about legendary goals and then told them what my legendary goal was, that it was legendary because no one had ever done it. I told them that legends don't ever create legendary results by themselves, so I let them know that they were going to be part of making this happen. We agreed that they would all work with me to support doing whatever I asked and needed to get to Gold in a record five months in the business. My oldest son shouted out, "That's this month!" I told him it would definitely be legendary to do this and I laid out the schedule for everyone. As I did so, the impossible suddenly looked probable. I scheduled time to work with at least two people in Tony's, the Brown's, and the Ford's, groups each week to help them achieve Brass this month. Glenna had agreed to work with Jerry and Sharon. Sara was already working with Maria and they were doing great. I asked the kids what they wanted as a reward for all the work that we were going to have to do this month. They told me that they had been working on earning a trip to the local amusement and water park by helping mommy already. So if they could go sooner by helping me, that would be the best reward. We had a group hug and a handshake and I went upstairs to change and get ready to meet with a guy in Tony's business.

The days turned into weeks and things were going along great. Jerry had implemented game plays in his new town and had recruited four new people personally; his new team was off to a great start using the success pattern as the structure for teaching them how and what to do. His game plays were picking up momentum and both his team there and here were doing well. Sharon was using the game as a recruiting tool two nights a week to help her introduce people to XL-8. She was also using it as her training tool on Saturday mornings for her training method. She got a copy of the success-pattern presentation that I taught in the business-development conference and used it as the structure for her trainings. People in both of their groups were engaged in taking the PEProfile, listening to the audio library, and using the simulator. What a blessing this system was to help everyone stay on track, even without local leadership there to help them. In fact, moving away seemed to have empowered both of them to take on a greater leadership role.

The local weekly business previews were working well for helping the teams here to introduce the business to many new people. Glenna was sure to have Jen, Cindy, and me host it every week and involve people in our groups with different parts of the meeting, like the introduction, presentation, or ending.

Our weekly game events were taking on a life of their own. It was fun to go. There were always prizes and life-changing, enlightening moments that happened for people. The live tables concept had grown into people using the game almost anywhere people would meet. Sara told me that she had seen people playing the game at the food court in the mall. And yesterday I saw one of the Ford's groups playing at the bookstore coffee shop. It was incredible to see people actually doing something to help their lives improve.

In my first leadership call it was suggested that we create a monthly *Residual Income*® tournament. People could use their player cards from the previous week's game and continue from where they left off. The person with the highest PEPs, residual income, and net worth could get some kind of recognition at the business-development conference at the end of the month. What a great idea. I was grateful for Glenna's advice to create this group in my organization.

Glenna's leadership meeting and call were inspiring. This group was supportive of everything that was going on and had innovative ways of producing results faster for everyone on the team. I presented the idea of giving recognition at the conference for *Residual Income*® game tournament winners, and it was accepted. Cindy was selected to do the success-pattern presentation at the conference, and Jen was invited to give her first conference presentation on contacting. I was going to announce the Improve Yourself awards, Jen was going to announce the Build a Team awards, and Susan was honored with announcing the Become a Leader portion. Glenna reminded us that tickets for the annual XL-8 super convention went on sale tomorrow and if people bought their tickets right then, they could save enough to pay for their hotel room. We all needed to make sure to promote the event.

Glenna told us that she had a goal of getting a thousand people there. She also made it clear that we needed to leave some time for Gary to make his announcement at the conference. We took turns trying to get Glenna to tell us what it was, but she was relentless in teasing us. Glenna was watching the overall growth of the organization and decided that Stephanie and Kim should host their own business-development conferences in their own hometowns.

Saturday trainings had become so large that it was necessary to split them into two groups, one in the morning and one in the afternoon. The good news was that it really didn't take more of any one person's time because of the way we had already started dividing up the work. Our people were increasing their PEPs, which were helping them get up to speed quickly. This helped them to prepare to effectively build a team and lead game plays or carry out other assignments as they were needed. We found out a few weeks ago that Sara was pregnant, which I feared would create a bit of a challenge for us. She had a very difficult time in her first month of pregnancy and I didn't see how anyone was going to be able to help Maria. However, it turned out that Maria was prepared to step up and help herself. She told me on our leadership call the other day not to worry because she had fifty PEPs and was doing great.

Javier was doing well. He got his PEPs over thirty in about ten days. And it seemed that everyone in town knew him. He was recruiting like crazy and what made me feel the most at ease about him was that he was telling everyone to follow the proven 3-Step Success Pattern. He had invested decades learning sales skills and almost no one could do what he could right from the start. So he was setting their expectations properly. As a result, his team was growing. He and Maria were hitting it off pretty well also. They seemed to be spending a lot of time together.

He was single and never married and she was a single mom with a couple of kids. I think this business has many benefits that I had never considered before. It's brought Javier and Maria together and has made Sara and me closer than ever before. Even in the midst of their budding romance, their businesses were growing at incredible rates.

By the end of the second week, Javier had already qualified as a new Copper and was set up to make it all the way to Brass this month. By the middle of the third week, Maria was already qualified as a Brass with three groups almost qualified as new Coppers, which would push her to Silver! Even without the help of Sara and the distraction of a new love interest, Maria's business was taking off. This was another testament to the success pattern and the support tools to help people accelerate their personal growth, which seemed to correlate into specific, tangible results.

Jerry and Sharon both decided to come to the conference. Glenna invited them to stay at her home. I picked them up from the airport and took them to Glenna's. She had made a trip to each of their respective towns to help them by doing a personal recruiting and training event. Since they made the effort to come, Glenna made sure to go out of her way to reward them with some extra nice pampering. They deserved it after all they had done to change the lives of so many people. She reminded me how lucky I was to have them. And then, like always, she taught me a lesson about the word *luck*. She said the letters stand for Laboring Under Correct Knowledge: luck! I agreed, and then left them alone to talk and have some face-to-face time. It was a great treat for them to be together in person.

This was going to be the best monthly business-development conference ever! I couldn't sleep knowing what was about to happen. I knew Jen was having similar success, and Cindy was starting to accelerate her team growth as well; she was only about two months behind Jen and me in team development.

Cindy pulled me aside at the last preview meeting and said she had given up her hard feelings about me and what had happened with the Fords and the Browns. She said that if they had joined her team, they probably would have quit the business by now because she would have taught them the ineffective "enroll, hope, and replace" strategy. I was excited for what this business does for people, including Cindy. Mostly, I was grateful for what it has done for me. As a whole group we sold about fifty more tickets than we had room to seat in the auditorium. If everyone came, we had agreed to put up chairs on the stage for the leaders and their spouses to make room. And this was with Kim and Stephanie holding their own events in their hometowns. What a great problem to have.

There were about twenty of us seated on the stage when the conference started. Because Stephanie's group wasn't there, neither was our normal host, who came from her group; she stole him to use in her conference. But I hadn't remembered talking about a replacement host or making an assignment about this in our weekly leadership meetings. I wondered who the host would be? Was this the surprise Glenna was talking about in regard to Gary? Just then Gary came out and started the meeting—with no fanfare or fancy introductions. Many knew Gary, and it was obvious to me that Glenna had not talked about this in leadership meetings because she wanted it to be a surprise, and it sure was. He did a great job. He was an accomplished presenter in his own right, and he had attended the previous three conferences, so he had a good example to follow.

The afternoon session was outstanding. Cindy talked about the three basic principles that make the 3-Step Success Pattern work, how starting from the start and learning to build personal effectiveness before building the team and to following the success pattern had changed her life and business. She talked about the difference between building the business using the "enroll, hope, and replace" strategy and the predictability, comfort, and peace that comes from embracing the 3-Step Success Pattern. Her presentation style was extremely compelling. I saw some people in the crowd wiping their eyes a few times when she was telling about her frustration in the beginning.

I had to start another notepad in this conference. Jen's comments were the first page of this new pad. I was sure that whatever insight she gave us would be just as valuable as the predictability page of the last one. She was going to speak about contacting. Cindy did a great job edifying Jen and then turned the time over to her. When Jen stood up, her group gave her a standing ovation, which led everyone else to follow their example. The cheering went on for more than a minute. It was overwhelming. I know it touched Jen's heart, and she deserved it for staying with the business for so long without the success she desperately desired. She spent a minute telling her story, briefly sharing the frustration of doing the business in an "enroll, hope, and replace" way. Jen then moved on to begin talking about what she called a core skill that everyone must master to have a strong and profitable business—contacting.

For many people who enroll in the business, contacting is one of the scariest, yet most important aspects of success. Jen told us that her fear and inability to contact had cost her literally hundreds of thousands of dollars. She even told about her experience helping me to enroll Jerry. She talked about our conversation after that meeting, and it was in that moment she decided that she would no longer let this hold her back. She continued by telling us, "Because we don't have a storefront for people to come to, the only way for people to become aware of you, the company, and our products is through personal contact."

It was awesome to learn from someone who had learned to be a professional. She continued saying, "When you are contacting people, the main thing to keep in mind is that you are looking for people who are dissatisfied with something. For example, some people don't have enough time or money to do the things they want in life. Others however, might have too many bills, or too many jobs. No matter what their pain, we have the solution!" She then told us that there are two purposes to contacting: (1) to find out why our prospects are dissatisfied, and (2) to set an appointment. She implored us not to make contacting into something it's not. She further explained that contacting is not a presentation or a selling event. It's an opportunity to meet new friends or reconnect with people we already know.

Jen explained that there are essentially four kinds of people: hot, warm, chicken, and cold. Then she described each of them for us. I wished that I had heard this when I first enrolled in the business. No wonder Jen's group was growing so quickly. She explained the groups starting with hot contacts. "They are the people in our lives with whom you could walk right into their house without knocking, like family and your closest friends. There won't be a lot of these people in your life. The good news about these people is that they know a lot about you. The bad news about these people is that they know a lot about you."

Jen said warm contacts are people who know you in some respect. They are people who know you by your first name or, if you briefly explained who you are, would remember you from some past experience. That is to say, you could call them and say, "Hi Suzie, this is Jen," and they wouldn't wonder who Jen is. Usually these are people you work with, neighbors, or those in your church or other organizational groups. This will be your largest list of people to talk with about XL-8.

Your chicken list is mainly comprised of people you hold in high regard and probably don't think would be interested in or need the business. By the time you effectively contact these first two groups, the chicken list people won't be much of a problem. You will have had plenty of practice and your PEPs will have increased so they won't be nearly as scary anymore.

Jen continued, "Last, there are cold contacts. These are people you do not know yet. You must initiate a conversation with this group of people. You can ask them a question to get the conversation started; or you can wear a button or lapel pin, or your attitude by itself can be a conversation starter. In the past few months we have had incredible trainings on asking high-yielding questions and connecting from the industry's top leaders. You will need those skills to be an effective contactor. But no matter which group of people you are contacting, remember that your single goal in contacting is to set an appointment to discuss the details of your solution to their pain."

In conclusion, she explained that we needed to understand the difference between having conversations with people and contacting them about how we can positively impact their life. "Conversations are interesting and almost always fun, but they seldom lead to anything besides conversation. Sometimes it is necessary to talk to our prospects a time or two before we try to make an appointment with them. But in the long run, conversations don't lead to any result for our prospects or us, other than reconnecting. I don't want you to go home and just have reconnecting conversations. I want you to go contacting when you get home.

"What I mean by that is you need to find out what's missing in people's lives and then inform them that there is a way for them to make their life what they want it to be, to get serious about changing circumstances that they don't like." She challenged all of us to get our conversion rates of contacts to presentations up to at least 60 percent, "You need to have at least six out of every ten people you contact agree to let you do some kind of presentation." She invited us to talk to her if we had questions. And if we wanted more in-depth information, we should listen to the CDs in the *Skills of the Million-Dollar Earners* audio library. Then Jen called Gary back to the stage for an important announcement.

He made sure everyone knew when the evening session started and encouraged us to be in our seats early because more people would probably be at the evening session. Then he told us about a new tool he had just completed that would make our game play events much more valuable. He said more people would be able to master specific skills and become master networkers faster, that a higher percentage of people would enroll as associates and more of our team members would be able to get their friends and family to events and game plays because of an increase in their effectiveness in event promotion, edification, and contacting.

"This new secret weapon is a book called *RIGged for Success*. It is guaranteed to help you understand how to use the *Residual Income*® game more effectively. It has different scenarios that show specifically how to set up the game to create different experiences. Some focus on product promotion, others on how and why higher PEPs equal higher checks, and others will help you understand the compensation plan. In all, there are forty different scenarios to use to help you more effectively recruit, train, and retain people on your teams!" He let us know that we could order them in the lobby after the meeting or from our upline, just as we ordered other tools. Gary then excused us until the evening session.

What an awesome explanation of contacting: short, sweet, and directly to the point. It was something that every networker should know, and, even better, something that we all could explain for ourselves! My whole team was excited. When we went out to eat, everyone was talking about his or her renewed enthusiasm about contacting. They felt like they already had the skill, but now that Jen had simplified their expectations, they felt relieved that the hard and scary job of contacting seemed more simple and do-able. All they were trying to do was to find out what other people wanted and make an appointment to see if they were committed to do anything about it. This afternoon session had been so valuable. I was always amazed that the evening session was better attended. From a business-building perspective, the afternoon session seemed more beneficial.

The evening session started with everyone in a festive spirit. When

Gary came out to get the meeting started, the entire leadership group was backstage waiting to come out and congratulate the award recipients. We had the traditional song, opening prayer, and veteran recognition, then he introduced me to announce the awards for the Improve Yourself phase. It was a bit nerve-racking to make sure to pronounce everyone's names correctly. I got great practice because there was a long line of people who all got to come onto and stay on stage for being part of the High Peppers Club, those with at least thirty, forty-five, and seventy or more PEPs.

A woman in Maria's organization had the highest profile score during the month. A man in Javier's group had the least amount of red areas in the Improve Yourself phase of the success pattern. A woman in the Ford's team earned the award for the largest improvement in PEPs during the month. I was able to announce the new *Residual Income*® game tournament winners: a man in Tony's business earned the first place prize and a woman in Jerry's group, here in town, earned second place. Over the course of the month, they both created a *Residual Income*® game net worth of over twelve million dollars! What an incredible lesson was taught in this activity. I finished my section by introducing Jen for her part of the recognition awards.

There were getting to be so many people in the group that recognizing them all for getting a minimum amount of people to the conference was becoming increasingly difficult. The grand prize was earned by Maria from my team. Of course there were a lot of people who were doing at least fifteen presentations. It was exciting to see how many people were taking action to build their business. Javier won the Personal Enrollments award. Winners' Circle was earned by twenty-two people on my team and another eight or nine from Jen's team, plus a few others. And for the first time in my business career I earned a place in this group. Someone in Jen's group earned the Brass Ring for the most personal production points. Jen turned the meeting over to Susan with an inspiring introduction.

Susan awarded me the Silver Star for team enrollments this month; there were over 180. She announced that Kim had earned the Golden Eagle award for team production points, although she wasn't able to be there to accept it because she was running her own conference. She then talked briefly about promotion levels, saying they were a measuring stick of great achievement. She started with the Copper achievers.

Thirteen people qualified as new Coppers on my team alone, including Javier, Jen, Susan, and Kim. All of them had new people as well and Amy (the waitress) also qualified as a new Copper. There were eleven new people who were promoted to the second level, or Brass, including Maria, Jerry, Sharon, and Javier, who got a huge applause because he had advanced not only to Copper, but also earned Brass. Amy followed Javier's lead by jumping right past Copper to Brass.

I had made a goal of helping three new people get to the third, or Silver, level. I wasn't sure until right before the conference if I had made it or not. But when Susan called out Tony, the Browns, the Fords, *and* Maria, I not only made my goal of three, but in fact I had four new Silvers! Maria was such a great surprise. She and Javier had advanced two promotion levels. The announcement meant that I had made it to Gold. Jen also achieved that milestone. There we were, two "rivals" shaking hands in congratulatory adoration for the other. What a great day this had been. Susan turned over the time to Glenna to recognize the Rhino Power Team promotion winners.

The stage was filled with people who all got to stay when she announced the winners for the Effective Business Builder gold, silver, and bronze awards. A woman in Susan's group earned the bronze award. Javier earned silver and Maria earned gold. Maria, who had never actually won anything in her life, was on the highest level of the podium as the Olympic theme played. It had been a great night for everyone. I was pretty sure that we had either outgrown this location or we would soon have to split up and have our own events.

When the stand was pulled out for Glenna to use for her presentation, she looked dramatically at her watch and even pointed to it to make sure that we all knew how long it had taken for the recognition part of the meeting. But she had such a big smile on her face that showed she didn't seem to mind shortening her time to present to allow all the attention to those who were making the growth happen. She took a few minutes to talk about an important topic that related directly to one of the causes of the team's incredible growth—focusing on others. More specifically, focusing on their needs, goals, and on their progress toward those goals.

She began by asking us if we knew what our greatest business asset was. "If you think it is an inventory of XL-8 products, you don't fully understand the business yet. The products and services we sell belong to XL-8 not you!

"People are your greatest asset—your prospects, customers, associates, upline, and downline! The most successful people in any business invest heavily in their greatest asset. In this case that means people! Successful business owners invest time with them, teach them, share with them, encourage them, and build them up. The people who choose to come with you on your journey are the most important asset of your business.

"Legendary college basketball coach John Wooden taught that winning was a natural result of flawless execution of the fundamentals of the game. And focusing on others is one of those fundamentals in this game. The first piece of advice my mentor gave me when I decided to get serious about this business was that; 'People don't care how much you know, until they know how much you care.' This changed my perspective on people, the business, and how to really build it.

"Residual income, security, and generational wealth can be achieved only when you help others discover, work effectively for, and achieve what they want. The more you give, the greater the value of your service to others, the more you will get. It's difficult to reach even your smallest goals without providing value to others. And the bigger your goals and desires, the more you will need to learn to focus on the achievement of others in your business.

"The problem is that most people have been taught to look out for number one. It's the 'what's in it for me' mindset that creates selfishness and competition. The world today teaches the only way to get ahead is by stepping on, or climbing over others. Some examples of this are, 'There can only be one winner,' or 'Second place is really only the first loser,' or 'Winning isn't everything, it's the only thing.' How many times have you heard comments like these? It's ironic because in this industry, the more you focus on what you want and the more you ignore what other people want, the less likely you are to get what *you* want. The reason why most people live a life of desperation and lack is that success happens when you focus on the needs of others, not yourself.

"You have witnessed right here on this stage people working in cooperation with each other to help each other succeed—even when they didn't have a direct vested interest in doing so. John Wooden's example applies to this business: If you focus on helping others succeed, if you help others get what they want, you will get what you want as a natural consequence. Ask yourself this question, 'What can I do right now, to create value for somebody else?'

"Make friends and become more likeable. The number one reason anyone buys from you or enrolls in your business is that they like, trust, or believe in you. I remember the first time I felt like I was building real security in XL-8 was when I saw a couple I recruited into the business standing on the stage at a national convention like the one we are going to have next month. They were on their way to the life they had dreamed of even before they got married. They told me that for the first time in their lives they were making money, they were having their needs met, and they were accomplishing their goals. They had become the kind of people others would follow because they had realized the power of focusing on others. They focused on helping others learn, practice, and apply the success pattern. By natural consequence, they began to get what they wanted, and in turn, so did I!" Glenna said triumphantly.

Steve noticed when she paused at the end of her presentation it was strangely quiet in a room that big and with that many people. Glenna broke the silence by thanking all of us for being there and for pursuing our passions, dreams, greater causes, and higher purposes. She made sure to invite us to the annual XL-8 super convention next month and to get the details from the leaders who would have the tickets. They could answer all the information about registration and travel. Then she said good night. I didn't want it to end, no one did. I had always been a big fan of the afternoon session, but this was incredible and, as Sara and I mingled with our team members, I realized that all the things we learned in the afternoon session helped us to create the results from this one.

After the event Gary and Glenna met backstage for a while. They looked at the numbers concerning recognition, enrollments, and residual income. Gary asked about the *Residual Income®* game tournament he had heard about. Glenna gave him the names of the top twenty people in the tournament, and Gary compared them to PEPs, team-building activities, and income. He commented that they were matched exactly! The top people in the tournament who were in the Improve Yourself phase had increased their PEPs the most. Some, in fact, not only got into the High Peppers Club, but they jumped over the thirty PEP group to the forty-five PEP group. Those in the tournament who were in the Build a Team phase either joined the Winners' Circle or were at the top of the enrollment list and advanced in the first few promotion levels.

Those who are in the Become a Leader phase had the most people at the event, progressed to more advanced promotion levels and earned the most residual income. Either the game helped them succeed faster or because they were already advancing, they were able to play the game more effectively. Glenna added some clarity to Gary's thought. "If they were already moving forward, then why such explosive growth over the past few months since we introduced the game?

"The game is obviously a critical tool to help everyone accelerate his or her journey through the success pattern. Even Jerry and Sharon had big increases in their businesses, and they weren't here with us at all. Yet they started new groups and those groups qualified as High Peppers, and both Jerry and Sharon advanced a promotion level. This game, Gary, let's people experience all the things that the PEProfile uncovers and they learn in the *Skills of the Million-Dollar Earners*, and lessons in the training meetings and on the conference calls. So tell me more about this new book you have. I think you called it *RIGged for Success*," Glenna asked.

"*RIGged for Success* is a set of essential tips, tactics, and techniques for using the *Residual Income*® game to create a specific result," Gary explained. "I wrote it to help our team get the most out of the *Residual Income*® game so they will be able to rapidly become master networkers. From the information I received from Susan, Steve, Jen, Tony, the Browns, the Fords, Kim, Sharon, and others, they needed a way to keep the weekly game plays fresh and interesting. There were specific skills they wanted to teach their groups in the Saturday training. Part of the solution came when they invented the idea of live tables and the tournament. I took their idea and looked at all the skills on the PEProfile and decided we could set up the game in multiple ways to help people learn specific skills and to have widely varying experiences playing the game.

"We wanted to help their prospects and associates to experience what it would be like to be successful in the business by making a sizable income and achieving their goals and dreams before they showed them the details of XL-8. They felt like using the game to help their prospects experience success and achievement was a great way for them to more fully understand what XL-8 was all about. By experiencing all aspects of the business, their prospects would be able to make educated decisions and take appropriate action—they would be more likely to enroll and actually do something.

"So I took some time and thought of some of the challenges people might have using the game to its fullest extent. There are sections for each of these important uses, such as how to invite people to a game play; use the game as a recruiting, training, and retention tool; set up the room to get the most out of the game; get started with a game play; accelerate the results people experience in the game; do a debrief after the game is over and calculate the value of the business they created during the game.

"Then I started to think of a wide range of ways we could adapt and adjust the game for different kinds of game plays, It became apparent that there are thousands of ways to play the game depending on what result a person is trying to create. The game can also be played generically, allowing the leader to let the teaching moments occur, as they always seem to, or emphasize specific skills and knowledge. There are forty scenarios that help accelerate the growth, effectiveness, and productivity of any team. Each of the scenarios is based on a topic that will help teach players how to be more effective in any phase of the success pattern. Leaders can use the scenarios by analyzing the results of their team's Personal Effectiveness Profiles to determine what issues are holding the group back and then set up the game with a specific focus. For example, leaders can focus on PEPs and why the education system is so important; contacting; the 3-Step Success Pattern; edification; team-building; goal definition and achievement; promotion levels; the compensation plan results; product promotion; customer service; building a names list; leadership and event promotion; or any of the critical skill topics. *RIGged for Success* contains a portion of the many possibilities and variations that could be used to help any individual or team prosper.

"Take Cindy, for instance, before she was using the game. Her results remained pretty much the same for those initial months, so we can easily say that her PEPs probably didn't increase much during that time. She was able to personally recruit new people, but she didn't understand the success pattern or how to help any of her people to progress, and they didn't last long in the business. Since she has been using the game, she has essentially doubled her PEPs from twenty-two to forty. She has more people than Doug ever had at one time when he was in the business, and hers are ordering and attending events and have increased their PEPs to be able to effectively recruit for themselves. Cindy has been promoted twice, and her residual income has jumped to an annualized $30,000, all in the past thirty to sixty days. It looks like she will be your sixth Gold leg.

"Cindy is learning, adopting, and teaching the 3-Step Success Pattern faster because she has been able to experience what building the business is like without it. Now with *RIGged for Success,* she will be able to help her team to duplicate and self-direct their efforts in areas that need improvement or strengthening. This is all because they will be able to fine tune each game play to help them target specific skills and knowledge," Gary concluded.

Glenna was resting her chin in her hands while Gary was explaining, and the more he talked about the uses of the book, the more excited she became. She sat up completely straight and when he finished, then she stood up and took a minute to gather her thoughts.

She said, "If I understand you correctly, the game coupled with *RIGged for Success,* the PEProfile, and the audio learning library is a complete self-directed business learning and building system that could be used in any group, no matter where they are or whether they had a local leader to help them. Is that right?" Gary confirmed what she so powerfully and simply explained. All at once it hit him. He had helped create the first of its kind training system in this industry, a system that would essentially guarantee predictability to building a strong and profitable business. "What I had envisioned when you came to see me those months ago was to help you change the industry in some significant way. And I think we have done it. Part of the solution was already in place, and we figured out how to make it complete. *And* we have demonstrated that it works to perfection." As they gave each other a business-like hug, Gary told Glenna how proud he was of her for taking the ideas they originally talked about and implementing them even though it was risky to do so. As they parted he said, "What a great day for us, those on your team, those in XL-8, and everyone in the industry!"

Early Sunday morning Steve picked up Jerry and Sharon at Glenna's house to take them back to the airport. "It was great to have the opportunity to see Glenna without the crowds and meeting schedules," he thought to himself. While they were getting their bags and the gift

Glenna had given them, I had a moment to share my gratitude for what she had done for me and asked her if there was anything she could think of that I could do better. She returned the thanks to me in her words, "for doing all the work." She told me I was doing all the right things and reminded me to make sure to love the people on my team—all of them, even the ones who aren't always loveable. She invited me to think about that on my day away from the hustle and bustle of work and the business.

On the way to the airport I told Jerry and Sharon how great it was to see them again, how proud I was of what they were doing in leading the way in their new communities, and how envious I was that they had stayed with Glenna. We were all really tired, so the short drive to the airport was pretty quiet, but I had to ask them what they had learned from hanging out with Glenna for two days. They told me she was exactly what we see on the stage and in the meetings. She really does love the people on her team. And she gets as excited when they succeed as when she succeeds. They agreed it was inspiring to see a person who "walks the walk" instead of being one way in public and a different way in private. What you see is what you get with Glenna.

On the way home from the airport I tried not to think about the business because I needed the weekly break from it and I wanted to concentrate on my family and church. But I couldn't forget the fact that I had set some legendary goals, and in every area I had achieved or surpassed them, including Winners' Circle, personal production points, team points, team enrollments, personal promotion level advancement, team promotion level advancements, team members at the conference, team members recognized on the stage, personal residual income, team member increases in residual income, and so much more. For a moment I became a bit overwhelmed with all that I had been blessed with. The crazy idea that I might actually be in line to make it to Platinum, along with Glenna next month, at the annual corporate convention even crossed my mind. As I pulled into the driveway I told myself just to relax and enjoy the incredible growth and success of our group for a minute before worrying about setting goals for next month.

15

Six Figures in Six Months

Late that night the phone rang. Most everyone knew that Sunday was not a day, or night for that matter, that we worked in our business. I answered the phone, it was Maria and she was excited. She wanted to talk to Sara, not me, but she was talking so loudly that I could hear her from five feet away. She first told Sara that Javier had proposed marriage to her! The wedding date had been set for the week after the super convention. Wow, I thought of this business as a relationship builder, but this is over the top! By the time they both got done talking about that, Maria had told her that she wanted to be at least a Gold in the business before the wedding.

She asked Sara if that goal was even possible for her. Maria knew that we were the first people ever in XL-8 to achieve Gold in five months, but she wondered if it would be possible for her to do it. Sara talked her through how closely we followed the three basic principles and the success pattern, that we made sure that all the new people understood it and were committed to follow it with precision. Once they knew how committed we were to learning and applying the success pattern in our business, for the most part, they had followed it as well. As a result, everyone progressed in a predictable manner toward his or her goals of success in the business. Maria said she would sit down with Javier and go over some goals that they believed in and were committed to, then she would call Sara back to go over them.

Almost the moment they hung up the phone it rang again. This time it was Javier. He apologized for calling on Sunday, but he had an important announcement. He excitedly told me that he had asked Maria to marry him. Of course I already knew, but I didn't want to spoil his surprise and so I pretended that I didn't know anything. This conversation was almost an exact copy of the one that Sara and Maria had just had. He acknowledged that Sara and I were the first people in XL-8 to achieve

Gold in five months, but he asked if it was realistic to think that he could achieve Gold in four months, and if it were, what specifically did he need to do to accomplish that? I told him the story of a man named Roger Bannister. Roger was the first man to run a mile in less than four minutes. He pursued this dream for many years. Many thought it was not even humanly possible to do it. But years after he made his goal he became the first man to run a mile in under four minutes. It was an incredible feat when he did it, but today it's commonplace for high school students to do it.

"So, the fact that I did it in five months made it possible for anyone. When you and others set out to do this, it will seem probable if you adhere to the success pattern and teach others to do the same." I asked him why he was asking, and he told me he was wondering because Maria was a Silver and had been enrolled four months. Then he said something that caught me off guard a bit. He told me that he had just skipped over Copper to Brass and he was considering the possibility of skipping over Silver and going for the Gold this month. I told him he should go for it. I congratulated him on his engagement and we hung up. In the back of my mind I was rooting for him, but at the same time I was thinking if he actually does that, he'd break my record. And then Glenna's words about leadership came to me and I quickly got over having to be the star of the show. In disbelief, Sara looked at me and I looked at her. Was it possible that both of them could have been thinking the same thing and called us almost at the same time? Their calls and the story of Roger Bannister made me think of legendary goals, and I started to imagine what my goals should be this month as I drifted off to sleep.

The morning sky had not yet begun to brighten when the electronic rooster awakened me. I barely opened one eye and could see the clock, which read 4:30 AM. I was having such marvelous dreams about standing on the stage at the super convention as a new Platinum. It was amazing to see twenty-five thousand people all focused on me and my story of going from schoolteacher to six-figure earner in six months, Gold in five months, and Platinum in six months. It was awesome. I talked about the word *predictability* and what it meant that first night at Glenna's house. Then I shared the success pattern just as I had at last month's business-development conference. Sara and the kids were with me on the stage and Sara was able to share what it meant as a mom, wife, and support partner to our team.

When I told Sara about the dream she said, "Maybe it's a message for you to follow." Until that moment I hadn't considered it as anything else but my imagination taking advantage of the silence of the night. But maybe she's right. As I thought about it, Tony called, and for the third time I had someone asking if I thought he could duplicate what I had done. When I hung up from the same success pattern explanation, Sara's words rang in my ears again, "Maybe it's a message for you to follow." When I got home from school Sara told me that the Fords and the Browns had each called and wanted me to call them as soon as I got home. Momentarily, I wondered if what I had considered a coincidence that morning would continue. Sure enough, they both expressed a desire to achieve the Gold promotion level before the super convention. Somehow what seemed really challenging and improbable last night now seemed conceivable. The fact that all these people saw me achieve something no one had ever done made it seem possible to everyone. When I hung up from talking to Mark and Robin Brown my whole attitude about Javier changed.

"Maybe, Mr. Sunshine, you could be a little more encouraging," I sarcastically thought to myself. "If Javier believes he can do it, maybe you can believe right along with him." I had only one appointment set up for this evening and it wasn't until later, so I took the opportunity to sit down at the kitchen table and write out my goals for the month. I had written goals so many times before and it always seemed easy to get them on paper. But tonight was different. I was unsure where to start. So many things were pointing to the achievement of the impossible that I started to believe they were actually possible. If Tony, Mark and Robin Brown, Ben and Pam Ford, Maria, and Javier all achieved Gold this month, then I would achieve Platinum. Platinum I thought, the pinnacle of XL-8, the level that Glenna had been trying to achieve for years. What made me think I could achieve it in just six months? I pondered. Then I asked myself, "Where is Mr. legendary goal guy now?" Back and forth this mental conversation went for a couple of minutes. Then I decided to write down my goals, whether they seemed achievable or not, and then share them with Glenna to do a kind of sanity check with her.

Glenna gladly met with me before the preview meeting. Maria and Javier were in charge, so neither of us had to prepare anything. She told me that it looked like I had used the success pattern to create my goals. She commented that most of them were team related rather than personal in nature. We started with my personal goals to increase personal PEPs to ninety or more, to do at least fifteen personal presentations and twenty team presentations, to personally enroll two new people and to create $10,000 in personal monthly income—annualized $120,000 personal income.

Then came the team goals: To have the team average for PEPs increase from twenty-four to twenty-eight; to have a team of at least five hundred people with fifteen or more associates at the Silver and Gold levels, combined with twenty or more serious builders; to have one hundred people on autoship and fifty recognized on stage at the convention. I wanted to have one hundred team members attend the conference and earn the Silver Star for team enrollments and the Golden Eagle for team production points; have one hundred people in the High Peppers Club— thirty, forty-five, or seventy plus PEPs; have the person with the highest profile score that month, and have the winner of the least amount of red areas in the Improve Yourself phase of the success pattern. I also wanted to have the person with the largest improvement in PEPs during the month, the most people enrolled in the Rhino Power Team, and the most to earn the Seminar at Sea promotion. My team goals continued: to have someone on my team earn all three medals for Effective Business Builder and to have the winner of the *Residual Income*® game tournament come from my team. Lastly, I wanted to promote twenty-five associates to Copper, ten new people to Brass, ten new Silvers, and five new Golds.

Glenna looked at the list, thought for a moment, and then expressed a couple of concerns. "First of all," she said, "I need to make sure that you don't expect to be recognized for some of these goals. XL-8 doesn't recognize people for all the things we do." She noted that there is no High Peppers Club, or person with the highest profile score, or the person with least amount of red areas in the Improve Yourself phase, the largest improvement in PEPs and there is no such thing as the Rhino Power Team at corporate. Also, there is no recognition for the most Effective Business Builder, or winner of the *Residual Income*® game tournament.

"These, of course, are great goals. I want you to pursue them and I will do a conference call and recognize people in these areas, but I need to let you know that your team members won't be recognized on the stage at the event for these achievements. As for the other team goals, help me see how you are going to achieve the team average PEPs goal, get at least five hundred people on your team with fifteen or more associates at the Silver and Gold levels, along with twenty or more serious builders, and have one hundred people on autoship who also attend the convention, earn the Silver Star for team enrollments and the Golden Eagle for team production points. I know I talked about legendary goals last month and you made some incredible progress. In fact, it was truly legendary, but these goals might be a little more than legendary. Let me see how you plan to approach them and then let's see what's really possible."

I explained, "My plan begins with having a weekly PEP call for everyone in the Improve Yourself phase, a separate call for everyone in the Build a Team phase, and a third call for everyone in the Become a Leader phase. This way we can improve skill and knowledge in the specific skills that are critical to the phase a person is in. I think we can get several months worth of training done in one month if we divide it up like this. With these calls, the only information a person is getting is pertinent to what they need to progress to the next step. Then I plan to change the way we do our Saturday trainings.

"I'm going to segregate people into different tables based on the success pattern phases and do the training using scenarios from *RIGged for Success*. Third, I am going to have personal coaching and counseling calls with the leader of each leg to help him or her take the most appropriate action and work with the people who are committed to progress. And last, I'm going to assume a leadership support role with associates in the Build a Team phase. Based on my counseling sessions with the leaders, I'm going to work directly with those who are progressing and want to advance to the Become a Leader phase.

"I'm going to become more personally involved in three-way calls, partnership presentations with individuals, and schedule and conduct follow-ups with those I personally show presentations to," Steve concluded.

"Hmm," Glenna said as she sat back in her chair. "The pace is not sustainable, but if you have the stamina to do this for a whole month it could create a huge explosion in your business. I do want to warn you though, you won't be able to do this month after month, and your team probably won't be able to duplicate this at all. But if you are committed to these goals, you can probably make it with this plan."

Sitting up in the chair and leaning toward the desk she said, "And then there are those five Gold level achievers. If you did this, that would make you a Platinum!" The way she said, "and then," and "if you," made me feel a little like Javier would have felt had he told me in person about his goal of skipping Silver and becoming a Gold this month. On the one hand, this is why I came to Glenna, to get a reality check on my goals. On the other hand, who was she to squelch my dream of doing what no one else had ever done? Maybe it made her mad that I would actually catch her by going Platinum at the same time she did. I know her better than that, so she must just be trying to help me be realistic about what I can expect, that the miracle of last month was just that—a miracle.

There have been many very talented people in XL-8 before me, and not one of them created the results I did. So I think Glenna was trying to help me see what was possible based on the skill and ability of the team and, without lowering my enthusiasm, help me continue to be the legend that the success pattern makes possible. So I asked her what I should do in regard to my goal for new Golds in the organization?

She told me it wasn't impossible because everyone who is now Silver on my team is perfectly set up to do it. "But in order to get the fifth leg over the hump, you will need to be careful not to push too hard. I heard that Maria and Javier are planning to get married right after the super convention. So, if Javier is planning a wedding and hoping to skip the first real leadership level in the compensation plan he, and you, might find this more difficult than it might seem. So if I were you, I would have a very candid conversation with Javier and Maria about their business goals and the wedding. I think you can achieve the other goals as I said before, with a monumental one-month-only effort. But I would evaluate the goal of five Golds based on your discussion with Javier and Maria.

"If they are not fully committed to the goal of getting her to Gold and the herculean goal of also getting him to Gold, then you can't do enough by yourself to help him skip Silver to get to Gold. So I would adjust your Gold goal to be four instead of five, and then get him to Gold the month or two after they get married. I know this might be a little hard to hear from me, but I want you to achieve these goals and I need to be as honest as possible. You need to know what will be required, and if you decide to do it, you will actually achieve the goals you set. Remember, I always want to create predictability in building the business," she advised.

Following Glenna's advice, I called Javier and Maria to explore their goals and plans for the month. Maria jumped right in and told me that she was planning to make it to Gold before they got married and when I looked at Javier he agreed. He continued by telling me that he wanted to be at the Gold level this month as well. Maria interrupted by saying that if they needed to postpone the wedding for a month to give them the best possible chance to both be at the Gold level, she would be willing to do that. Not that she didn't love Javier, but she did want to make sure he knew that she was just as devoted to his success and happiness as she was to her own. Javier looked a bit shocked at Maria's declaration. And while he was thinking about what to say next, she asked Javier to move the wedding date one month later.

She had been thinking about this for a few days now and moving the date would give them more time to plan the wedding with less stress. It would afford them the opportunity to really focus on building the two organizations. I couldn't believe what I was hearing. I told them I would support whatever decision they made and that I didn't want them to feel like I was pressuring them to do something they might regret. Javier said that when Maria made a proposal, she didn't do it lightly. The goal for double Gold was in place, and they would pursue it with all they had. On my way home I thought that if they were making this a priority in their life, then the legendary goal of creating five Golds this month was not even a decision that had to be made—it was already made.

On my leadership call I made the announcement that we would be doing a teleconference each week on Wednesday, Thursday, and Friday evenings. The Wednesday call was for anyone in the Improve Yourself phase, the Thursday call for anyone in the Build a Team phase, and the Friday call for those in the Become a Leader phase of the success pattern. Everyone agreed that this would be a great idea. Pam Ford added that if the call were recorded, then people who had a scheduling conflict would be able to at least listen to a replay of the call.

Immediately they began to promote the calls and with great results. I think each of them was excited to have another way of accelerating the progress of their team members. Of course, the majority of our people were in the Improve Yourself phase, and we had over one hundred people on the first call for people with less than thirty PEPs. On the Thursday call we had almost seventy and, surprisingly, we had thirty-six on the Become a Leader call. I suspect that some who were in the Build a Team phase listened to the leadership call as well. Because of the way we set up the calls, they were well received by the team.

All of the attendance numbers for each call grew as the month went on. The calls were set up as a thirty-minute teaching segment on one of the critical skills taught by me, and then a thirty-minute question-and-answer session. We had each of the Silvers on a panel to answer questions that came in. These calls were fun and valuable because there wasn't anything that served as a distraction to the team members listening. It was much easier to talk to a group where they were essentially in the same place in the success pattern. They got specific training on what steps to take next and practice on how to take those steps.

This idea was equally well received at our training meetings on Saturdays. We put the zero to thirty Peppers at their own tables, the thirty-one to forty-five Peppers at different tables and then the forty-six and higher Peppers with their own group. On our leadership calls we decided which scenario from *RIGged for Success* we wanted to use for each group. Then each leader facilitated a game play using that scenario. It was amazing to see the growth of each person. In a couple of hours, focusing on the specifics of each phase of the success pattern, people were having incredible break throughs. The record-breaking growth we had experienced over the past months was shifted into supersonic speed. We started calling our Saturday meetings "Supersonic Training."

This was becoming so successful that David McKay, Glenna's upline Double Platinum, came unannounced to the third Supersonic Training. He purposefully was a few minutes late so he wouldn't interrupt the proceedings. He watched while each group played the game in their own little world. It was kind of like watching a casino in Las Vegas, where one section was for playing cards, another was for roulette, and others were for dice games. The energy was unbelievable, and we never finished in the two hours that we had scheduled; no one wanted to leave! David took me aside afterward and asked what kind of special set up we had to have to make this happen. We told him we had been playing the game every Saturday since he was there the first time. We were just using the scenarios in Gary's book to focus on a different topic each week in each phase of the success pattern. He asked how he could get one or more of us to do this for his other groups. I told him I was focused on a legendary goal this month, but I would love to do it after the super convention—if he had his groups segmented into the phases of the 3-Step Success Pattern.

The first two ideas I had for accelerating recruiting, training, and retention were working beautifully. The third idea about partnering with individuals who were trying to advance was a lot more challenging. Supersonic Trainings didn't take anymore time than we were spending already. And the focused teleconference calls only added a couple of hours to the workweek. But the partnering idea took a lot more time and effort. I think this is what Glenna saw when she said this pace is not sustainable. I was working with a different group every night and sometimes two groups. This meant I had to become a master scheduler and record keeper to make sure to keep track of everyone I was talking to and what the next steps were for each of them.

I developed some really good habits during this time. I wrote down information about each person I presented to and followed-up with on a small card for future reference. I never failed to review the card before my next call or visit to make sure I knew who I was talking to, what we had talked about the last time, what they wanted that they couldn't get doing what they were doing now, and what the goals were for this meeting. This one single habit saved me many times. I was showing fifteen presentations per week and doing all the follow-ups as well. There were so many people and conversations, that it would have been impossible to remember who anyone was or what they had wanted. There were many times that I parked in front of someone's house and couldn't remember their name or anything about them. I pulled out the information card and then I had the names and everything about the prospect right there. And in most cases I then remembered the names, faces, and dreams when they opened the door or answered the call.

I was chasing my dream of going Platinum like a maniac. There were nights when I couldn't even remember what day of the week it was. Besides the help I was giving to my team members, I was also enrolling people personally. I had to remind myself that Glenna told me that this was not a pace that I should, or even could, sustain for more than one month. I was in a prime position to create more than just job-dropping residual income. I was actually creating generational wealth for my kids. My goal for retiring from teaching was at the Gold level, but I had already achieved this so I upped the ante a bit by making the goal for retirement the Platinum level. I was still personally recruiting because Glenna had told me stories of leaders only having a few leaders on their teams and those leaders managing them or holding them hostage. This happened because they knew that the bigger organization was being propped up by those few leaders. I decided I never wanted this situation to happen to me.

I decided early on that I would always lead by example. And this example meant that I needed to continue to enroll new people. Besides, it kept me connected to people who were just discovering or rediscovering their dreams. I loved the feeling of inspiring people and helping them to move forward to purposely live their lives and pursue their dreams. I had a great team with incredible people, and I didn't want to do anything to jeopardize those relationships. But I also wanted them to know that they were not in control of my future—I was. I also wanted them to do the same when they were in my position. The best way to create security was to have everyone sharing the features and benefits of XL-8 and the leadership of our team.

The week before the super convention we decided to meet as a leadership team at Amy's restaurant for a planning session. I told them to invite everyone who was going to qualify at the Brass level or higher this month. I was a few minutes late because I had been following up with a couple in Javier's group. When I walked in, there was an embarrassingly loud cheer from the team members who were already there. I was a bit shocked. I had set a goal of creating ten new Brass and ten new Silver associates. Along with the leaders I already had, this group should have been about twenty-five people. But there were over fifty! Maybe I hadn't been clear with the leadership team. Maybe they had invited anyone who held any promotion level. Tony could see that I was surprised by the number of people there and he pointed out that the team was growing and people were progressing without my noticing; I had been so busy helping everyone else that I hadn't been able to track the specific results very closely.

The leaders had taken care of everything, including getting Amy to take care of us. Most everyone had already reserved hotel rooms and was going to drive to the event in a caravan of cars. I wanted to make sure everyone was clear on what achievements would be recognized at the event and what things they would be rewarded for there. After the event on a huge conference call, everyone on Glenna's team would be recognized to the extent that it was feasible. No one seemed to worry too much about the fact that some would have to wait to be recognized a little later than they normally would. I also wanted to make sure we had a plan for sitting close to each other, like we did at the business-development conferences. The Silvers had this worked out so their teams knew where to meet and sit.

At the end of the meeting I did a small training on event promotion and the debriefing conference call I planned to have after the super convention. This way all of us could hear what others learned and took away from the event. Right when I finished, Amy came up and said she had an announcement to make. She told us this would be her last week at the restaurant. She had almost doubled her income from the restaurant in XL-8 and was quitting at the end of the week. She would be starting her new life at the super convention. The cheer I got when I came in was nothing compared to the ovation that Amy received. It was an awesome way to complete the night.

When everyone left, Amy told me that Doug had been in earlier that afternoon. When she told him that she was quitting because of her success in XL-8 he seemed pretty upset. He asked how she had learned about the company and why she didn't enroll with him. She told him he had never brought it up, that the day he had been there with Glenna was when Glenna contacted her and began helping her start living the life she always wanted. "Instead of congratulating me, he growled and stormed out. It bothered me until you guys came in and the feeling of warmth and belonging immediately came back. Even though I am not on your team, I thank you for making me feel like I belong to the group."

On the way home I was grateful for everyone on the team, for the number of people at the meeting, for their passion for achieving their dreams and goals, and for their commitment to follow the predictable pattern of success. I was grateful for Glenna and her willingness to reach out and help put a system in place, one that could make the business produce the promise we all had heard countless times in the meetings, on the stages, in the books and on the CDs.

16

The Event!

We drove fourteen hours as a group to get to the convention center. We left pretty early in the morning so we could get there in plenty of time to rest, talk, and prepare for two days of meetings that started the next day. The convention was to be held at the basketball arena at State University. My launch to my dreams was connected to the place where all this began after all. The arena seated over twenty thousand in the stands and apparently another three to five thousand on the floor.

I was looking forward to being with twenty-five thousand other XL-8 associates. We got checked into the hotel, which was no small undertaking. We agreed to meet at the pool in an hour to start putting a seating plan together, decide what sessions to attend, talk about where to eat, and so forth. We categorized each of the classes into Improve Yourself, Build a Team, or Become a Leader. That made it easier for everyone to choose what to attend. When Sara and I got to our room we already had messages on our phone.

One was from Mike Black, the Marketing Director at XL-8. He invited me to come to a leadership meeting that night at the convention center. I was planning on a quiet night with Sara, but if the company called me specifically, I supposed that Sara and I should probably go. Glenna left a message welcoming us to the convention and also invited Sara and me to the leadership meeting that night. I also had a message from David McKay; he said he wanted to set up a time to meet with me privately to discuss our training methods. He wanted to learn exactly how we were able to go from zero to the highest promotion levels in just six months. And the last message was from Jay Olsen, XL-8's founding associate and only Triple Platinum. He urgently needed to talk to me about the event and some logistics. He left me his cell phone and urged me to call as soon as I got the message. It was astonishing! I sat on the bed for a few minutes lost in my own thoughts.

What were all these messages about? The company's biggest leaders were calling me. I thought I was going to be able to sit, listen, and learn from the top leaders in the company for the next few days, just as I had in that first preview meeting and business-development conference. But this was turning out to be something quite different from what I had expected. Sara went for a walk to get the kinks worked out from a fourteen-hour drive while I returned the messages. I called Mr. Olsen and he told me I needed to meet him before the leadership meeting. He had a few things to discuss with me about my involvement in the convention and he wanted to make sure I understood how the company wanted me to participate in the convention.

"Participate," I asked, "what do you mean?" It would all make sense after our meeting he said. I agreed. Of course the meeting at the pool now needed to be more business-like than casual. I arranged some time to meet with David McKay as well, but that time would be during the convention itself. I did ask about the leadership meeting invitation from Mike Black. "Oh, Mike has been asking about you since you set the record for qualifying at the Gold level. He wanted to meet you and discuss your success," he said. There was something in the evasive way he told me that made me think this was something more than a casual meeting. And on top of that was the meeting I was having with Jay Olsen before the leadership meeting. Something was going on, I just didn't know what.

When Sara got back I told her about the unexpected meetings and she got a little anxious. "The corporate leaders want to talk to us? What do they want to talk about? I'm not dressed. I need to get my dress ready, fix my hair, and do my nails." I interrupted her by giving her a hug. Her reaction was unusual. She was always so calm and collected. I told her that they probably always did this to the new Golds at the convention. They just wanted to make sure that we knew about our simple assignments and other duties. And David had been to a few events and told me a few weeks ago that he wanted to meet with me. We had spent a lot of time with Glenna and she was probably just like the rest of the leaders, so she needn't worry about whatever this was. I may have calmed her down on the outside, but her nerves didn't seem any more settled on the inside. We went to the pool and she spent the entire time working on her nails.

The meeting at the pool was unbelievable. I knew I had distributed over one hundred tickets throughout the team, but it didn't sink in that I had achieved one of my goals until we were at the pool and I saw over one hundred of our team members present! There was hardly a place to stand. I made sure to spend a few minutes thanking them all for coming and for doing something about making their lives what they wanted them to be.

We talked for a few minutes and strategized about how to get the most from the event for everyone. We went through the schedule of classes and breakout sessions and talked about each one. Everyone made his or her own event plan and I told them that Jay Olsen wanted to meet with Sara and me and that we had to go. Tony kiddingly asked if they were going to have me speak or sing and dance. I told them I thought it was a casual meeting to let me know what my ushering or ticket-taking assignment was going to be. We shook hands, gave hugs, and they all joined in kidding us about taking over the show.

When we got to the convention center for our meeting with Mr. Olsen, we saw Glenna walking up to the same door Jay had told us to go to. What a great surprise. A man who had a Gold lapel pin from XL-8 met us. He checked our names on his list and gave us directions to where Mr. Olsen was meeting people. I assumed that he would be giving out our assignment like the guy who had just met us. But why would Glenna be here? Certainly she wasn't going to get an assignment like ours, she was a Platinum now.

The door was open and inside sat Jay Olsen. I had heard Glenna talk very respectably about him a few times. Glenna shook his hand and they exchanged a business hug. I reached out to shake his hand and when he had my hand, he pulled me to him and gave me a big bear hug; he was quite a bit gentler with Sara. Then he asked us to sit down. He talked about the honor and responsibility of participating in the convention. And when he mentioned the importance of poise and relate-ability as a speaker, I thought he was talking only to Glenna.

I figured he would give Glenna her assignment and then Sara and I would get ours. He told Glenna that he wanted her to talk for thirty minutes on listening, and then he turned and looked straight at me and said that he wanted me to talk for ten minutes about the success pattern. Then he turned to Sara and invited her to talk for a few minutes about being involved in the business as a mother. I couldn't believe what I was hearing. I felt like the coach had just put me in as a pinch hitter in the bottom of the ninth inning with the bases loaded, two out, and the season on the line. I had been in this position before. I had put kids in this position before, not wanting to think about the fact that the whole game or season was on the line.

My hands started to sweat and my mind raced. I felt like Sara had a few hours earlier when she found out about this "trivial meeting." I asked him why he had chosen us. Glenna told me that only Platinums spoke on stage at these events. Then he handed the latest monthly business report to me. When I looked at it I had remembered that Javier had changed his travel plans so that he could do two more presentations before he left. One appointment was with the Barkleys, the people who Glenna and I had visited after we enrolled Tony, and the Jacobsens. So he was going to be flying in later tonight.

He had enrolled both people and had signed them up on autoship. Apparently Javier was able to overcome my lack of voicemail skills from a few months ago. His last-minute success had put him over the top to become a Gold level associate. And this had in turn made us Platinums! Sara and I jumped and danced around the room until we remembered where we were. Then the reality set in of standing in front of twenty-five thousand people and talking. Jay gave us another congratulatory handshake and hug and as he did, it started to rain in that room. Or at least is seemed to. In all reality, it was the tears in my eyes.

How had Glenna been able to keep the secret? Was David's meeting just a diversion, or did he really want to meet with me. And now Mike Black's invitation to the leadership meeting made sense. These were all very subtle ways of telling us that we had made it. Glenna gave me that same congratulatory hug that my father had years ago at my wedding reception. It was awesome. I'll never forget the look that Glenna had in her eyes. She was so proud.

Mr. Olsen asked us if we had any questions, and before I could ask any, he told us that in the leadership meeting we would be given more specific instructions as to speaking times and logistics. Then he invited us to go with him to the leadership meeting. As we walked, I was getting nervous, like you do on the first day when you're the new kid in a new school. When we saw the group on the stage at one end of the arena and all the empty seats, it was breathtaking. My mind flashed back to playing in front of big crowds and dreaming of a moment like this.

We made our way down the stairs to the arena floor and as we got closer, everyone turned to look at us. David McKay turned and started to clap. Glenna and Sara started to cry. Glenna had waited for this moment for a long time and finally it was here. She was part of the elite XL-8 club. Sara realized that she was going to have to talk in front of all those seats, only they wouldn't be empty when she spoke. I was in awe. It was like I had hit a grand slam as the pinch hitter that Jay had made me feel like a few minutes earlier. Now I was rounding third base and was headed home to my teammates as the conquering hero. Outside of marrying Sara and the births of my children, this was the proudest day of my life.

We went through the entire convention schedule during that meeting. Assignments were made and every minute was accounted for. About halfway through the meeting Jay left for a little while. I didn't think anything of it at the time, except that it had created a little distraction. This meeting seemed pretty important and after all he was in charge of the convention. Glenna was assigned to speak tomorrow and the rest of Friday's schedule was confirmed. Saturday morning was organized and then we went through the announcers of each of the recognition areas. Just as we finished Jay returned.

He walked in with Javier and Maria. I couldn't believe it. Jay had managed to have Javier picked up from the airport and Maria from the hotel to be here for this meeting. He interrupted the meeting to welcome and recognize the new record holder for time to become Gold in XL-8. He introduced Javier and Maria and shared their unique circumstances of meeting in the business and building two groups to Gold at the same time. In fact, Javier had become Gold only a few hours earlier.

He suggested that they be included in the schedule to tell their story. Everyone agreed and one of the Platinums proposed to give up his spot on the agenda so that Javier and Maria could share. Now I knew how Glenna felt as she welcomed us to the leadership team an hour or so ago. Because of their circumstances and our circumstances, it was agreed that they would speak just after the recognition segment on Saturday evening and Sara and I were on just after them. I was overflowing with thoughts and emotions, so much so that I couldn't think straight. I am pretty sure that I didn't hear anything in the meeting from then on.

When we got back to the hotel there were people everywhere. There was a sea of XL-8 associates in the parking lot, the driveway, the lounge, the lobby, at the pool, and everywhere. Tony saw us come in with Ben and Pam Ford, and Mark and Robin Brown stood up and started to clap and cheer. I figured they were just being polite like they had at Amy's restaurant last week. But when Tony announced in his coaching voice to everyone within a mile, "Welcome the newest XL-8 Platinum Associates!" everyone joined in. How had they found out? Sara and I sheepishly acknowledged everyone with a smile and a wave. Much to my surprise it started to rain again, only inside the lobby of the hotel. An overwhelming feeling of gratitude came over me. And the one I would have wanted most in the world to share this with was right here by my side.

Tony invited us to sit with him for a minute. I later remembered when we sat down, that the Browns and Fords both disappeared. Pam Ford came back and whispered something to Tony, he nodded, and then suddenly became very tired and told us he was going to bed. We walked to the elevator together and he shared that Maria had told them that Javier had made it to Gold and that the company was picking them both up to go to the convention center. "We put two and two together and figured that qualified you as a Platinum. And whether the company was able to recognize you that quickly or not, we certainly were going to."

We had rooms on the same floor and so we continued to walk together. As we got closer to our room, I became aware of more and more people. There was a sign on our door and when we went in, there were balloons and paper banners everywhere. It looked like my house when I got home from the state baseball tournament. Behind us was a huge group of people cheering and clapping. That crazy month of going and going all seemed worth it now. So many lives had been influenced and changed. We invited the Fords in for a minute and told them how much all this had meant to us. We thanked them for all that they had done for us and for the people they were helping; to take control of their own futures. We told them that they all needed to get a good night's sleep because the next few days were going to be unbelievable and probably exhausting.

The super convention was in many ways like our business-development conferences, only much faster paced and each session had teaching and testimonial segments. There were only Platinum level speakers who each told how to do certain aspects of the business and why their topic was important as part of the system to building a strong and profitable business. The sheer number of people—twenty-five thousand instead of five hundred—was awe-inspiring. There were professional bands and high-profile guest speakers talking about success in every endeavor. It was a party atmosphere with intense business presentations from XL-8 corporate executives, including the president, the marketing director, vice president of product development, and the director of customer services as well as the top performing associates in the company. The enormity and complexity of this event made our local business-development conferences seem like child's play. I knew how much it took to put on a local event, so this must have taken an astronomical amount of work and planning.

Glenna's turn came and the host introduced her as a brand new Platinum and the crowd went crazy with cheers and applause. The music came up and Glenna appeared on the stage. Her assignment was to talk about listening, and I was eager to hear all that she had to say. It was a subject I thought I was already pretty good at. But as usual, I learned a lot as she talked. She began by asking us a question, "Have you ever had the experience that the person you were talking to wasn't listening to you but seemed to be formulating his next question or statement before you finished talking? How did this make you feel?"

She spoke so forcefully when she told us, "When you don't listen to others, it makes them feel like you really don't care about their point of view or opinion." I was so engrossed in her presentation I forgot that I was in an arena with twenty-five thousand other people. It was as if she were speaking directly to me. She said the biggest communication challenge people have is listening too little and talking too much. She added, "You never learn anything when you are talking. You can't learn what your prospects need, want, or care about while you are talking. You must learn to listen and truly understand what they are saying from their perspective, not yours.

"For you to provide solutions to your prospect's problems, you must first know what they are. You must build rapport with them, and they must get a sense that you are interested in resolving their discomfort. If you listen carefully to your prospects, they will tell you exactly what to say and do to get them to take action. For some it will be the value of your products and services they need initially. For others, it will be the opportunity of your business to create income and possibly more time. No matter what they are dissatisfied with, XL-8 probably has the solution for it."

Glenna went on to say, "Your pain is not necessarily their pain. Your prospects are not particularly interested in what the products, services, and business opportunity have done for you until they know how your products and services will alleviate their specific challenges. You may want more time and money. They may want better health and peace of mind. If you approach your prospects with the fact that your products and services gave you more of what you wanted, but exclude how the benefits will help them get what they want, they will not engage, either as customers or as associates on your team."

She briefly talked about the difference between hearing and listening and gave us ten things to do to improve our listening. She also listed the ten roadblocks that keep us from being able to listen, and most importantly, she taught us a three-step cycle that enabled our prospects to tell us how to sell to them. She told us that she had discovered how to talk about the secret to listening while she was taking a shower this morning. "When I was reading the three-step wash, rinse, repeat instructions on the shampoo bottle, it occurred to me that the process for successful listening is very similar to washing your hair. Instead of wash, rinse, and repeat, a great listener should ask, listen, and repeat. The formula for failure seems to be number one, talk, and then number two, talk more. Some people have mastered talking to the point where they can talk people in and out of the business in the same conversation.

"So, if you want to sell more of what we offer, the success formula is ask, listen, and repeat. Why? Because people don't buy your product or service; they buy what the product will do. They buy the product of the product. People who buy drills don't want drills, they want to make holes. People don't buy insurance because they love insurance companies or insurance agents; they buy insurance because they want to be covered in case of an emergency.

"This listening process will help you clearly understand what result your prospects, customers, and associates want. Once you have invested the time and effort in understanding, you will have the opportunity and information to make a powerfully accurate recommendation of the appropriate products and services because you know what they need and why they need it."

She added, "In order for people to really take us seriously and ultimately take the action called for, they need to know three things: can they trust you, are you good at what you do, and do you care about them? The ask, listen, and repeat cycle helps our prospects to get a clear positive message about all three of these questions and, in turn, they will take our recommendations."

She concluded by telling us that we have one mouth and two ears and that we should use them in that proportion. "Solve their problems— not yours," she implored us. "If you ask high-yielding questions to get them to talk, they will tell you what they need and how your products and services can help them to meet those needs. I hope you are all in business on purpose." She reminded us that the main purpose of business is to get and keep customers. "Becoming a master listener will help us better understand what our prospects, customers, and associates want and need, and the key to effective communication is to be interested, instead of interesting!" She told us that the *Skills of the Million-Dollar Earners* audio library had incredible details on this subject. Glenna encouraged all of us to get the set this weekend while we were at the convention and listen to it on the way home.

I never knew there was so much to know about listening. She had raised the bar of the quality of speakers at the event. I became a little more anxious about what I was going to say tomorrow. I looked at Sara, but she seemed to be more relaxed than ever about her assignment. Glenna seemed to give her a sense that she could do it if she just shared from her heart instead of memorizing a bunch of talking points.

Between sessions I met with David McKay while Sara had lunch with the ladies in our group. I wasn't sure what David wanted to hear. I drew out the 3-Step Success Pattern that Glenna had developed from what he had given her. I reiterated that the underlying principles that made it all work were the start at the start, build personal effectiveness before building the team, and to follow the proven pattern that creates predictability. It was an expansion of what he had taught to Glenna.

I told him we also used the PEProfile and have people listen to the audio library CDs that match the skills they need to work on from the profile report. I explained that we used the *Residual Income*® game to practice the specifics of what people need to know based on the success pattern phase they are in, to put action to the specific skills in that phase. I also told him that Gary had written a kind of guidebook or resource manual called *RIGged for Success* to help us get as much as possible out of the *Residual Income®* game. David was familiar with it because the manual was what we had used the morning he came and visited us.

The system was incredibly simple and anyone could duplicate it. Even if they weren't present with the leader, they could succeed if they used the system that Glenna and Gary had put together. I used Jerry and Sharon as examples in my group. They had both become Silvers and they each had four or five people at the Brass level and a few who would be Silver in the next few months. David nodded his approval and invited me to his next regional event in three months to share this with his teams. We shook hands and I went back to the hotel to meet Sara.

The evening session started with a prayer and the singing of the national anthem, just like our local conferences. It was inspiring to hear twenty-five thousand people sing the national anthem. Then they invited everyone who was currently or who had served in the military to stand up. The audience applauded and cheered. It was an amazing feeling to stand again with those who had served the cause of freedom.

The host welcomed us and announced that this was a very special evening. To get it started off properly, we all needed to show our excitement and appreciation for the one person without whom none of this would be possible. He edified Paul Richardson, the president and founder of XL-8, and then turned the time over to him. Paul talked about the vision and mission of XL-8, and then we heard from Mike Black and other corporate executives. The evening concluded with Jay Olsen, who talked about how a single person could make a significant difference in the world and about the concept of leverage.

By the time the evening ended, I was worn out but ecstatic. I had a pretty good idea of what I was going to say tomorrow when I presented the success pattern. I had an outline to follow from the business-development conference a few months ago. The explanation that I gave to David McKay was a perfect refresher to remind me of what I had already practiced in that conference presentation. I wanted to meet with the group, so we decided to meet briefly by the front door to talk for a minute about the day. We made sure that everyone was clear about how to navigate tomorrow and what classes they wanted to attend. A little while later, a tired but excited group headed back to their rooms.

Saturday began perfectly. The morning was going well until the sound engineer asked me for slides or visuals for my presentation. I suddenly realized that I didn't have anything to show during my speech. However, in my planner I always had the napkin copy of my success pattern that Glenna had drawn for me. I was a bit embarrassed at how crude it looked. He smiled and said that it might be better this way. "It might make it more real that you carry it around with you and that it can really be used everyday in building the business." He was the first person in the world I gave that napkin to, and for some reason I felt like I should remind him that it was very important to me and to please make sure that I got it back. He told me he would personally see to it.

The classes and presentations that we heard in the first session were outstanding. They taught classes on commitment, work habits, goal setting, products, company and industry knowledge, making a list, the compensation plan, contacting, presenting, asking for the business, and customer service. It was fantastic to have my team being taught from the company's foremost experts on each topic. I was glad that everyone was getting great knowledge. I couldn't help but think that if each presenter used the *Residual Income*® game, his or her students would get even more value by experiencing the use and results of their topic.

In between sessions Sara and I went back to the hotel room to put the final touches on our presentations and practice a bit. Sara lay down on the bed and in about one minute she was fast asleep. I practiced a couple of times and then reminded myself that I had done this before; that I wasn't reciting the Gettysburg Address or the preamble to the Constitution. I was going to be talking about something that had become so embedded into my mind that I knew it better than most things I had taught the kids in my classroom. I lay down beside Sara and all the reasons I was building the business in the first place came flooding into my mind as I drifted off to sleep. We were awakened by the phone ringing—it was Tony. He wanted to know if we wanted to go to the meeting together. He called a few minutes before the wake up call I ordered to ensure that we didn't sleep through the convention. It felt good to get a little rest before the meeting.

The host started the evening session by talking about the importance of goals, achievement, and recognition. He encouraged us all to welcome those who were being recognized for great achievement between now and the last super convention. He started with the Winners' Circle award, then he invited everyone who had achieved the Copper level to line up on the left side of the stage. There were three Platinums on the stage with microphones and each person got to come on the stage, tell who they were, where they were from, and who their Gold upline was. By my count, there were twenty-seven new people from our team who were recognized. That didn't count everyone else who had achieved this before this event. It was also the first time we got recognized on the big stage as well. It was fun—another goal achieved. I gave Sara a high five. It took almost ten minutes to do this one promotion level. Then they repeated this for the associates who achieved Brass.

While we were standing in line to go on stage for this recognition, Sara looked at me, smiled and said, "We made it!" We had eleven new people at the Brass level. It took less time for this, but it was inspiring to see all the people who had achieved the second level in the business. Then came what the host called the first career making level. He said that most people who achieve Silver can make XL-8 a career if they choose to because of the money they make at this level. He invited them to come to the left of the stage and said each one of them would have the opportunity to have a minute to talk about what the business meant to them. It was awesome to hear how people's lives had been changed by the business even at the Silver level. We had had a goal of ten new Silvers and we had exactly ten.

We also got to go on stage for this recognition level. The major benefit of this was that we got to speak for a minute to get warmed up for our presentations later on. We were three for three. It was awesome. Not so much because we were achieving our goals, but because most of the people who were being recognized from our team were saying that their Gold level upline was someone else on our team. It seemed better that our leaders names were being said from the stage than our own. I felt like this meant that others were stepping up to leadership, which meant that I would never have to worry about being everywhere all the time ever again.

When the new Golds were announced, they were told to tell who their upline Platinum was and that they could talk for two minutes. There were only about fifteen people who were recognized at this level, and five of them were on our team! Our fourth goal achieved. We were able to hear from Maria, Javier, Tony, Ben and Pam Ford, and Mark and Robin Brown. Our name was called as the upline Platinum five times in a row! I think I realized one of the things that made me feel great was having people tell how we had positively affected their lives.

And when we got our turn, we had a chance to tell everyone there how much Glenna had meant to us, that none of this would have been possible without her. Finally, the new Platinums were announced.

There were four new Platinums and two of them were in David McKay's group. He was able to introduce Glenna, Sara, and me. We each got to talk for a few minutes about what it meant to us to reach the highest level in XL-8. Glenna thanked David for his help and encouragement over the years. Sara thanked Glenna and congratulated David on having at least one Platinum with a Platinum in their business. I also wanted to take just a minute to thank Gary, who had created part of the system that was responsible for making it possible to enroll in the business six months ago and to be on the stage as a new Platinum today. When we left the stage, the crowd roared. I felt like I had just won the World Series. All the memories and experiences from the day that I decided not to go to State University until today all seemed to make this moment worth while. But I didn't have much time to relish the feeling. Sara and I were rushed backstage to get ready for our presentations in a few minutes.

When we got off the stage, the host announced a band that played for about twenty minutes and then Javier and Maria had an opportunity to tell their story. As a part of their introduction, the host said that Javier had broken the record for fastest to make it to Gold. When he said that, I started feeling a little jealous. I had broken the long-standing record, but Javier came right behind me and broke mine. However, the feeling quickly left when I remembered how grateful Glenna had been with me when we went Platinum at the same time she did. This was a sign of stability and security that people were breaking records. Javier and Maria were awesome as they told their story of meeting, building two different groups, and both achieving Gold in the same month; to top it off, they announced as they concluded, that their wedding would be two weeks from today. The crowd cheered as loud as they had the entire event. Then to our surprise, the host came out and let them introduce us. They did an awesome job of edifying us. In the moment we came on stage I was feeling a little ashamed for the jealousy I had felt a few minutes earlier.

Sara spoke first. She began by talking specifically about her concerns when we first enrolled in XL-8. "I was worried about the time Steve was spending away from the family and the money we were investing," she shared. "But more than that, I was concerned that with all the other things I had to take care of as a mother and wife, that this would be just one more stress and, quite frankly, I didn't need it. I wanted to be able to provide a safe place for my children and for them to be happy.

"I secretly longed for some security, not to have money-making decisions for me all day every day. I wanted to be able to take the kids to buy clothes and not worry about every penny; to be able to go to church and pay tithing and not have to hope that there would be enough money at the end of the month to eat," she said a bit teary eyed. "I wanted my husband who had been working his guts out not to have to be stressed about money every minute of the day and night.

"And now because of XL-8 and the support we have had from David McKay, Glenna, the hard work of my husband, and what he is going to talk about in a few minutes, I can go grocery shopping and buy whatever my family needs. We have a college fund for the kids now. I can donate to and volunteer at the humanitarian group at the church. I don't have to feel bad when I buy a new dress or use my gym membership. My bathroom is now remodeled and the kitchen is next. But one thing I want to share with you ladies out there: next week one of my greatest goals will be met, I am going to have a housekeeper come and do the things we all love to hate about running a home! And I'm going to use the time I used to spend cleaning and cooking to be with my kids and Steve.

"Was it worth it? You better believe it! Will you do it? I don't know. Only you get to decide that. I will tell you that it can be done because I live with a man who has done it. So I would encourage each of you to listen and learn from my man and my kid's hero, Steve."

Everyone stood, applauded, and cheered in complete appreciation for Sara's honesty and heart-felt comments. She stole the show for sure! The applause went on for at least two or three minutes. "How do you follow that?" I asked as I tried to restore order. But it did take a few more minutes before I was ready to begin.

I assumed that very few people in the crowd knew about the success pattern and even fewer had implemented it in their business. So I planned to keep my presentation very simple. Looking out at twenty-five thousand people was an incredible emotional rush. And following Sara made this even more challenging. I talked about the first meeting I went to and how Glenna had talked about the business being predictable. I talked about why predictability was important and the sound man put up the 3-Step Success Pattern that Glenna had drawn on the napkin; it really got to me. I was determined not to let it rain again, not now, not in front of this audience. As I struggled to regain my composure I shared that most people say that this business is a matter of luck and chance instead of being predictable.

As I wiped the tears from my eyes I told them that I used to believe that also, until Glenna drew this diagram on a napkin one night at a restaurant and explained that this is what made the business predictable. "No matter what happens or where you are in the business-building journey, if you have this map, you will know exactly where you are and what you need to do next to achieve the success you desire."

3-STEP SUCCESS PATTERN™

IMPROVE YOURSELF	BUILD A TEAM	BECOME A LEADER
0-30 PEPS 14-30 Days	31-45 PEPS 60-120 Days	46-70 PEPS 10 Leaders
*20 Critical Initial Skills	*20 Critical Building Skills	*10 Critical Leadership Skills
Time Focus	Time Focus	Time Focus
95% on personal effectiveness	15% on personal improvement	10% on personal improvement
5% on recruiting	50% on recruiting	15% recruiting
Action Items	30% on training new people	65% training people to become leaders
1. Get associate#	5% on retention	10% on retention
2. Enroll on product autoship or autopay	Action Items	Action Items
3. Have tickets to next event	1. 20-30 hours per week commitment	1. Full time/professional commitment
4. Take the PEProfile	2. 8-10 personal contacts per week	2. Training using team PEProfile results
5. Gain a firm knowledge and testimony of company and products	3. 60% conversion rate on contacts and personal presentations	3. Enroll 2 new personals each month
6. Memorize contacting scripts	4. 90% conversion rate of follow-ups	4. Promote 1 new leader per month
7. Make an effective list of 200 names	5. Take PEProfile quarterly	5. Training system using R.I.G.
8. Subscribe to education system	6. Register team for education system	Goals
9. Have personal improvement plan	Goals	1. Increase PEPs to 70+
10. Participate in R.I.G. (Residual Income game)	1. Increase PEPs to 45+	2. Score green or yellow in leadership skills
Goals	2. Score green/yellow in team-building skills	3. Increase team PEPs average to over 30
1. Increase PEPs to 30+	3. 15-25 associates on team	4. 250+ team members
2. Score green or yellow in first 20 skills	4. 3-5 committed to leadership track	5. 15 or more leaders
3. Enroll 1-5 customers/associates	5. Break even and then earn at least $2,500 in residual income	6. 20+ serious builders
4. Receive products for FREE		7. 100 people on autoship or autopay
		8. 100 in education system and events
		9. 50 recognized on stage

I explained each section of the success pattern, PEPs, and the idea of focused time. I taught them about the Personal Effectiveness Profile, the *Skills of the Million-Dollar Earners* audio library, the *Residual Income*® game and our newest tool, *RIGged for Success*. I told them that using these tools in conjunction with the success pattern one month ago, I had set the record for fastest associate to achieve the Gold level. And because I taught this to all my associates, the new record now belonged to someone on my team. His and my own personal success were based around this business model. I thanked them for pursuing their dreams and passions and for doing something about their circumstances instead of just sitting around complaining. I closed by inviting anyone who wanted more information about this to come and see me or certainly counsel with their own leaders to learn more about it.

The host came back on stage, thanked me, and asked everyone if they wanted to go Gold in the next four months or Platinum in the next six months. They went crazy as he said that we have just seen two couples who have done that, and he challenged everyone on his team to learn how to get and use the 3-Step Success Pattern, the Personal Effectiveness Profile, the *Skills of the Million-Dollar Earners* audio library, the *Residual Income*® game and *RIGged for Success*.

The convention went on for another two or three hours, but I was so relieved and emotionally drained that I couldn't remember anything else. I sat there with Sara and went over my goals from my notebook. Goal by goal I gave myself one point for every one I achieved. I told myself that if I got more than fifteen points, I was going to Javier's dealership when we got back to buy that Jag I had driven with him a few months ago. I was creating enough income now to afford that as my Platinum reward.

- I had a goal of increasing my PEPs to ninety or more and I did it, one point.
- I was to do at least fifteen personal presentations and twenty team presentations, two more points.
- I wanted to personally enroll two new people, that's four points.
- I wanted to create $10,000 in personal monthly income and I was way over that now with all the Platinum and leadership bonuses, five points.

- The team average for PEPs increased to twenty-eight point five, that's six points.
- I had 564 people on my team now, seven points.
- I had fifteen Silvers combined with Golds this month alone, eight, nine points.
- And I had more than twenty people who were on track to go Silver next month so I would consider them to be serious builders, ten!
- I had over one hundred people on autoship. And,
- More than fifty recognized on stage here, eleven, twelve.
- And I know that more than one hundred members of the team came to this event, thirteen.
- I did earn the Silver Star and the Golden Eagle, fourteen, fifteen.
- I had more than one hundred people in the High Peppers Club, sixteen. Ding, ding, ding! Yes that will be one beautiful new dark sapphire convertible Jaguar, thank you very much. Sara is going to look so great driving that around town.
- I am sure that I had the most people enrolled in the Rhino Power Team and earning the Seminar at Sea promotion, seventeen.
- And the biggest legendary goal of all was to go Platinum.

So that's eighteen points for sure and possibly seven more depending on whether I have the person with the highest profile score this month, the winner of the least amount of red areas in the Improve Yourself phase, the person with the largest improvement in PEPs, the people who earn any of the three Effective Business Builder medals on my team or the winner of the *Residual Income*® game tournament. And now that I think of it, I should win the most improved PEPs this month. I had an increase of over twenty-five. So that's nineteen, with a possibility of six more points.

I could feel the wind blowing in my hair at that moment as I drove that dark sapphire convertible Jaguar home and pulled into the driveway. "I think I will drive it to school just to make a point to Mrs. Jones." During the last presentation I realized that I still had one goal to take care of. It was one of the most important personal goals that I had made when I got into the business. I asked Sara for the checkbook and I wrote a one thousand dollar check to Sara's dad to repay him for the money he had sent us to help pay for groceries, clothes, or whatever else we couldn't afford.

When I wrote his name in the "Pay To The Order Of" line on that check a great calm came over me. This business had been more than a blessing to us. It had literally changed our lives and would make a difference for generations to come—not only for our family, but for all those who had already joined the team and for those who would join it in the months and years to come. Just think of the message that could now be honestly shared in the living rooms of the world: six figures in six months! By the time the speaker had finished and the check was written it began to rain in that arena and there was nothing I could do or wanted to do to stop it.

17

Time Flies When You're Having Fun

The next year went by like lightening. Sharon had grown the business to the Silver level, which is exactly what she wanted it to be and made between four and five thousand dollars per month. She had some Golds in her group and a Platinum. Jerry was promoted to superintendent of schools in his town and maintains his Silver level. He has five Golds in his group and a $50,000 income to go along with his $90,000 school district income.

Cindy and Amy are now Golds. Cindy's annualized income is over $130,000 in addition to her real estate income. And Amy spends her time with her kids and volunteers in the parent-teacher organization at the school and at the local homeless shelter.

Kim, Stephanie, Susan, Jen, Tony, Ben and Pam Ford, Mark and Robin Brown, and Maria and Javier are all Platinums. Kim, Stephanie, Susan, and Jen are holding their own monthly business-development conferences. Tony retired from teaching and coaching, moved into Glenna's neighborhood, and is building a swimming pool in the backyard. Maria and Javier got married and have been featured in three industry magazines.

Doug, the *hopium* salesman, is eating at a different restaurant, still thinks he knows more than Glenna, has enrolled in a different company, and the last time I talked to him he's still making one to two thousand dollars per month using the "enroll, hope, and replace" strategy.

Sara and I are on our way to Double Platinum. We hold our own business-development conferences. Sara had a baby girl, wrote a book about leadership and being the perfect support partner, and does women's business conferences.

Glenna made Gary a partner in her business. She is paying him a percentage of the money she earns from Steve, Cindy, and Amy's business as compensation for helping her to create their success. Gary has retired from his traditional training career. He is leveraging the relationships he developed over the past months with the leaders in his interview group and has begun a new career as an industry speaker and success coach.

Time really does fly when you are having fun. We are so excited to be backstage at the XL-8 super convention. It's a great time to pause and reflect on our work and accomplishments over the past year and to renew our relationships with friends and family members in the business. Once again, we have been learning from the company's top performers and tonight we have the opportunity to hear from a new industry star about my favorite subject, the science of predictable business building.

The arena is rocking, the lights are blindingly bright and the crowd is in a frenzy as the band comes off the stage. Glenna is the host of this part of the event and she continues to encourage the mayhem by clapping with them for a few minutes. When she stops clapping, people start to sit down and she begins introducing the next speaker. She starts by saying that only a few months ago this man's life was completely different from what it is today. And it is this business that is responsible for his opportunity to share with us. He recently retired from his corporate career as a teaching guru and Fortune 500 corporate trainer. "Help me welcome to the stage the inventor of the *Residual Income*® business-building simulator, personal effectiveness coach, and mentor to six-figure earners all over the world—Mr. Gary Kirk!"

It's mayhem all over again, everyone is cheering and clapping. Gary is one of the main reasons they have come to this convention. They want to hear from the person who perfected the success pattern by combining the Personal Effectiveness Profile with the audio library and inventing the *Residual Income*® game to create real predictability in the business. "I am delighted to be here tonight with you all," Gary says as he motions everyone to sit down.

"What I am going to share with you briefly tonight is how each of you could create a six-figure income in the next six months if you choose to pay the price and religiously follow a proven pattern that creates predictability in this business. In the next few minutes I will teach you through the stories of real people in this industry and in this company, like Glenna Hanks who advanced to the highest level in her company once and then for a second time in the past year.

"Like Steve and Sara Thoms, who created six figures in six months
and now have dozens of people in their business who have also done
it; like Ben and Pam Ford and Mark and Robin Brown who enrolled,
listened to their upline mentor, and have now created security and
generational wealth; like Maria and Javier who met through the business
and have been able to build an incredible lifestyle with each other and
are teaching others to do the same; and Jen, who struggled for so long
in the business but persevered and finally learned the success pattern.
And, lastly, I want to share with you the story of Cindy, who started her
career in the traditional way—enrolling, hoping, and replacing people
on her team—until she realized the success pattern was like the magic
potion for predictability in this seemingly luck and chance business.

"How did they all do this, you might be asking yourselves? Well
at the fifty thousand-foot level, Glenna taught her team to follow the
leader and implement the predictable 3-Step Success Pattern, and she
taught them to do the same for their teams. Let me begin by telling you
that traditionally there are only two ways to tell if you are succeeding
in this business.

"One of the ways is by counting how much money you make
each month. The other is by looking at how many people you enroll
each month. Of course, making money is the very reason most of you
enrolled in the business, and enrolling people is one of the principle
ways that you get paid. But it's not the best way to keep score when
you begin your journey. Your journey to job-dropping residual income,
financial security, and generational wealth started the day you enrolled.
But the chances that you had enough personal effectiveness, or PEPs,
in the critical skills in this business that will create the results you want
when you enrolled are pretty low.

"Just like any other profession, you shouldn't start counting
success based on bottom-line results, like enrollments and paychecks,
until you have the ability to create those results. That's what makes
the 3-Step Success Pattern so powerful. You can actually see where
you are in the business process and get critical insight on the specific
skills you need to improve to be effective at doing the work that
produces the results you want—like income, freedom, and life style.

"So keeping score in this business in the beginning by using
enrollments and income as the measuring sticks does not work. People
with low PEPs don't enroll many people—they can't! They can take

their sponsor with them and, if their sponsor has over thirty PEPs, they will enroll new people, but the low-PEP associate working by himself simply lacks the skill and knowledge to create life-changing residual income. So pay special attention to the Improve Yourself phase of the success pattern for the things that apply to most people when they enroll.

3-STEP SUCCESS PATTERN™

IMPROVE YOURSELF	BUILD A TEAM	BECOME A LEADER
0-30 PEPS 14-30 Days	31-45 PEPS 60-120 Days	46-70 PEPS 10 Leaders
*20 Critical Initial Skills	*20 Critical Building Skills	*10 Critical Leadership Skills
Time Focus 95% on personal effectiveness 5% on recruiting	Time Focus	Time Focus

Action Items
1. Get associate#
2. Enroll on product
  autoship or autopay
3. Have tickets to
  next event
4. Take the PEProfile
5. Gain a firm knowledge
  and testimony of
  company and products
6. Memorize contacting
  scripts
7. Make an effective
  list of 200 names
8. Subscribe to
  education system
9. Have personal
  improvement plan
10. Participate in R.I.G.
  (Residual Income game)
	Action Items	Action Items

Goals
1. Increase PEPs to 30+
2. Score green or yellow
  in first 20 skills
3. Enroll 1-5
  customers/associates
4. Receive products
  for FREE
	Goals	Goals

"Income and enrollments are a few of the ways you keep score when you get to the Build a Team phase. And rest assured that if you increase your PEPs to at least thirty or more in the Improve Yourself phase, your effectiveness in the Build a Team phase is essentially guaranteed and it's going to be huge, mostly because you will be taking purposeful action in its proper sequence, and you will be incredibly effective at the tasks you do each day in your business. So consider the business characteristics in the Build a Team phase of the success pattern, and recognize that they do require skill and knowledge to be effective. That's why higher checks come from higher PEPs.

3-STEP SUCCESS PATTERN™

IMPROVE YOURSELF	BUILD A TEAM	BECOME A LEADER
0-30 PEPS 14-30 Days	31-45 PEPS 60-120 Days	46-70 PEPS 10 Leaders
*20 Critical Initial Skills	*20 Critical Building Skills	*10 Critical Leadership Skills
Time Focus 95% on personal effectiveness 5% on recruiting	Time Focus 15% on personal improvement 50% on recruiting 30% on training new people 5% on retention	Time Focus
Action Items 1. Get associate# 2. Enroll on product autoship or autopay 3. Have tickets to next event 4. Take the PEProfile 5. Gain a firm knowledge and testimony of company and products 6. Memorize contacting scripts 7. Make an effective list of 200 names 8. Subscribe to education system 9. Have personal improvement plan 10. Participate in R.I.G. (Residual Income game)	Action Items 1. 20-30 hours per week commitment 2. 8-10 personal contacts per week 3. 60% conversion rate on contacts and personal presentations 4. 90% conversion rate of follow-ups 5. Take PEProfile quarterly 6. Register team for education system	Action Items
Goals 1. Increase PEPs to 30+ 2. Score green or yellow in first 20 skills 3. Enroll 1-5 customers/associates 4. Receive products for FREE	Goals 1. Increase PEPs to 45+ 2. Score green/yellow in team-building skills 3. 15-25 associates on team 4. 3-5 committed to leadership track 5. Break even and then earn at least $2,500 in residual income	Goals

"The more traditional ways of keeping score apply to associates who are in the Build a Team phase. These new areas of activity are added ways of telling where you are in relation to financial goals related to residual income that comes not only from enrollments, but from retention as well. Of course, enrollments are a critical element to business. Your goal in this business is not only to get customers and associates. True residual income comes from getting—and then keeping—customers and associates. The glue that keeps customers and associates in your business is your ability to teach others to create success so they can build and maintain their own businesses with or without you. The challenge is that very few people know how to do this effectively. And hence there is the Become a Leader phase of the success pattern.

3-STEP SUCCESS PATTERN™

IMPROVE YOURSELF	BUILD A TEAM	BECOME A LEADER
0-30 PEPS 14-30 Days	31-45 PEPS 60-120 Days	46-70 PEPS 10 Leaders
*20 Critical Initial Skills	*20 Critical Building Skills	*10 Critical Leadership Skills
Time Focus 95% on personal effectiveness 5% on recruiting	**Time Focus** 15% on personal improvement 50% on recruiting 30% on training new people 5% on retention	**Time Focus** 10% on personal improvement 15% recruiting 65% training people to become leaders 10% on retention
Action Items 1. Get associate# 2. Enroll on product autoship or autopay 3. Have tickets to next event 4. Take the PEProfile 5. Gain a firm knowledge and testimony of company and products 6. Memorize contacting scripts 7. Make an effective list of 200 names 8. Subscribe to education system 9. Have personal improvement plan 10. Participate in R.I.G. (Residual Income Game)	**Action Items** 1. 20-30 hours per week commitment 2. 8-10 personal contacts per week 3. 60% conversion rate on contacts and personal presentations 4. 90% conversion rate of follow-ups 5. Take PEProfile quarterly 6. Register team for education system	**Action Items** 1. Full time/professional commitment 2. Training using team PEProfile results 3. Enroll 2 new personals each month 4. Promote 1 new leader per month 5. Training system using R.I.G.
Goals 1. Increase PEPs to 30+ 2. Score green or yellow in first 20 skills 3. Enroll 1-5 customers/associates 4. Receive products for FREE	**Goals** 1. Increase PEPs to 45+ 2. Score green/yellow in team-building skills 3. 15-25 associates on team 4. 3-5 committed to leadership track 5. Break even and then earn at least $2,500 in residual income	**Goals** 1. Increase PEPs to 70+ 2. Score green or yellow in leadership skills 3. Increase team PEPs average to over 30 4. 250+ team members 5. 15 or more leaders 6. 20+ serious builders 7. 100 people on autoship or autopay 8. 100 in education system and events 9. 50 recognized on stage

"Leadership is not just a matter of having someone on your team. You *become* a leader, you don't inherit the position. Long-term success is built on developing leaders, not just associates. So even if you were able to use your mentor to enroll a few people in the beginning, it is your growth, example, and personal development that attracts and inspires others to grow and succeed with you. To be a leader you must become the kind of person who not only attracts people to the business, but the kind of person who also attracts leaders to it.

"Use the success pattern to get new customers and associates started right, instead of just getting them started. The 3-Step Success Pattern helps everyone see the cause and effect by targeting personal improvement and its effect on the results you get from working in your business. It also shows how residual income really works, opposed to income from single transactional sales like enrollments. It's the model that makes the industry of best opportunity and makes it the industry of predictable opportunity.

"Every day people ask me what the secret is of this business. And every day I tell them the same thing. Sometimes I even whisper it in their ear. The secret is that there is no secret. And when I do that, many are surprised and some are even disappointed. The secret is something personal. It's the critical skills and knowledge that you probably don't even know about yet. And that's why you need to take the Personal Effectiveness Profile. If you do that, then and only then can I or your upline mentor tell you exactly what the secret to success is *for you*! Then and only then can we tell you exactly what you need to do next to begin your journey to the life you dream of and are passionate about.

"As a special gift to you as a future member of the Rhino Power Team and a serious business builder, I am giving you a free access code to take the PEProfile for yourself. You are the authors of your own success story. Go ahead, turn the page to find the access code on the inside back cover of this book. Use the code as the key to begin writing the next chapter of your life, one that is filled with the dreams you envisioned when you enrolled in the business.

"Take care of yourself and those you meet every day. They are counting on you to help them achieve their greater causes and higher purposes. I look forward to meeting each of you as you come by and see me at the booth. Have a great night; I'll see you at the top!"

About the Author

Clay Stevens is a twenty-five year veteran in network marketing and has extensive personal experience in direct selling. This experience combined with his expertise as an instructional designer has been the foundation for the comprehensive training system presented in *Six Figures in Six Months*.

He developed the 3-Step Success Pattern to resolve the dilemma of predictability in an industry that is generally thought of as luck and chance. The three bedrock principles from which this success pattern originated provide context and experience for anyone who wants to build a strong and profitable business in less time with less frustration.

Mr. Stevens is an industry mentor, a Fortune 500 corporate trainer, and a personal effectiveness coach. He also holds three degrees in training and instructional technology, which have enabled him to develop two of the most effective tools to come to direct sales since the audiotape: The *Residual Income*® training simulator and the Personal Effectiveness Profile, both of which help sales teams learn, practice, and apply the critical skills necessary to succeed in building relationships, learning critical skills, and creating duplication to create personal wealth.

Mr. Stevens has written four books on effective training methods and owns four patents for instructional methodologies and game-development technologies. He has also won national awards for multimedia training programs. He founded Ri Training to help new associates, veterans, and leaders solve the three biggest problems in network marketing: recruiting, training, and retaining people on their team.

Glenna's Tool Box